Ferdinand Toennies

ON SOCIOLOGY: PURE, APPLIED, AND EMPIRICAL

THE HERITAGE OF SOCIOLOGY

A Series Edited by Morris Janowitz

Ferdinand Toennies

ON SOCIOLOGY: PURE, APPLIED, AND EMPIRICAL

Selected Writings

Edited and with an Introduction by

WERNER J. CAHNMAN AND
RUDOLF HEBERLE

THE UNIVERSITY OF CHICAGO PRESS

CHICAGO AND LONDON

ISBN: 0–226–80607–3 (clothbound)
0–226–80608–1 (paperbound)
Library of Congress Catalog Card Number: 70–127822

THE UNIVERSITY OF CHICAGO PRESS, CHICAGO 60637
The University of Chicago Press, Ltd., London

Printed in the United States of America

Contents

Introduction

I

THE PRESENT VOLUME on Toennies differs from other volumes in the *Heritage of Sociology* series. The wide range of Toennies' work and the sheer extension of it, in combination with the difficulties of interpretation and the fact that very little thus far has been available to English-speaking readers, made it advisable to devote two volumes of this series to Ferdinand Toennies. The first volume assumes the pattern of a "Reader," presenting selections from Toennies' sociological writings with brief connecting texts. A second volume will contain papers on various aspects of Toennies' work along with a documentation of the relation of his work to those of Marx, Spencer, Durkheim and Weber.

In addition, the first volume differs from other volumes in the series because it represents more than what is still alive of a classic author's work. While Durkheim's, Simmel's, and Max Weber's writings are largely known to American social scientists through translations, such is not the case with Toennies, Charles P. Loomis' meritorious translation of *Gemeinschaft und Gesellschaft* (1940) notwithstanding. To be sure, Toennies was well known to the founding fathers of American sociology—we will return to this point later—but they read German fluently and needed no translations. However, the close contact with German literary and scientific developments which they had maintained was fatally weakened in the wake of World War I. Consequently, when Toennies collected some of the most important of the numerous papers, articles, and reviews which he had published previously in scholarly journals in the remarkable volumes of *Soziologische Studien und Kritiken* (1924, 1926, 1929) and in *Fortschritt und Soziale Entwicklung* (1926) and when he finally completed his *Einfuehrung in die Soziologie* (1931), these publications failed to make an impact. Soon afterward, the Hitler catastrophe engulfed Toennies' entire work. It follows that the pieces which we have translated come to American social scientists as a substantially new thing, and are likely to mark the emergence of Toennies as a major contributor to the heritage of sociology.

It is only seemingly contradictory to what has been just stated that *Gemeinschaft und Gesellschaft*, even without the clarification which Toennies provided in his later writings, has become one of the most influential books in modern sociology. Out of these two title words, along with Durkheim's "solidarity" and "anomie" and Weber's "bureaucracy" and "charismatic authority," one could construct the edifice of sociological conceptualization, even if all the other pieces were lost. But, as Hans Freyer has observed, the influence which Toennies' slim volume has exerted all around the globe, the German-speaking countries included, has remained "anonymous and almost subterranean" in character: everybody talks about *Gemeinschaft und Gesellschaft*, but hardly anybody has read the book from cover to cover, and those who have read it have, more often than not, largely misunderstood its message. The most frequent misunderstanding is the one of "misplaced concreteness." The sociostructural terms *Gemeinschaft* and *Gesellschaft*, along with their social-psychological counterparts "essential will" and "arbitrary will," have been taken as classifications of factual realities when, indeed, they are meant to be comprehended—thought of, as it were—as "normal" concepts or "ideal-typical" constructs; not as concretely distinguishable categories but as intellectually distillable elements of a society (a *"Scheidung,"* not an *"Unterscheidung,"* to use Toennies' own words). To quote oneself (from W. J. Cahnman and A. Boskoff, *Sociology and History*, p. 110), one can say that "thus, a 'family,' 'clan,' 'village,' 'friendship' may serve as approximate examples of *'Gemeinschaft,'* but they are *'Gemeinschaft'* only to the extent to which they coincide with the ideal conceptual image of *'Gemeinschaft.'* 'City,' 'state,' 'industry,' 'public opinion' may serve as examples of '*Gesellschaft*' in the same way. In other words, viewed in the light of normal concepts, actual societies, especially of the '*Gesellschaft*' type, are always mixed." Similarly, "essential will" and "arbitary will" are pure types of volition; they are aspects of a total psychic reality, not mutually exclusive concrete parts of it.

In Germany of late, the misunderstanding has been carried even farther. In the 1920s, but especially after 1945, in the light of the Hitlerian *Goetterdaemmerung*, Toennies was thought of as being a romantic, in the sense of posing as a *laudator temporis acti* when he was actually a disciple, in part, of romantic philosophy in his emphasis on will and emotion as a substratum of, but not a substitute for, the rationality which is inherent in the human condition. He was accused of idealizing *Gemeinschaft* when he merely stressed its raw pristinity and unreflected innocence as against the deliberate calculation of advantage and disadvantage and the weighing of ends against means in *Gesellschaft*. He was pilloried as the seducer of youth because *Gemeinschaft* became the catchword of the exuberant protest of the youth movement against the false pretensions and the mechanized life style of bourgeois society; he was even made responsible for unwittingly blunting the edge of opposition against the abuse by the Nazi demagogues of such a conglomerate term as *Volksgemeinschaft*; by the same token, Toennies could have been made a "precursor"—a favorite term of *post factum* semiwisdom—of National Socialism because he saw in socialism (of a very different kind, to be sure) a hope for the future. I refrain from mentioning names at this point, except for the one of Ralf Dahrendorf. What he has to say about Toennies (in *Gesellschaft und Demokratie in Deutschland*, pp. 151 ff.) deserves reference because it is so typical of the misinterpretation of Toennies as an enemy of "modernity" as to be almost a caricature of it. Dahrendorf, in his interpretation, does precisely what Toennies, in his writings, does not, namely, to confront "a beautiful *Gemeinschaft* of emotions in the past" with "a heartless contractual *Gesellschaft* in the present"; after thus confounding concept and reality, he concludes that the bogeyman whom he has put up never existed and that *Gemeinschaft*, if it ever existed, wasn't as "agreeable" as he thinks Toennies had made it out to be, because it contained "illness and early death, hunger and war, dependence and humiliation" along with a presumed "harmony" of feelings.

No doubt, these evils, like many others, are ever present, and they are disturbing wherever they are found, but they are not, as Dahrendorf erroneously assumes, "the outcome of human essential will"—they are the negation of it. Dahrendorf further assumes erroneously, as far as the interpretation of Toennies is concerned, that an "authoritarian political order" is identical with *Gemeinschaft*, and he then assures his readers that this Don Quichotesque windmill is not "rational" when Toennies, in fact, discerns both authoritarianism and fellowship in *Gemeinschaft* as well as in *Gesellschaft*, but ascribes increasing rationality to the processes of *Gesellschaft*. Dahrendorf caps the confusion when he alleges that Toennies' intention is "to devalue contract and conflict, law and human autonomy." In Toennies' view, the positive value of *Gesellschaft* consists in pitting law and contract against the element of conflict that is inherent in human autonomy. Dahrendorf inadvertently is correct when he finds *Gesellschaft*, historically speaking, nearly identical with "modernity," but incorrect when he thinks that this is a statement *contra* Toennies. Toennies sees the shadows in the development of modern society which—surely—we all ought to be aware of, but also its inexorable necessity. As the reader of this volume will soon come to know, Toennies affirms the value of rationality as the mark of maturity and the essence of the scientific spirit. Psychoanalytically speaking, the recently fashionable German disparagement of Toennies, of which Dahrendorf is a pronounced example, may be recognizable as a displacement of guilt feelings, but that does not decide the issue. However, Toennies' comment from the first preface of *Gemeinschaft und Gesellschaft* (1887) would seem to be justified: "I shall not be responsible both for erroneous explications and for presumably clever applications. People who are not trained in conceptual thinking better abstain from passing judgment."

It must be admitted, though, that Toennies does not make it easy to fully comprehend his famous treatise. This has much to do with his style of writing, but also with the nature of his conceptualization. Toennies does not write in the approved scientific fashion, starting with hypothesis, proceeding to proof, and ending with conclusion. Rather, he presents his case after the manner of a musical composition, with two doubly intoned *leitmotivs* (essential will—*Gemeinschaft;* and arbitrary will—*Gesellschaft*) and intricately intertwined variations on the fourfold theme. In addition, he intertwines conceptual analysis with factual explication in such a way that the reader cannot always be sure whether the author refers to a "normal concept" or to a historical trend. It would be adequate to say that Toennies presents a theory of sociation that is universally valid, but that he uses this theory to illuminate the course of modern history. As a result of the multiple composition of Toennies' thinking, his style of writing is full of assumptions, allusions, and polemical asides. But the nature of his conceptualization and the thrust of his argument are clear if one considers the totality of his work in addition to the youthful work of genius that is *Gemeinschaft und Gesellschaft.*

Toennies divides the total field of sociology into general and special sociology. By general sociology, he refers to areas of inquiry that are sociologically relevant without, in his view, belonging to sociology proper, such as social biology (chiefly, physical anthropology), demography, and social psychology. These subfields, which are now securely included within sociology or anthropology, are of no more than passing interest to Toennies. His enduring interest belongs exclusively to what he calls special sociology. He subdivides special sociology into pure, applied, and empirical sociology. Pure sociology, frequently characterized as theoretical sociology, is more precisely designated as philosophical sociology: it deals with pure concepts, static norms, basic ideas, and their interrelationships. These concepts, norms, and ideas refer to human volition, and are requisites for the understanding of social structure. Applied sociology, which is likewise theoretical in nature, applies the static concepts of pure sociology to the dynamic processes of history. It has been labeled a philosophy of history, but is actually a sociology of history or, in contemporary parlance, a theory of social change. Empirical sociology, or sociography, aims at the accurate description and analysis of human relations. It uses chiefly quantitative methods, but also interviews and other tools of detailed investigation. Whenever possible, it strives for mathematical clarity of relationships. It follows that pure and applied sociology, while conceptually distinct, are not easily kept apart in analysis: pure ideas must be illustrated by reference to historical reality, and social processes must be understood in the light of pure ideas. But the relation of empirical research to pure theory is more complex.

In order to understand the nature of this connection, one must be aware of the multiple points of departure in Toennies' thinking. He starts from a natural law conception of man and the state which had been most radically formulated by Thomas Hobbes, and also by Spinoza, and which is most virulently expressed in the writings of the classical economists, and he finds there the model of *Gesellschaft;* but he complements the rational procedure of natural law with the empiricist and experientalist approach of the historical schools of law and economics, of romantic philosophy and the theory of evolution, and he derives from them, as well as from older sources, the model of *Gemeinschaft.* Man by nature is a social being in *Gemeinschaft* and an initially asocial being in *Gesellschaft;* but *Gesellschaft* makes for social relations through convention and law. In his paper on "The Nature of Sociology," Toennies says that both theses, that man is a social being, and that he is an asocial being, are correct and that they complement each other; yet, in his paper "A Prelude to Sociology," he adds that it would be inaccurate to say that the organic (historical) and the mechanical (rationalistic) view are both "right" and that they are to be combined in a synthesis; the organic view, he means to say, precedes the rationalistic view logically and historically; *Gesellschaft* is derived from *Gemeinschaft* in the same sense in which arbitrary will is derived from essential will, reflection from emotion. Yet it must be remembered that all of these are not categories but elements, and that they are "things of thought"; in the life that is lived, they are never found pure and alone. It must further be understood that essential will is not identical with drive or instinct. Volition always involves thought; but it makes a difference whether thought is in the service of vital processes or whether thought gains independence, as it were, and pursues its own ends.

The latter point is of decisive importance for the understanding of the sociology of Toennies. Many deliberations, of which we can indicate only a few, must be anchored here. One can see a number of reasons, apart from those mentioned above, why Toennies' sociology was widely misunderstood. What he had to say appealed to neither party in the *Methodenstreit:* he emphasized the primacy of life over thought, yet he delineated the victorious progress of rationality which he considered to be a psychological and historical necessity. With Hobbes and Spinoza, he held that scientific inquiry proceeds from cause to effect; but, with Schopenhauer, he believed that as the external world is moved by causality, so the internal world is moved by will, and that social processes must be understood from the inside out, that is, as conditioned by the varieties of human volition and their contradictory indications. This makes Toennies a dialectician and a phenomenologist and brings him near to the organic view of the symbolic interactionists, who reached similar conclusions from different points of departure. Toennies would have endorsed Cooley's sentence, "The imaginations which people have of one another are the solid facts of society." But he would have added that imagination must be seen as turning into action through the agency of the human will. We will have to say more about these linkages of thought in the second volume.

The present volume should do away with the notion that Toennies thought of *Gemeinschaft* as "good" and *Gesellschaft* as "bad"; his repudiation of value judgments in scholarship is as pronounced as Max Weber's, and it is documented already in the preface to the first edition of *Gemeinschaft und Gesellschaft;* it has been repeated on later occasions. The present volume also ought to do away with the related notion that Toennies assumes a world without conflict. Rather, what he means to say is that social relations, as envisaged in pure sociology, are positive, affirmative relations, either of the *Gemeinschaft* or the *Gesellschaft* type, or at least predominantly of one or other type. Negative, or hostile, relations are acknowledged, but they are designated as being asocial, or even antisocial, in character; in a pure *Gemeinschaft,* they are nonexistent *ex definitione;* in a pure *Gesellschaft,* they are neutralized by the legitimately exercised power of the state. Hostile relations, such as crime, delinquency, marital discord, strikes, lockouts, riots, wars, and, even more so, the radical negation of social bonds that occurs in suicide, are therefore pathological. To use medical analogy, *Gemeinschaft* and *Gesellschaft* as well as their psychic correlates essential will and arbitrary will, like health, are normal concepts or "things of thought"; they must be assumed. But manifestations of pathology, hostility, illness, and death are actual occurrences; they must be researched. They are deviations from basic assumptions; they are social problems. A statement of this kind marks the place of empirical sociology in Toennies' scheme of special sociology. Toennies himself used the term pathology in his paper "Sozialwissenschaftliche Forschungsinstitute" (*Forschungsinstitute—Ihre Geschichte, Organisation und Ziele,* Hamburg 1930) and elsewhere; one is therefore justified in saying that Toennies' published work as a whole uses not so much a dichotomy of *Gemeinschaft* and *Gesellschaft* as a trichotomy of *Gemeinschaft, Gesellschaft,* and pathology. There are pathologies of *Gemeinschaft* and pathologies of *Gesellschaft.* Clearly, these are not found in pure sociology, but they intrude into applied sociology, and they constitute the dominant theme in empirical sociology. Methodologically, pure sociology, dealing in essences, uses a phenomenological approach; applied sociology, analyzing processes, a dialectical approach; and empirical sociology, investigating social problems, a positivistic approach. If this is understood, the three sociologies of Toennies, although they speak in different tongues, will be seen as closely interrelated and as a unit in thought.

II

Ferdinand Toennies (26 July 1855–9 April 1936) was born on the parental farm in the county of Eiderstedt in Schleswig-Holstein, Germany; he spent his childhood there and, after his father's retirement, in the nearby town of Husum, always within sight and sound of the North Sea. His mother's family—her maiden name was Mau—hailed from East Holstein, and was predominantly a family of Protestant ministers and of scholars. His father's family was of Frisian origin. The Frisian people, who inhabit the northern provinces of the Netherlands as well as a coastal rim in Germany stretching from the Dutch to the Danish border, have maintained themselves as an independent peasantry, free from feudal domination, from the early Middle Ages until modern times. It would not be correct, however, to think of Toennies as being of peasant origin in anything like the accepted meaning of the term. His father grazed meat cattle that were shipped to markets in Hamburg and in England; in addition, he had an interest in a provincial bank. But it is correct that Toennies throughout his life remained emotionally tied to "the gray town by the sea," as Husum was called by the poet Storm, whom Toennies knew and adored, and generally to land and folk in Schleswig-Holstein. Although a scholar's scholar, he had an easy way with the common people, a trait that made him a perfect interviewer.

His father's means enabled Toennies to study philosophy, history, classic languages, and archaeology, and, later, economics and statistics at the universities of Jena, Bonn, Leipzig, Berlin, and Tuebingen; at the latter university, he received a doctorate of philosophy in the field of classical philology in 1877. In 1881 he became a *Privatdozent* at the University of Kiel (in philosophy) on the strength of a first draft of what was six years later to become his famous book *Gemeinschaft und Gesellschaft*. He lived in Kiel and Hamburg and later in Eutin, a small town between Kiel and Luebeck, but did little teaching, partly because he did not enjoy the formal obligations connected with teaching, partly because his independence of mind, his socialist leanings, his support of working class movements, and—apparently—his membership in the Ethical Culture Society made him persona non grata with the powerful chief of personnel of the central university administration in Prussia. He became a full professor (appointed to a chair of economics) only in 1913, but applied for emeritus status already in 1916; however, as emeritus, he resumed teaching, this time in sociology, from 1921 to 1933, when he was summarily dismissed by the National Socialist regime. His erratic career notwithstanding, Toennies enjoyed a high reputation as a scholar.

From 1909 to 1933 he was a member of and president of the *Deutsche Gesellschaft fuer Soziologie,* which he founded together with Georg Simmel, Werner Sombart, Max Weber, Rudolf Gold-scheid, and others. He was a co-founder and first president of the *Societas Hobbesiana* (Toennies was a Hobbes scholar of the first order), a member of the *Verein fuer Sozialpolitik,* the *Gesellschaft fuer Soziale Reform,* the *Institut International de Sociologie,* the English and Japanese sociological societies, and a honorary member of the American Sociological Society, among others. Toennies attended many international scholarly congresses, but he was especially at home in England. From his youth, when he searched British archives for Hobbes manuscripts, to his old age, he remained an admirer and disciple of English scholarship; as far as the social sciences are concerned, he repeatedly testified to his indebtedness especially to Herbert Spencer and Henry Sumner Maine.

Toennies was not a liberal in the sense of the Manchester liberalism of the nineteenth century; nor was he a supporter of the sham splendor and vainglory of the Hohenzollern empire. He was a democrat, a republican, a freethinker, a socialist of a kind, and a devoted supporter of the labor movement; he was intensely interested in trade unions, consumer cooperatives, and adult education, especially workers' education. One can say that he was conservative in temperament but radical in conviction. Although he believed that a scholar should not be a member of a political party, he eventually joined the Social Democratic party in 1932, in view of the rising threat of the Nazi movement. He wanted to stand up and be counted. We will publish examples of his anti-Nazi articles from this period in the second volume.

Toennies' contacts with, and his influence upon, American sociology constitute a fascinating topic which can be referred to at this point only in a cursory manner. Toennies was most appreciative of Lewis H. Morgan's *Ancient Society,* which he called "a standard work of sociology"; he was especially impressed by its congruence with the basic tenets of Marxism. Marx and Engels, as well as Morgan, emphasize the importance of human relations at work and of technology; and so does Toennies. Among the fifty-five non-German authors (along with thirty-six from Germany and Austria) whose work Toennies reviews in Volume III of *Soziologische Studien und Kritiken* are nine American authors; the most important names, apart from Morgan, are Small, Ward, Giddings, Walter Lippman, and Mark Baldwin. Toennies' contacts with Albion W. Small seem to have been especially close. He was invited to participate in the Congress of Arts and Science of the Universal Exposition in St. Louis, Missouri, in 1904, apparently at the initiative of the exposition's vice-presidents, Albion W. Small, the founder of the department of sociology at the University of Chicago, and Hugo Muensterberg, the German-American psychologist at Harvard University. Among the American social scientists whom Toennies met at St. Louis were Charles A. Ellwood, William I. Thomas, and Edward A. Ross. The paper which he read at St. Louis, "The Present Problems of Social Structure," was published in *The American Journal of Sociology* in 1905, and is reproduced in this volume. Toennies was among the early editors of that journal.

Toennies' work was well known to Robert E. Park. Toennies is quoted three times in Park's and Burgess' influential *Introduction to Sociology*, and Park's dichotomy of "family" versus "marketplace" clearly is an adaptation from Toennies, turning what had been an ideal type into a real type—a very Parkian procedure. Park himself acknowledges (in *The Problem of Cultural Differences*, 1931) that the dichotomy of "sacred" versus "secular" societies is directly derived from Toennies' concepts of *Gemeinschaft* and *Gesellschaft*. Two of Park's foremost students, Howard Becker and Robert Redfield, later have elaborated on this dichotomy and on the related dichotomy of "folk" versus "city." Generally, however, Toennies' influence had turned subterranean: he was quoted and even utilized without quotation, but not read. The familiar misinterpretation of Toennies' basic theorems, that they idealized the country and pilloried the city, appealed to many American sociologists in the 1920's. To those who actually read and—at least in part—understood Toennies belongs Louis Wirth, whose paper on "The Sociology of Ferdinand Toennies" appeared in the *AJS* in 1927. Surely, Louis Wirth's paper on "Urbanism as a Way

+ Folk Culture of Yucatán.

of Life" (1938) is inspired by a Toenniesian conceptualization. By way of contrast, Robert M. McIver's references to Toennies in his books on *Community* (1929) and *Society* (1937) seem to be far off the mark. Pitirim A. Sorokin's treatment in *Contemporary Sociological Theories* (1928) is more perceptive, although it is marred by Sorokin's mannerism of finding everything a later author says "adumbrated" in earlier authors. Albert Salomon's brilliant obituary of Toennies in *Social Research* (1936) went largely unnoticed, and so did Karl J. Arndt's and C. L. Folse's translation of Toennies' article "The Concept of Law and Human Progress" in *Social Forces* (1940). An effective breakthrough came with Talcott Parsons' "Note on Gemeinschaft and Gesellschaft" in *The Structure of Social Action* (1937). Both Albert Salomon's article and Parsons' "Note" (the latter with a notable addition acknowledging that the "pattern variables" are derived from Toennies' basic concepts) will be reproduced in the second volume. We refrain here from referring specifically to Rudolf Heberle's various papers and articles on Toennies. With Charles P. Loomis' translation of *Gemeinschaft und Gesellschaft* under the title *Fundamental Concepts of Sociology* (1940), we enter into a new phase. Its effects were delayed, however, by World War II and its aftermath; they become manifest only now.

III

Else Brenke's bibliography ("Schriften von Ferdinand Toennies aus den Jahren 1875–1935" in: *Reine und Angewandte Soziologie—Eine Festgabe fuer Ferdinand Toennies zu seinem 80. Geburtstage* (Leipzig: Hans Buske, 1936), although not entirely complete, contains over six hundred items, the harvest of a lifetime. To be sure, many of these items are popularizations of scholarly papers, some are repetitious. But even if half of the six hundred publications are laid aside, there remains a stupendous output of scholarly productivity to choose from. In order to decide on the selections that were to go into the present volume, the first consideration was to exclude those publications that were already easily accessible in English, especially *Gemeinschaft und Gesellschaft* (ed. Chas. P. Loomis, now available, under the title *Com-*

munity and Society, as a Harper Torchbooks paperback), *Custom* trans. F. A. Borenstein, 1961) and the paper translated by Arndt and Folse in *Social Forces* (1940). However, we included the St. Louis Exposition paper of 1904, because it could hardly be considered easily accessible, and two brief passages from *Gemeinschaft und Gesellschaft* (using Loomis' translation, but modifying it in part), because they are indispensable for the argument which our selections intend to present, yet likely to be overlooked by the casual reader of the Harper Torchbook edition. We then gathered the selections into four major parts. Part I deals with the formation of Toennies' "pure" concepts, meaning normal concepts and ideal-typical constructs, especially the basic types of *Gemeinschaft* and *Gesellschaft*. Particular attention is given to the emergence of the ideal type concept from Toennies' interpretation of the philosophy of Thomas Hobbes. Part II deals with the elaboration of these concepts in papers which Toennies published in the years 1899–1924. It is very difficult, if not impossible, to grasp what Toennies meant to say in his classic book of 1887 without an intimate knowledge of these four explanatory papers. Part III, then, presents Toennies' mature treatment of pure sociology in selected chapters from *Einfuehrung in die Soziologie*. What had been presented rather poetically in *Gemeinschaft und Gesellschaft* is here scientifically clarified and at the same time elaborated. Part IV deals with empirical sociology, but in an unsatisfactory and sketchy way owing to the fact that almost all of Toennies' numerous papers on topics of empirical sociology are very long, full of tabulations, and hardly excerptible. However, to make good for the omission, a paper reviewing Toennies' total output in empirical sociology (or sociography) will be offered in the second volume. Part V deals with applied sociology, that is, chiefly with the theory of social change and the theory of public opinion; public opinion must be understood both as an element of social change and as a result of it. Toennies' theory of social change, which was never systematically elaborated by Toennies himself, likewise will be treated in the second volume.

A few things must be said about the principles which guided the translation. To translate Toennies requires a great deal of sensitivity. He assumes that the reader has a considerable knowledge of the philosophical, sociological, and historiographical literature in the major European languages, and he writes a very personal and rather discursive style. In addition, description and analysis, assertion and polemics are often intermingled. Without a subtle sympathetic insight, one can easily read out of a Toenniesian sentence a meaning that the author never intended to put in. At times, one passage is understandable only if one remembers another passage that is complementary to it. Consequently, all translations had to be checked and rechecked repeatedly, occasionally almost to the point of a retranslation. The terminology had to be brought in agreement with current sociological usage. Passages that were too brief had to be expanded somewhat while others that seemed to be verbose had to be curtailed—all this without violating the basic requirement of faithfulness to the author's intentions. We can assure the reader only that we have tried to do our best, not that we have entirely succeeded.

Toennies' terminology is another matter. As a rule, we have not translated the key words *Gemeinschaft* and *Gesellschaft* although occasionally we have said "community" and "association." Wherever we said "communal" and "associational," we have put the words *Gemeinschaft*-like and *Gesellschaft*-like in brackets. By "community," the reader must not understand a territorial or administrative entity, but what is held in common, what makes for cohesion, what provides bond among men. Occasionally, the meaning of the word "community" comes near to the one of "communion," as in intimate friendship and similar relations that are beyond question. Of course, initially the local community, the community of blood and the community of minds and hearts were one and the same thing, but this unity has been lost. Only fragments of community exist in our life, making for widespread uneasiness and a sense of alienation. We have translated *Gesellschaft* as "association" rather than as "society," because in the word "association" the meaning of choice and purpose comes clearly to the fore while "society" is generally understood as referring to an overall entity; and we ought not call the part by the same name as we do the whole. It is, however, interesting to note that not so long ago (for instance, with Hegel), "civic society" referred to the economic nexus as against either the intimate "family-society" or the supreme power of the state. Now the market aspect of human relations is all-pervasive.

The psychic correlates of *Gemeinschaft* and *Gesellschaft*, *Wesenwille* and *Kuerwille*, are rendered as "essential will" and "arbitrary will." This differs from Loomis' usage of "natural will" and "rational will" because this usage might be conducive to something like Wundt's mistaken interpretation of *Wesenwille* as an instinctual drive and therefore as devoid of rationality. Rather, "essential" refers to the unity of life and thought, while "arbitrary" refers to the emergence of thought as an independent agent, with the effect that means and end may cleave apart.

Some Toenniesian terms have to be translated flexibly. For example, *Beziehung* usually is to be translated as "(social) relation" or "interaction" and *Verhaeltnis* as "relationship," but this does not hold in every instance—quite apart from the occasional usuage of *Verhaeltnis* in the very concrete sense of "affair" or "liaison." By and large, *Verbindung* ("union") is based on essential will, and *Verein* ("association") on arbitrary will, while *Verband* refers to any "organized group"; yet, *Verbindung* and *Verband* at times are used interchangeably. *Gebilde* and *Bezugsgebilde* are frequently, but not always, to be translated as "social structures" or "institutions." Still more complex is the case of *Herrschaft* and *Genossenschaft*. *Herrschaft* is translated as "dominion," "domination," "authority," "control," depending on the context, but *Genossenschaft* can either be rendered as "fellowship" or, in the case of a *Konsumgenossenschaft*, as "cooperative"; the adjective *genossenschaftlich* may be translated either as "cooperative" or as "egalitarian." It must further be understood that *Genossenschaft* is typically *Gemeinschaft*-like, while *Herrschaft* can occur either in *Gemeinschaft* or in *Gesellschaft*. Frequently, in order not to mislead the reader, we have put the German term in brackets beside whatever English translation was preferred in a particular instance.

The translations are by Carola Toennies Atkinson, A. B. Ashton, Werner J. Cahnman, Ursula Fritzsche, Rudolf Heberle, E. G. Jacoby, and Kaethe Mengelberg. Carola Atkinson, with the assistance of Rudolf Heberle, translated the chapters from the *Introduc-*

tion to Sociology; A. B. Ashton translated *Progress and Social Development;* Werner J. Cahnman *My Relation to Sociology,* the first preface to *Gemeinschaft und Gesellschaft, Power and Value of Public Opinion, The Concept of Gemeinschaft, Prelude to Sociology,* and, together with Kaethe Mengelberg, the second preface to *Gemeinschaft und Gesellschaft* and *The Divisions of Sociology;* Ursula Fritzsche, together with Cahnman, *Historicism, Rationalism, and the Industrial System;* Rudolf Heberle, the chapters dealing with empirical sociology; and E. G. Jacoby, the selections from Hobbes, *The Nature of Sociology,* and the concluding piece from *The Spirit of the Modern Age.* However, all translations were checked by Cahnman and rechecked by Heberle, to ensure the necessary unity of style and interpretation. The editors assume full responsibility for whatever miscarriages may have occurred.

The editors worked together in perfect harmony; both selections and translations are our common responsibility. Parts I and II of this Introduction were written by Cahnman but approved by Heberle; Part III as well as the linkage text are a cooperative product. It must be revealed, moreover, that there were two assistant editors without whose help the arduous work that is now behind us could not have been completed: Franziska Toennies Heberle and E. G. Jacoby. Franziska Heberle provided the personal touch in our ongoing conversation as well as the index; E. G. Jacoby (of New Zealand), apart from his participation in the business of translation, fashioned the selected bibliography and kept up a continuous correspondence with the editors. Jacoby not only is a student of Toennies; his knowledge of every nook and cranny of Toenniesiana is so superb that it would have been plainly impossible to proceed without him. Gisella L. Cahnman, fortunately an exceedingly busy person herself, had to endure her husband's unavailability most of the time. Cahnman's students at Rutgers University tolerated frequent references to Toennies in the theory and social change classes. Morris Janowitz was a patient and generous general editor. Also, the financial assistance of the Rutgers Research Council is gratefully acknowledged. The most important person in the entire enterprise, the prospective reader, cannot be characterized. It is hoped, however, that he will be satisfied.

I. Formation of Concepts

EDITORS' NOTE. *The chapters combined in Part I under the heading* Formation of Concepts *are decisive for the understanding of Toennies' sociology. Most of them were written early in life; but we are fortunate, indeed, to have from Toennies' pen an autobiographical piece, written late in life, "when the shadows of the evening are falling"; this is an acknowledgment of his spiritual ancestry and a clear statement of his mature scholarly convictions.*

The first and the second prefaces to the significant work of his youth, Gemeinschaft und Gesellschaft, *written in 1887 and 1912, respectively, are likewise indispensable if one wishes to comprehend and evaluate properly the philosophic background, the scientific intention and the polemic aim of this slim but influential volume. These prefaces were not included in Charles P. Loomis' translation, and are published here in English for the first time.*

The importance of Toennies' Hobbes *studies for the formation of his concepts cannot be overrated. We are referring to these studies in a special prefatory note in connection with the chapter on* Normal Concepts.

1

MY RELATION TO SOCIOLOGY

I WISH to characterize briefly my relation to sociology.
I had been early engaged in philosophical studies, and approx-
imately since 1877 these were centered on Thomas Hobbes, especially on his writings about the philosophy of law and government.
From this point of departure the path led generally into the English
literature about these matters, and within a short time this showed
me the way to Herbert Spencer. From Spencer I turned back to
Auguste Comte. Now, I had before me the two great authors in

Translated from "Mein Verhaeltnis zur Soziologie," *Soziologie von Heute:
Ein Symposium der Zeitschrift fuer Voelkerpsychologie und Soziologie,*
ed. Richard Thurnwald (Leipzig: C. L. Hirschfeld, 1932), pp. 103–22.
Considerably abridged, especially regarding the controversy with L. v.
Wiese who had critically commented on the foundations of Toennies'
sociology in *Koelner Vierteljahrshefte fuer Soziologie,* vol. 4.

L. v. Wiese had attacked Toennies on three points: first, that Toennies
thought of *Gemeinschaft* as "good," *Gesellschaft* as "bad," which constituted an impermissible value judgment; second, that no concrete phenomenon could properly be described as either *Gemeinschaft* or *Gesellschaft;* third, that social relations could be of a negative as well as a
positive character. The gist of Toennies' reply to the first criticism is included in the selection that follows. His reply to the second criticism was
that he thought of *Gemeinschaft* and *Gesellschaft* as heuristic principles
or "normal concepts" (*Normalbegriffe*), with "ideal types" as their objects. It is fairly obvious that v. Wiese misinterpreted Toennies' position
with regard to points one and two; but the controversy with regard to the
third point cannot be resolved in a similarly clearcut manner. L. v. Wiese's
position makes good sense from a positivistic point of view while Toennies'
way of seeing things is voluntaristic in character.

sociology; Albert Schaeffle was linked to them as a German sociologist of some importance. Indeed, Schaeffle's *magnum opus,
Bau und Leben des sozialen Koerpers*, like Spencer's work, is entirely conceived in the organicistic manner, even if it is more specific as far as the working out of the analogies is concerned. These
analogies interested me very much at this time, and they made me
try *pari passu* to enlarge and deepen my knowledge of biology. In
the philosophy of law I received a strong impetus partly from
R. v. Jhering, partly from Sir Henry Maine. In addition, I occupied myself with the specifically German literature of rational natural law, starting with Pufendorf, as well as with the historical
school of law and the romantic writers, who denied the validity of
natural law and supplanted it. For instance, at this time (ca. 1881),
I read with vivid interest Adam Mueller's *Die Elemente der
Staatskunst.*

I decided to comprehend the true meaning of natural law as
well as the intentionally destructive criticism of it; consequently
I reached the point where I could form for myself a picture of the
entire pervasive effect of rationalism and the principle of scientific
reasoning which is derived from it. As a result of all this, I attempted to understand (*verstehen*) psychologically all non-rational
and somewhat less than rational modes of thought and I concluded
that they could never be absolutely unreasonable (*unvernuenftig*),
that they must carry their own meaning and that this meaning ultimately was reducible to human volition. I arrived at the generalization that what is social emanates from human willing, from the
intention to relate to each other, a together-willing (*Zusammen-
wollen*), as it were; and I set myself the task of penetrating to the
essence of this willing.

The study of scientific socialism contributed considerably to
the clarification of my thinking. I was fervently devoted to socialism
in these years: as early as 1878 I had read assiduously the first
volume of Karl Marx's major work, *Das Kapital;* Rodbertus and
his interpreter Adolf Wagner stimulated me for years afterward.
At the same time, I was interested in ethnology. Among the works
which impressed me deeply I should like to mention especially
Bachofen's *Mother-Law* and an American publication, Morgan's

Ancient Society. I might have mentioned a number of other works of this kind, particularly those of English and French authors who attempted to penetrate into the supposedly earliest phases of the social life of mankind, for instance, Hearn's *The Aryan Household* and Fustel de Coulanges' *La Cité antique.* Only much later, I got acquainted with and appreciated the works of the German jurist Leist.

From these studies and thoughts derived the book *Gemeinschaft und Gesellschaft,* whose first edition bears the subtitle: *A Treatise of Communism and Socialism as Empirical Forms of Culture.* I intended to say thereby that one ought not to see in these oft-quoted slogans mere phantasies, that is, cleverly reasoned ideals and utopias, but manifestations of actual social life. Regarding communism, this was nothing new, because such concepts as original (early) communism and agrarian communism were frequently used already at that time. What I thought to elaborate, in addition, was that another concept which likewise was often mentioned as a characteristic feature of modernity, namely, "individualism," was nothing but an ideal limiting point in the grand process which leads from communism to socialism, from *Gemeinschaft* to *Gesellschaft.* In this sense, I had said already in the preface to the first edition that there is no individualism in history and culture, except as it emanates from *Gemeinschaft* and remains conditioned by it, or as it brings about and sustains *Gesellschaft.* And on the last page of the text it is said: "The whole development . . . can be conceived as a trend (tendency) from the original (simple, familylike) communism and the (rural-urban) individualism which emanates from it and is based thereon, to the independent (metropolitan-universalistic) individualism and the thereby determined (national and international) socialism." In stating it this way, I meant to say that the germs of socialism are contained already in the whole matter of formal contracts and especially in the association, so that what was involved in the parallel progress of civic society and governmental institutions (*Staat*) essentially was an enhancement of the political factor, that is, the government. In this connection, I thought both of the societal development which makes this enhancement necessary and of the "law" of the increase of governmental responsibilities of my learned protector Adolph Wagner. Always did I see in the entire historical development since the middle ages the gradual setting free of rationalism and its increasing dominance as inherently necessary processes, and especially as processes of the human mind as will. From early youth I had been led by Schopenhauer to comprehending in will the core and essence of what is human, but I never fully appreciated the metaphysical generalization and the impermissible enlargement of the concept of will which is implied in Schopenhauer's philosophy. Rather, I soon returned to the concept of will as something specifically human, as *appetitus rationalis*. For a long time I have in my thoughts tried to work out the difference within the reasonable will which would correspond to the difference between *Gemeinschaft* and *Gesellschaft*. Finally, I arrived at the following formula: "Since all mental effect, because it is human, is characterized by thinking, I am discerning will inasmuch as it contains thinking and thinking inasmuch as it contains will." I first called these concepts essential will and arbitrariness (*Wesenwille* and *Willkuer*), but replaced the latter term in the third edition by the term arbitrary will (*Kuerwille*), because of the very different and somewhat contradictory meaning which is attached to the term arbitrariness.

The theorem to which I have recently attached decisive weight for the comprehension of the entire theory has not yet been sufficiently clarified in the book, namely: that relations and associations must always be understood as autonomous, except if they are imposed from the outside. In other words, relations and associations must be understood as existing in the will of those that are related and connected by it. They are immediately present only in the consciousness (*Bewusstsein*) of the participants; this is particularly so in the case of secret societies. In the second place, to be sure, relations and associations exist also with regard to other persons and their particular relations and associations, and these other persons recognize their existence by certain characteristic features, if and when they intend to enter into a relation or association with them; this is conditioned primarily by the existence of relations and associations of a similar kind. The most important example is the recognition in international law of a state and its government by other states and their governments; these are most important events in political history. However, the same thing occurs in simpler and more private spheres, for instance, in the recognition of a union by the managers of a large-scale enterprise or the leaders of an employers' association, by which act the workers' association is recognized as actually existent and capable of entering into negotiations, precisely as in international law recognition regularly is followed by the assumption of diplomatic relations. Also, among the students at an academic institution mutual recognition of their respective associations is of similar significance.

My work in pure sociology—as I later called it—was put to rest for about two decades because theoretical problems met with very little understanding in that period. As I had been strongly interested since the days of my youth in demography and moral statistics, I devoted myself to investigations in these fields, especially in criminology. But I returned to the conceptual world of pure sociology soon after the beginning of the new century, that is, as soon as the atmosphere had become more favorable. In a paper about "The Nature of Sociology" (*Das Wesen der Soziologie*, Gehe Stiftung, 1907), I searched for a common concept for social relations (*soziale Verhaeltnisse*) and associations (*soziale Verbaende*), and for a mediating concept between them, and I thought that "social will" might be such a concept. Soon, however, I realized that "social will" is a heterogeneous concept because it doesn't refer to a concrete entity while concrete entities, in turn, come into existence only through social will. In this way I arrived at the concept of a social collective, or social collectivity (*Samtschaft*). A social collective is an enlargement of social circles, and a social circle, such as a family or a circle of friends, is to be understood as the objective unity of a multiplicity of social relations. Collectives, however, I conceive of as being of firmer texture and longer duration although, like relations and associations, they are immediately given in the thinking and willing of their members. An example is a social estate or—almost an ideal type of a collective—a political party. This makes the difference between collective and association very clear: a collective as such is unorganized, for instance, a country's nobility or, to be sure, a party; however, a collective can bring forth a formal organization, as may be observed frequently. Other examples of large-scale, unorganized collectives are a people, a society, Christendom, Protestants, Freethinkers, and others; finally mankind, at least as an idea.

After I had thus differentiated between three kinds of social entities, I might be asked why I have not combined these in the concept of the group, after the manner of other respected sociologists. I believe I have good reasons to reject the term group. The use of that term reveals unawareness of, and deviation from, the basic idea which underlies my theory of social entities, namely, that they ought to be seen and analyzed from the inside out; this does not apply to the merely external formation of groups or crowds. I observe a group of people on a street, if a dozen or more persons gather at the place of an accident or on the occasion of a brawl.[1] To be sure, it is possible to look upon phenomena of this kind sociologically; but they are not per se sociological, or social, entities. Perhaps it would have been more serviceable to use the term social configurations (*Gestalten*). I have preferred the term social entity (*Wesenheit*) for two reasons. First, I wanted to avoid the misunderstanding that the term configuration had anything to do with *Gestalt* psychology. Second, it seemed to me that the term entity pointed more decisively to the requirement of emphasizing the subjective foundation of all human associations—and this is the cardinal point of my theory.

I first developed the essential points of my entire theory in the treatise "The Divisions of Sociology" ("Einteilung der Soziologie"). With slight modification I hold on to the position taken in that treatise. It is the basis of my *Introduction to Sociology* (*Einfuehrung in die Soziologie*), which is going to appear in 1931. This *Introduction* refers almost exclusively to theoretical, or pure, sociology because pure sociology contains those concepts and theories which characterize sociology as a particular branch

1   Contemporary sociology does conceive of a group in psychological terms, that is, as an "inside-out" relation, while it regards a crowd as a mere aggregate.—EDS.

of scientific knowledge. However, I distinguish between pure, applied, and empirical sociology, and devote to the two latter branches a brief chapter at the end of the *Introduction*. Further, in view of the fact that scientific usage attaches a much wider meaning to the term sociology, I thought it convenient to designate this wider meaning, which includes social biology and social psychology, as general sociology, as distinguished from special sociology, which is sociology in a more specific sense. Pure sociology, then, marks the point of departure in special sociology. . . .

At this point,[2] I might say a word about the voluntaristic explication of social structures (*Gebilde*), which has been subjected to doubt by L. von Wiese. He does not want to hear anything about taking one's point of departure from the motives of men; he maintains that "nothing can be said about such generalities." I must admit that this opens up an abyss between us. The objection against my pointing to a people (*Volk*) as an example of a collective runs like this: one could find in all kinds of places numerous individuals who preferred belonging to another people, if they had the choice. I regret to have to consider this objection as invalid. The reason for the misunderstanding is that von Wiese refuses to recognize the principles which are basic for the formation of my concepts—normal concepts—and their objects—ideal types. He says that my "mode of thinking which is rooted in my native soil," namely, that a deep harmony existed between man's essential will and the conditions under which he had grown up, was nothing but an ideal, a mere fiction that was stubbornly maintained by moralists and politicians; "but it was not always in agreement with reality." I have not considered it as an "ideal," but as an ideal, or constructional, type. Consequently, it goes without saying that not all phenomena which may be named after it can actually be subsumed under it; it would seem obvious that our earth is a very particular kind of sphere and yet we use this mathematical normal concept to describe it. . . .

As far as the concepts of *Gemeinschaft* and *Gesellschaft* are concerned, it ought to be understood that I don't apply them to the

---

[2]   The sequence of the following sections has been reversed.—EDS.

development of a culture in such a way—as L. von Wiese seems
to assume—that the former, as a period of youth, is described as
"good," the latter, as a period of senescence, as "bad," with the
consequence that what is good in youth is seen as derived from
Gemeinschaft while the evil quality of senescence is derived from
Gesellschaft. If anybody should have talked in this manner, all I
can say is that he's certainly not been my pupil, for the simple reason that I consider such a way of putting it to be thoroughly erroneous. My own opinion is very different. I do not know of any
condition of culture or society in which elements of *Gemeinschaft*
and elements of *Gesellschaft* are not simultaneously present, that
is, mixed. Moreover, although *Gemeinschaft*, too, arrives at higher
and nobler forms of human relations, it is correct to say that *Gesellschaft* is the essentially variable element which enhances culture
but also transforms it into civilization—to use, once again, these
two concepts, which occur in this sense already in the preface to
the first edition of *G. & G.;* by the way, Franz Oppenheimer emphasizes the same contradictions. The decisive factor in the emergence of *Gesellschaft*, that is, the causative factor in the tremendous revolution that culminates in *Gesellschaft*, is economic
in nature, namely, trade. In my opinion, trade in its development
is nothing but the capitalistic system. My evaluation of this system
does not essentially differ from the one of a thousand socialists,
before me, with me, and after me, and if I differ, I do so only in
the sense that I am perhaps more seriously engaged in the objective analysis of the totality of the capitalistic development during
the last few centuries. I do not disregard the tremendous consequences of trade, which connects places and peoples, or the
achievements of trade regarding the liberation and growth of the
individual forces of will and mind. Especially do I recognize that a
consequence of trade is science; and with the battle of science
against ignorance, superstition, and delusion I sympathize from
the depth of my soul. In this respect I have never wavered: if this
is not always clearly discernible in *G. & G.*, in spite of what was
already on my mind at the time when it was written, then the reason for it must be sought in the limitations of this work. I have
dated notes from these and still earlier years which clearly demon-

strate how I thought and felt in my youth. Another testimony is my intensive occupation with thinkers like Hobbes and Spinoza. Of romantic enthusiasm, I have permitted just as much to influence me as I felt was objectively warranted, especially from the point of view of esthetics; in this sense I have looked upon Adam Mueller with considerable benevolence, but, to be sure, not with exaggerated admiration. If romanticism becomes a personal philosophy, it must lead the Protestant and the freethinker into the lap of the *una sancta catholica*, because in that case he seeks emotional tranquility and esthetic satisfaction more than truth. The opinion that I should be capable of such a manner of thinking has always made me smile, if not to say laugh. However, I do think that even in the event—which I believe would be the most favorable regarding the present civilization—that this civilization could be gradually transformed into a socialistic organization of society, the end nevertheless would be inescapable. It would not be the end of mankind, nor would it be the end of civilization or culture, but it would be the end of the particular civilization or culture that is marked by the heritage of Rome.

2

PREFACE TO THE FIRST EDITION

OF *GEMEINSCHAFT UND*

GESELLSCHAFT

THE CONTRAST of the historical and the rationalistic interpretations of living phenomena has in the course of the nineteenth century permeated all aspects of the sociocultural sciences.
This contrast coincides essentially with the attack of empiricism
and critical philosophy upon the stable system of rationalism, as
it used to be represented in Germany by the Wolffian school of
thought. To gain a renewed understanding of these varied approaches is therefore of no small import, if one intends, as I do, to
arrive at a new analysis of the fundamental problems of social life.

It is paradoxical to say that empiricism, in spite of its decisive
triumph over rationalism, at the same time is complementary to
it in a formal sense. This is particularly noticeable with regard to
Kant's theory of knowledge, which, claiming to reconcile the contradictions, is as much modified empiricism as it is modified rationalism. This is noticeable already with regard to Hume's pure
empiricism; for Hume, too, does not inquire whether a general
and necessary cognition of facts and causality actually exists;
rather, he deduces conceptually the impossibility of such a cognition in much the same way in which Kant subsequently believed to
be able to deduce its actuality and consequently its potentiality.
Both employ a rationalistic approach, but with opposing results.
Hume had presupposed empiricism with reference to perception,

Translated from Vorrede zur ersten Anflage (1887) of *Gemeinschaft und
Gesellschaft*, according to the new edition (Darmstadt: Wissenschaftliche
Buchgesellschaft, 1963), pp. xv–xxv. The last two paragraphs have been
omitted.

in the sense that cognition appears as the effect of objective qualities and existential situations upon a carte blanche of the human mind; according to Kant, perception, like thought itself, is a product of the subject's activity, even if the existentiality and coeffectiveness of the objects remains granted. Following Kant, one might say that the coincidence with respect to truth is conditioned by the identical nature of the instruments of cognition which, beyond forms of perception and rational categories, are nothing but idea-complexes. More specifically, the instruments of cognition are associations of perceptions and images with names and judgments, as far as the comprehension of facts is concerned. However, if we look for the cause of given effects, we must assume definite concepts concerning the nature of *agentia* (essences, objects, or forces) and concerning the manner in which they become effective, so that one can select necessities and certainties from a wide range of potentialities. According to a Humean empiricism, however, such certainties cannot be reached otherwise but through the acquired knowledge of regular temporary sequences, so that, indeed, all associations of an equal kind are confirmed through repetition as habits and can be interpreted as necessary, that is, causal factors. Thereby, causality is removed from objects and transferred to man, not different from the way this is done by Kant, when he says that causality is a category of reason. Kant does not accept, however, Hume's explanation of causality from the mere experience of the individual. The Kantian formulation, whereby causality is an a priori of experience, truly points to the direction of an explanation in greater depth. For the psychological regularity which Hume has discovered must be supplemented by, and even justified through, the idea of a spiritual entity, or mind, endowed with forces or tendencies that appear as aptitudes in the process of becoming. Physiologically, the differentiation of human thought from the *consecution des bêtes* can be comprehended already from the nature of the human cerebral cortex, by dint of which the active coordination of received impressions is necessary, grows and takes shape, and must be understood as a definite relation between a total configuration of impressions and the particular impressions which occur at a given instance. For the total configuration is the absolute a priori; it can be conceived only as involving the totality of nature through as yet ill-defined general relationships, of which some gradually become clearer through the development and the actions of the brain and the sense organs, that is, through the comprehending mind of man. Each sequential experience, like any other activity, takes place in a totality configuration and through the organs which belong to that configuration. However, this results in a *regressus in infinitum*, leading back to the origins of organic life which, if conceived psychically, might as well be understood as the incorporation of experience. This follows from the recognition that every kind of action and of suffering (because suffering is only an aspect of action), or life itself, is experience, just as experience, in turn, is either action or suffering. Action involves organic change; it leaves tracks of one kind or another, be it in the same or the opposite direction as the tendency of the growth and development of the organism, or even indifferently defined. This is what is known as memory. More specifically, memory is the continuing labor and force of sensual impressions, which are evident in the shape of coordinated complexes, that is, of fixed emotions which are themselves the product of memory.

Every possible transformation of an organ is, to be sure, conditioned by its nature and by its place in a total configuration, that is, by the manner in which the organ in question is predisposed and likely to accept, or not to accept, the change. It is in this sense that I propose (in the second book of this essay on *Gemeinschaft und Gesellschaft*) the unity of, as well as the differentiations between, liking, habituation, and memory as elementary modifications of will and spiritual force in each and every mental production. This proposition extends to the problem of the origin and the history of human cognition. In other words, all this is merely an explication, partly following Spinoza and Schopenhauer, and partly the biological theory of descendence; it is an interpretation of the idea by means of which Kant has, indeed, overcome Hume. From the correctness of this interpretation derives not only the fact that, but also the reason why, we cannot think of what is in being otherwise than as being in action and of what is becoming otherwise than as acted upon; these are antecedent, and even eternal, functions which are imprinted in the very structure of our cognitive processes, that is, our power of reasoning. Not to be able to do otherwise is a necessity upon which our feeling of certainty is founded, because being active per se and being active according to one's nature is one and the same thing, in line with the formal rule of identity.

If it is true that human beings form a natural community of thought because causality is within us like sense organs and if, as a consequence, we necessarily attach names to subjects and objects (what is acting and what is acted upon), then whatever differentiates these phenomena can only be the result of thought—thought about what are the subjects that are acting, that is, the truly real entities. Peoples, groups, individuals differ in this regard, even if there is wide agreement that the active principle in nature is expressed in mythological and poetic imagery. Linguistic forms are testimony to that fact. To be sure, the differentiation between dead (that is, only acted upon) phenomena and those that are alive (meaning those that are acting) is an early acquisition of thought; nevertheless, what prevails is the idea that nature is a living thing, that action is voluntary, and that gods and demons participate in it, along with visible subjects. However, if ultimately world and fate are put into the head and the hand of a unitary God who has created them out of nothing, maintained them according to his pleasure, and endowed them with rules and laws according to which whatever happens appears as regularity and necessity, then, all subordinated wills and liberties in nature, including man's own free will, are made to disappear and tendencies that cannot be deduced from received external action are understood only as inexplicable inclinations and forces. In that case, even the *liberum arbitrium indifferentiae* is being reconstructed in the shape of such an inexplicable force and mysterious quality, not so much as a fact of experience but as a necessary assumption which is designed to exonerate the omnipotent and omniscient from the responsibility of having initiated the violation of his own rules and regulations.

This entire mode of looking at things, like the idea of a unitary divine will, already belongs to a manner of thinking which on principle is opposed to religious faith and folk belief, even if it continues to bear the vestiges of its origin from these sources. These principles develop to the point where they are capable of resting upon themselves and to appear altogether independent of the opposing principles whence they sprang while, at the same time, they encounter principles of their own kind that have freely unfolded themselves in those areas that are the natural domain of thought. The reference here is to scientific thought. Now, scientific thought, where it appears first and in undisputed purity, has nothing to do with the causes of phenomena and still less with human or divine will; it derives from the skills of comparing and measuring quantities, as a generalized auxiliary technique, such as doing sums, calculating, computing; in other words, as techniques of separating and combining, dividing and multiplying given quantities. These operations can easily be performed in thought because thought has prepared an orderly system of names and designations for them, so that no differentiation in the perceived objects disturbs the thought-induced posing of identical and arbitrarily combinable units. Insofar as the operation of such a system requires a hold on some objects, the calculator chooses, if possible, objects that are identical, conveniently calculable, and easily manageable; if they are not at his disposal, he will construct them and endow them with the desired qualities. To be sure, one finds innumerable configurations in nature that resemble each other to a larger or lesser degree with regard to their perceived qualities, to the point where they can be designated as equal; and be it further granted that it is natural to identify them with a name; nevertheless, the identification becomes artificial and arbitrary inasmuch as names are consciously formulated, the individual differences not only neglected but deliberately excluded from consideration and virtually destroyed for the purpose of creating a usable and as nearly as possible perfect equality. However, all scientific thought, like mathematics, must strive for equality to make measurement possible, the reason being that measurement is to arrive at general statements and precise relations, of which equality, in turn, serves as a measuring rod. In this regard, scientific equations are like measuring rods in such a way that actual relations between actual objects are comprehended in relation to them. They are service-able in the economy of thought. What in innumerable actual in-stances would have to be calculated again and again is being cal-culated once and for all in an ideally constructed instance and merely applied subsequently; regarding the ideally constructed instance, all actual instances are either identical or stand in an ascertainable relation to it and consequently to each other. In other words, gen-eralized or scientific concepts, statements, and systems may be compared to tools by means of which we gain knowledge or arrive at least at assumptions in particular given instances; the pro-cedure is to insert particular names and conditions in lieu of those of the fictitious and general instances: the procedure of syllogism. In a variety of ways, this procedure is used in applied science (as thinking in analogy to the principle of sufficient reason) and in pure science relative to a system of names (a terminology), which is represented in its simplest form by a system of numbers (as thinking in analogy to the principle of identity). For all pure sci-ence refers exclusively to constructions of thought (*Gedanken-dinge*), such as a generalized object or a quantity (for purposes of pure calculation) or the extensionless point, the straight line, the plane without depth, the regular bodies, when relations between spatial phenomena are to be determined. Similarly, imaginary events in *time* are considered as type-constructs of actual events, such as the fall of a body in a vacuum whose velocity is calculated as a unit in space measured in an arbitrarily measured unit of time, as equal or changeable, according to certain assumptions. As a rule, the application turns out to be more difficult the more the merely thinkable general instance differs from observable par-ticular instances, especially as they grow in complexity and irregu-larity. If separate bodies, through movement, assume momentary spatial contact, we arrive at the scientific concept of causality as a quantity of performed labor (contained in movement) which equals another quantity of labor, namely the effect, and conse-quently is interchangeable with it, according to the principle of the identity of action and reaction; this becomes a pure concept after each and every connotation of reality and productivity has been eliminated from the concept of force. In some such manner emerges the great system of pure mechanics; the applications of this system are the concrete natural sciences, especially physics and chemistry.

However, besides and within this scientific view of causality, a philosophical view develops and maintains itself, enhancing as well as critically evaluating the scientific view. It is an organic view as against a mechanical one, a psychological view as against a physical one; according to this view, nothing exists except productive force, the actual and permanent unit of a conservative system of general energy, from which unit all its peculiarities are derived, both as aspects and as effects. All natural laws are serviceable to the principle by means of which the universe is maintained, as all laws that are traceable to mechanics are serviceable to the principle by which the life of an individual or a species is maintained—and it is in individuals and species that "law" becomes reality. The more science, on the one hand, extends its methods to living organisms, the more it must become philosophic in this sense. Conversely, a philosophic view of nature, which would be oriented on the principles of simplicity and necessity, can descend to varied, relative and quasi-accidental truths only to the degree to which it coincides with scientific principles. Such a view must demonstrate life and all its phenomena with the help of type-constructs which are formed in analogy to general ideas, because the derivation of the particular from the general is the essence of life.

All science, and consequently all philosophy as science, is rationalistic. Its objects are things of thought (*Gedankendinge*), that is, constructions. But all philosophy, and consequently all science as philosophy, is empirical, in the sense that to be is to act, existence to be comprehended as movement and the potentiality, probability, necessity of change as the essence of actuality, the nonbeing as the truly being, in brief, dialectically. The empirical and the dialectic methods require and complement each other. Both are concerned with tendencies that meet each other, contest each other, and combine among themselves, which means that they can be understood and become known only as psychological realities. The empirical as well as the dialectic method are confirmed in general and individual psychology because we know that human will is our own will and that human life and fate is a totality consisting of individual wills, the fact that individual wills are always and inexorably conditioned by other natural phenomena notwithstanding. The facts of general psychology are manifested in an actual historical culture or civilization, that is, in human social life and its creations.

History per se, as a collection of facts, is neither science nor philosophy. But history is both science and philosophy to the extent that we are capable of discovering in it the regularities of human existence. History is a totality of events whose beginning and end are accessible only to highly indistinct assumptions. One might say that we are no more in the dark about the future than we are about the past. What we experience as present, we must first observe and attempt to understand. However, a difficulty arises at this point. A large part of the work in this field, whose phenomena are as manifest and as mysterious as those of nature itself, is diminished in its value on account of the difficulty which we encounter in approaching the subject matter in an unbiased way and according to the principles of exact theoretical procedure. The subject, that is, the researcher, is too close to the objects of observation. A great deal of effort and training, perhaps even an innate power of cold reasoning, is required in order to view the phenomena of history with the same remote objectivity with which the natural scientist views the life processes of a plant or an animal. Even a learned and critical public does not, as a rule, desire to learn how, in the view of an author, things are, have become the way they are, and are likely to develop, but rather how, in his opinion, they ought to be; for one is accustomed to observe that one's conception of what ought to be determines one's recognition of what is and has been, and even one's expectation of the future —something which, to a degree, may be unavoidable—but one does not want to admit that the deliberate avoidance of this ever present danger is the very essence of the scientific attitude. One expects and almost demands the point of view and the violent rhetoric of partisanship rather than the imperturbed logic and tranquility of the impartial observer. Consequently, in contemporary social science, and especially in Germany, what is actually a partisan controversy is made to appear as a divergence in pure theory.

One can tolerate such partisanship as a manifestation of opposed tendencies in negotiations relative to legislation and administrative practices, where the representatives of competing interests and social classes, with more or less *bona fides*, may present themselves as advocates of antagonistic convictions and doctrines which in actual fact are nothing but technological principles of politics. Occasionally, divergencies of this sort are deeply rooted in moral sentiments and subjective inclinations; but passions of this or any other kind must not be permitted to disturb the objective evaluation of facts as they are. For example, the weight which is attached to the antagonistic doctrines of individualism and socialism and to their adequacy for the comprehension of what actually occurs in modern industry and commerce appears to me comparable to what would happen if medical practitioners were to transfer allopathic versus homeopathic therapeutic methods to physiology. In view of all this, it would seem important to free onself from all foggy usages of this sort; one must take one's stand outside the phenomena and, as with telescope and microscope, observe structure and processes which inside a culture or civilization are so very different from each other, researchable in general and in large dimensions as in particular and in small dimensions, in the same way as in *natura rerum* the course of heavenly bodies and the life processes of elementary organisms. In the universal view, history is nothing but an aspect of the fate of a planet, that is, a chapter in the development of organic life made possible by the gradual cooling of the earth. In a narrower view, history is the environment and condition of my daily life; it is everything that occurs before my eyes and ears and is known as human action and interaction.

These deliberations are brought to a focus in empirical and dialectic philosophy. The necessities of life, the passions and activities of men are the same empirically and dialectically. The rational disciplines, likewise, refer generally to the same phenomena. These disciplines assume absolutely separate and rationally or arbitrarily acting individuals; they attempt to analyze, on the one hand, the ideally conceived relations and combinations of their wills and, on the other hand, the changes in material conditions that occur by means of commercial contact. The former, attentive to the formal consequences of relations between isolated individuals, is represented by pure jurisprudence or natural law; the latter, devoted to the material aspect of these relations, is represented by political economy; the former may be compared to geometry; the latter to abstract mechanics. Both approaches, if applied to social reality, are all the more fruitful, the more developed and complex human activities and relationships have become in the wake of the advancement of culture. In spite of this, "organic" and "historical" views have been put forward in opposition to both natural law and political economy. The present theory [of *Gemeinschaft* and *Gesellschaft*] attempts to absorb these theories and to keep them in a state of dependence. But in this respect, as in others, the theory has not been able to do more than indicate the variety of approaches rather sketchily. The complexities of the subject matter are overwhelming. The schemata of thought that have been proposed ought to be judged more with regard to their utility than with regard to their correctness. Only further analysis in the future will show how useful the theory really is, and I wish myself strength and encouragement to that effect. I shall not be responsible, though, both for erroneous explications and for presumably clever applications. People who are not trained in conceptual thinking better abstain from passing judgment. However, I am persuaded that such abstention, as well as any other, ought not to be expected in this time and age.

   I could write a special chapter about the influences to which I owe the furtherance of my ideas. I could mention a number of them in the field of the social sciences. Some of the more important names are occasionally quoted. I should like to mention, though, that the great sociological works of Comte and Spencer have accompanied me on my way. Both have their weaknesses, the former more in its prehistorical foundations, the latter more in its view of history; both see the evolution of mankind too onesidedly and directly conditioned by man's intellectual progress.

I further ought to mention that I have followed eagerly the efforts of Albert Schaeffle and Adolf Wagner in their important books. However, both of them, in my opinion, have not come up to the profound political insight of Rodbertus regarding the pathology of modern society, which theorists as well as legislators, all good intentions notwithstanding, can do little else but modify. I do not conceal, moreover, that my analysis received lasting impressions—stimulating, informative, and confirming—from the very different works of three excellent authors, Sir Henry Sumner Maine, Otto von Gierke, and Karl Marx. Sir Henry Sumner Maine (*Ancient Law, Village Communities in the East and West, The Early History of Institutions, Early Law and Custom*) is a philosophically trained historian of law with a very wide horizon. It is to be regretted, however, that he puts up an unjustified resistance against the inordinately informative insight with which Bachofen (*Mutterrecht*) and Morgan (*Ancient Society*) have penetrated the prehistory of the family, the community, and institutions in general; Maine's optimistic judgment of modern society I do not hold against him. I have always admired Gierke's erudition (*Das deutsche Genossenschaftsrecht, Johannes Althusius*, etc.) and respected his judgment, although regarding the economistic approach to society, which I consider most important, I have found little in his writings that I could have used in my own work. In this regard, Karl Marx is the most remarkable and profound of the social philosophers (*Critique of Political Economy, Das Kapital*). I am emphasizing Marx all the more eagerly because he has never been forgiven the supposedly utopian fantasy whose definitive refutation was his very pride. The idea which I express the following way: that the natural and for us past and gone, yet always basic, constitution of culture is communistic, the actual and the coming one socialistic, in my opinion, is not foreign to those historians who understand their own work well enough; but only the discoverer of the capitalistic mode of production knew how to make the idea thoroughly clear. I see in all this an interconnectedness of facts which is as natural as life and death. I might find life enjoyable, death regrettable: but joy and sadness are resolved in the contemplation of divine fate. I am altogether unique in my terminology and in my definitions. One thing, however, is easy to comprehend: there is no individualism in history and culture, except as it emanates from *Gemeinschaft* and remains conditioned by it, or as it brings about and sustains *Gesellschaft*. Such contradictory relation of individual man to the whole of mankind constitutes the pure problem.

3

PREFACE TO THE SECOND
EDITION OF *GEMEINSCHAFT*
UND GESELLSCHAFT

THIS TREATISE, first published twenty-five years ago, has persistently, although slowly, gained a not insignificant influence on the growth of sociological theories in the German language areas and beyond (in Italy, Denmark, Russia, and America). And this has happened in spite of very unfavorable, even adverse, circumstances. The book was meant for philosophers. Although such men as Paulsen and Hoeffding stressed its significance, and even Wundt characterized it as rich in thought—and although Ueberweg-Heinze's and Vorlaender's histories of modern philosophy considered it worth mentioning, contemporary philosophy on the whole remained silent. The new concepts here propounded were not even regarded as worthy of criticism or possible refutation.

The deeper reason for this is the relationship of philosophy to the problems of ethics. There is, to be sure, no lack of books on ethics, and in particular the three heads of the newest philosophical wisdom, whose names were mentioned, happen to have published such books, and they met with great success. These books, of course, did not ignore the problems of contemporary social life or those of the evolutionary history of mankind; they have inquired into these very seriously. Also the publications of Eucken and Barth may be mentioned in this connection.

Yet everyone knows, and knows it as a significant fact, that

Translated from Vorrede zur zweiten Auflage (1912) of *Gemeinschaft und Gesellschaft*, according to the new edition (Darmstadt: Wissenschaftliche Buchgesellschaft, 1963), pp. xxvi–xxxviii. The last two paragraphs have been omitted.

sociology is not accepted at German universities, even at a side table of philosophy; sociology is deliberately excluded from its symposia.

The cause of this exclusion is not a dislike of the name which, in fact, is used more and more by philosophers. It is an aversion to the subject; philosophy, especially the leading academic philosophy, does not feel equal to a thorough and radical treatment of these problems. The reasons for this sentiment are more than accidental.

The growth of modern philosophy has been closely bound up with the growth of the natural sciences. Two hundred years ago the Aristotelian scholastic philosophy with the corresponding theological doctrine of morality, law, and society still prevailed. The eighteenth century brought modernization, at least in Protestant Germany, as did the Revolution in France: the universities followed the bourgeois movement and its political progress.

In addition, the philosophy which attached itself to the mechanistic conception of nature included a doctrine of law and a theory of society, which, in fact, were considered the principal elements of ethics. The tendency of this "practical" philosophy was of necessity antitheological, antifeudal, antimedieval. It was individualistic and therefore, according to my terminology, associational rather than communal in nature.

The great and historically significant contributions of this philosophy are the rationalistic, "natural rights" theory of law and the "political economy" of the physiocratic school which is intimately connected with it. The latter was continued by the "classical" English school of political economy. In the preface to the first edition of this treatise I compared the former to geometry and the latter to abstract mechanics.

Both the doctrine of natural law and political economy contributed greatly to the formation of the rapidly developing modern society and the corresponding rapid growth of the modern state. Both developments took place under the banner of revolution—the great French Revolution, which destroyed the Holy Roman Empire, and the smaller revolutions which followed in France and Germany—here partly through the action of the Prussian monarchy, which was revolutionary in origin and drive; these revolutions, which continued throughout the nineteenth century, provided powerful impulses to capitalism and to a legislation which essentially served the purpose of capitalism.

All revolutions, however, evoke powerful countermovements; restorations and reactionary tendencies follow these repercussions with evident necessity.

The "restoration of the political sciences"—a designation which includes the historical school of jurisprudence—wanted to finish off the natural-rights doctrine and, above all, the rational and individualistic construction of the state as a contract. It succeeded in doing so, at least in Germany—particularly as regards the "academic" representation of these doctrines. For in England, the theory of legislation and the analytical jurisprudence of Bentham and Austin deliberately reverted to Thomas Hobbes. In the Latin countries, in Russia, and in America, the natural-rights doctrine continued more or less to be acknowledged as the liberal philosophy of law.

But even in Germany, the philosophy of law was not altogether neglected although it receded to the background as an academic discipline. The historical school which was initiated by the skeptic Hugo and the Catholic romanticist Savigny, as well as by the Protestant-conservative system of Stahl, who was of Jewish descent, reverted to Schelling's originally pantheistic but increasingly fantastic philosophy of nature. Also the philosophy of law of Krause and his more successful disciple Ahrens was pantheistic, although with a somewhat more humanitarian, cosmopolitan, Masonic bent. But the philosophy of Hegel had a much earlier and more powerful impact, even in developing and adapting Schelling's thoughts: in natural law, as expressed in "The Philosophy of Right" (1820), Hegel intends to unfold the nature of the objective spirit which, starting from free will, posits its abstract object in the law and rises to morality, the idea of which assumes reality in the state.

What made this system significant was that it undertook to conceive the modern social structures—society and the state—as spiritual-natural entities. That is, to demonstrate them as necessary, instead of simply rejecting them as being based on theoretical errors, as was the inherent tendency of romanticism and historical jurisprudence and, indeed, restorative and reactionary thought. On the other hand, in the Hegelian system—its reference to "world history" notwithstanding—all historical insight, as well as any theory of real relationship between individual will and social groups, is blotted out. Hegel's philosophy of right is not only an interpretation and construction but also a glorification of the state, and for him the state which realizes the moral idea is the existing state, that is, the Prussian state of the Restoration period which, however, cannot altogether deny its radical past. Hegel's theory of the state, therefore, is as ambiguous as this conservative absolutism; its ambiguousnes became evident in the Hegelian school of thought. The Hegelian left wing led from the officially approved, quasi-absolutist, liberalism to democratic liberalism and beyond, yet without academic acceptance.

Parallel with the decline of Hegel's philosophy runs the replacement of the old Prussian concept of the state—cloaked in the conservative *Deutsche Bund*—by the idea of German unification, which Prussian thought for a long time had held in scorn; paradoxically, as with so many historical fulfillments, it came about in such a way that the idea of the Prussian state became its forceful tool.

During this epoch philosophy lost the spiritual, that is, the ethical-political leadership of the German nation. Its fate was the fate of a liberalism, which by the epithet "national" indirectly expressed that it had chosen subordination in principle and that it considered itself less called upon to lead the more radical elements than to adjust to the reactionary ones.

This mentality remained in contact with enlightenment only in the area of the natural sciences, but even this only to the extent that it carefully avoided conflicts with official religiosity. This was especially true after 1878, when the struggle between the state and the Roman Catholic Church (*Kulturkampf*) had been abandoned and a tolerant-friendly relationship even to the papal church had been made an article of the national creed.

The deeper-lying connections with the general social development are easily discernible. The development of large-scale industry had started in Germany after 1840, in constant interaction with the neighboring countries, France and England; the labor movement and with it the socialistic-communistic doctrines knocked at the gates.

They knocked also at the gates of the universities. Economics predominantly was a practical political doctrine. It had essentially supported capitalism and free competition. "Laissez-faire" was its slogan. To be sure, German scholarship attempted to attribute to political economy a historical character and thus contributed to breaking the dogmatism of the Manchester school. Ethical motivations spoke strongly in favor of the struggling working class. Academic socialism (*Katheder-Sozialismus*) entered the stage. The name had not been invented by its supporters, but they felt confident enough to adopt it. Political economy, which had already, in England, incurred the odium of materialism—through the passionate eloquence of Carlyle and Ruskin's ethically and aesthetically tinged accusations—now appeared in the garb of German idealism, which considered it fitting to appeal primarily to the sense of duty of the propertied classes.

Foremost among the men who thus created a new social-political consciousness were scholars like Schmoller, Brentano, Knapp, each of them active and influential in his particular way. Adolf Wagner and Albert Schaeffle asserted with considerable success the demand for methodical strictness and systematic generalization in the great controversy of socialism versus capitalism (or individualism). Wagner, under the influence of a genuine socialist (Rodbertus), pleaded for the extension of governmental action, for the legal theory of all private property, for the predominance of social economic over private economic concepts. Schaeffle ventured upon a description of "The Structure and Life of the Social Organism" (*Bau und Leben des Sozialen Koerpers*) in a similar spirit, but with greater philosophical ambition. He agrees with Herbert Spencer—in fact he was strongly influenced by him—in the "organicistic" interpretation of sociology. But whereas Spencer arrived at the postulate of an administrative nihilism, Schaeffle advocated administrative universalism. Yet, both conceived of the development of civilization in the light of the evolution of all life, that is, of descendence theory, drawing conclusions which, although perhaps irrefutable in their basic elements, soon carry the mind onto the slippery ice of assumptions which hover between fear and hope. Auguste Comte, on the other hand, intended to establish sociology on a positivistic foundation, by deducing the definitive and correct structure of social life and politics from a definitive and correct theory, according to the law of evolution of human thought, the law of the three stages. A certain relationship to Hegelian dialectics is unmistakable in this. Generally, the idea of a creative synthesis of the practical tendencies of the time characterized progressive thought in the nineteenth century.

Ever since the seventeenth century, all enlightened scholars had adhered to the notion of an evolution of civilization from barbarism and savagery and of men from brutelike conditions, replacing the belief in paradisiacal origins and glories. This approach had been obscured by Restoration and romanticism and consequently had to be regained through Darwinism; yet, essentially, the approach is not so much an application of a biological theory of evolution as the latter is a generalization from it. In Hegel and Comte this essential independence from the biological theory is still clearly evident.

What distinguishes Comte is that, under the powerful influence of Saint-Simon, he takes a critical position toward progress, modernity, and liberalism. The romanticists, the defenders of tradition, of the Middle Ages, and of authority, did the same. But Saint-Simon and Comte take this position on the basis of progress, of modernity, and of liberalism. Without wanting to return to faith and to feudalism, they recognize the prevalence of a positive and organic order during the Middle Ages, and they likewise recognize the essentially negative and revolutionary character of modernity without repudiating science, enlightenment, and freedom but, on the contrary, affirming and emphasizing these all the more.

Such is also the inevitable position of socialist theories toward the problems of culture. A socialist theory, in this context, does not mean a theory making certain value judgments about capitalism, private property, and the proletariat and postulating a certain policy or even a new social order. Socialism in this sense merely means a theory which does not simply validate the implicit and accepted value judgments of liberalism and of the dominant view in social philosophy but places itself outside and above the contrast to which this view, without realizing it, remains naïvely confined.

Socialist theory takes a critical position toward things as they are and their development; that is, as a theory, it is primarily cognitive, contemplating, observing.

Herein lies the permanent significance of the *Critique of Political Economy.* For political economy in its classical form, which is retained even in its historical-ethical modification, meant to describe and establish the allegedly normal social organization, that is, one that is based on individual liberty and equality of acquired rights. In other words, it is based on the unlimited inequality of property and on the cleavage of society in the class of propertied owners, on the one hand, and that of the proletariat, on the other.

In contrast to these assumptions, the following insights are fundamentally important: (1) that most of traditional culture has existed and flourished without these allegedly normal conditions, as without railroads, telegraphs, and automatic devices; that, on the contrary, common property by all the people, at least of the land, and private property of the means of production by industrial laborers has been the rule historically, and to a large extent they still are; (2) that even "present society is not a solid crystal but an organism, capable of change and constantly in a process of change." (Karl Marx, *Das Kapital*, preface to the first edition, July 25, 1867).

Furthermore, it is an indispensable element of "scientific socialism" that political conditions, or even the scientific, artistic, and ethical tendencies, are not primarily the initiating factors of social movements, no matter how much they may be coeffective; rather, the initating factors are the crude material needs, sensations, and feelings of the workaday life which are differentiated by social conditions, and therefore shape up differently in different strata and classes; this relatively independent variable has a definite effect upon political conditions and cultural trends, even if, in turn, it is constantly promoted or retarded and always significantly modified by their influences.

Ethnological and sociological research ("from Bachofen to Morgan," as I put it in the preface of this treatise in 1887) and furthermore the rivers and rivulets of economic and legal history had combined in the direction indicated under (1). This is why I turned with rapt attention to the enlightening lectures of Henry Maine, and why I was infinitely enriched by Gierke's *Genossenschaftsrecht*, a work in which he subjects the legal as well as the cultural economic, social, and ethical aspects of cooperative institutions to a learned and profound analysis in order to explain the formation of law and to demonstrate the indissoluble relationship between law and culture.

More closely connected with my special studies was the same author's *Althusius*, through its discussion of the theories of the state that are based on natural law. For I had taken my departure from Hobbes, to whose biography and philosophy I had devoted diligent studies in the years 1877 to 1882. I owe the stimulation for these studies to Paulsen[1]; with Paulsen and with all those who know and have studied that great thinker, I admire the energy and consistency of the Hobbesian construction of the state. However, when I traced the powerful influence of Hobbesian concepts in England and elsewhere, down to the nineteenth century, I was astounded by the decline of this rationalistic and individualistic philosophy of law, which in the eighteenth century had been accepted as the pinnacle of wisdom. Really, should theories be considered worthless and meaningless, the core of which had been accepted as correct by men like Kant, Fichte, Feuerbach; theories which had been basic for all of modern legislation, for the emancipation of the peasants as for freedom of trade, by their influence on political economy and administration; theories which had been

[1]   Friedrich Paulsen, like Toennies of Frisian descent, professor of philosophy and education at the University of Berlin, was until his death in 1908 connected with Toennies in intimate friendship; cf. Olaf Klose, E. G. Jacoby, Irma Fischer, *Ferdinand Toennies-Friedrich Paulsen, Briefwechsel 1876–1908* (Kiel: F. Hirt, 1961).—Eds.

basic to the system of Bentham, so influential in England and beyond?

The void created by the elimination of the doctrines of natural law and its political philosophy had been filled by historical jurisprudence, the organic theory of the state, and a groping eclecticism, in which again and again theology emerges as the most self-assured element, and one that could be certain of the acclaim of the powers that be.

The theological foundation of law and social corporations (*Verbaende*) is historically highly significant, but otherwise scientific thinking is concerned about it only because it has to overcome it. The purely historical view operates without concepts and is therefore not knowledge in a philosophical sense. The only debatable theory of this kind is the theory of the "organic" nature of law and the state, which has been connected with theology since ancient times. Recently it has reappeared, partly in connection with the philosophy of nature to which theology soon reasserts its relationship (Stahl), but partly also in the new garb of biological analogy. This is a reciprocal matter: biology aims to explain and interpret the natural organism by means of comparison with the facts of social life, as sociology does in converse fashion with regard to "social organisms."

I never denied that some analogies of this kind are well founded. They result from phenomena which are general and common to all life, as unity in diversity, as the interaction of parts with each other and of these parts with the whole, that is, the tendencies which we recognize and designate, on the one hand, as differentiation of organs and functions, on the other hand, as the division of labor.

However, I never could make sense out of the assertion that the state, the local community, or any human cooperative "is" an organism, even if a man like Gierke affirms this conception with the whole weight of his idealism; he did it as late as 1902 in an excellent lecture on "The Nature of Human Corporations." External and internal experience, he says, suggest the assumption of effective corporative units; he adds that some of the impulses which determine our actions originate from the communities (*Gemein-*

schaften) penetrating our individual selves; that the certainty with which we feel that our self is real comprises the fact that we are subunits of more complex life units, even if we may not find these in our consciousness and can infer only indirectly, from the effects of the community within us, that social wholes are of a physical-mental nature. Consequently, Gierke assumes that the law of human corporations represents an existential system for socially determined living beings, comprising the entirety of social law, with the legal concepts of constitution, membership, juridical person, executive organ, and the act of free will, all of which creates a corporate personality—and this not by way of contract, but as a creative act of the community.

In contrast to this, I make a stricter distinction between natural corporations, the significance of which for social life is indeed eminent, and cultural or artificial units, although the latter may proceed from the former.

To be sure, the former, too, exist *in* and *for* our consciousness, but not essentially *by* our consciousness, as do the properly and truly social relationships and associations. For I claim this insight to be the fundamental sociological insight: that, aside from the real units and relationships between men, there exist units and relationships posited by and depending upon their own will, and therefore essentially of an ideally conceived character. They must be understood as created or made by men, even though, in fact, they may have attained an external objective power over the individual, a power which always is and means the power of united wills over single wills.

I saw the great meaning of rational natural law in the fact that it attempted to comprehend anthropologically the entities which so far had been interpreted predominantly in a theological manner, explaining these seemingly supernatural structures as creations (*Gebilde*) of human thought and will.

Yet I never doubted that this was not an explanation of general validity. The historical school of jurisprudence, whose favorite was the common law, and which appealed to the natural sense of justice and the quietly working forces of the folk culture (*Volksgeist*), had at that time received many new confirmations

by the extensive studies of primitive agrarian communism which
—after von Maurer, Haxthausen, and others—just then were combined by Laveleye. Other endorsements came from the interpretation of the legal structures of clans and families, whose basic
features, similarities as well as differences, were presented by comparative jurisprudence. Especially, the elements of the Aryan institutions became visible and transparent. Leist's fine works dug
deeply into the problem, to my intense satisfaction; prior to that,
The Aryan Household, by the Australian Hearne, had made a
great impression on me. Also the writings of Post were useful to
me; Lyall's *Asiatic Studies* introduced me to the still alive Indian
clan and informed me about the relation between state and religion in China. With this was combined the profound impression
of Fustel de Coulanges' *La Cité antique*, Bachofen's *Mutterrecht*,
Morgan's *Ancient Society*, and others.

All these works furthered and deepened the insight into the
distinguishing features of modern society and the modern state,
which concepts I had found propounded with absolute validity in
Lorenz von Stein's significant analysis. Added to this was the new
theory of society, which R. von Jhering outlined in his unfortunately fragmentary *Zweck im Recht*; (vol. I, 1877), a work proceeding in wholly rationalistic fashion, so that this work appeared
to me as a "renewal of the natural rights doctrine." I also considered A. Wagner's profound discourses on the philosophy of law
(in his *Grundlegung*, vol. 1, 1876) as such a renewal despite (or
because of) their state-socialistic tendencies. Already at that time
I shared that approach to practical policy, but the theoretical construction did not appear to me satisfactory in every respect.

The idea of writing the present book began to mature when in
1880 I came across a passage in Maine's *Ancient Law*, which I
have quoted in German (cf. Loomis' translation, p. 182). The
contract is there described as the typical legal transaction and as
characteristic for all rational legal relationships and these, again,
as the confirmed expressions of all rationally conceived social relationships; consequently, then, society and the state have likewise
to be conceived as contracts between individuals, that is, as based
on their free and conscious will. However, not all legal relation-

ships and corporations can be construed according to this formula, especially not the initial and continually effective familial ones. Are they nothing but enforced ("military") relations, as they appeared to Herbert Spencer? Obviously not. They, too, are affirmed by free will, even though not in the same manner as those relationships and agreements which are clearly and distinctly conceived as means for the complementary and coinciding purposes of the individuals. In which way? That was now my problem.

From here originated the theorem of *Gemeinschaft* and *Gesellschaft* and, inseparable from it, that of essential will and arbitrary will. Two types of social relationships—two types of the formation of individual wills—but both to be derived from one and the same point of departure, namely, the relation between the whole and its parts, the ancient Aristotelian contrast of organism and artifact in which, however, the artifact itself ought to be understood as in its essence more or less related either to the organic or the mechanical aggregate. All social forms are artifacts of psychic substance, and their sociological conceptualization, therefore, must be a psychological conceptualization at the same time.

Hoeffding, himself a psychologist with a bent toward sociology, attracted to it by his interest in ethics and the philosophy of religion, wrote about this book that it combined sociology and psychology in a unique way by showing how social development is essentially connected with, and has its counterpart in, a corresponding evolution of human mental faculties.[2] Wundt, who also considered these concepts worth mentioning, supposes that my distinctions of the forms of will probably correspond to "the more common one of simple or instinctual will and composite will or choice."[3] My answer (*Archiv fuer systematische Philosophie* IV, vol. 4, pp. 487 f.) was:

For me, instinctual will is only the germinal form of essential will; the latter comprises not only composite will of the most complicated kinds, but essential will unfolds and realizes its nature as *human* will only through composite will; for I never have called the "natural in-

2   Mindre Arbejder, p. 144, Copenhagen, 1899.
3   Logik II,[2] p. 599.

stincts" of men their will; rather, I conceive human will always as *appetitus rationalis*. As *appetitus*, moreover, I conceive not so much the urge (or resistance) to do something as the positive or negative attitude to the object (the *Nicht-Ich*), which forms the basis of the urge to act; this relation becomes essential will only if it is accompanied and coeffected by thought. I repeat: essential will is realized only in the composite will—for I thus interpret the whole realm of ideas of a creative personality, such as an artist or ethical genius, namely, as the expression of his essential will. But I thus interpret as will every free act, inasmuch as it evolves from the essential tendencies of the actor's mind, feeling, or conscience. Therefore: by essential will in its social determination and by *Gemeinschaft* I understand and analyze what Hegel calls the concrete substance of the *Volksgeist*, something rising so far beyond the "social instincts" that, in fact, it determines and supports the whole culture of a people.

Political economy largely leads its own life, apart from philosophy. Yet, political economy always has been searching for a relation to philosophy and often has vividly expressed the desire for a philosophical foundation. During the twenty-five years which have gone by since the publication of this book, this has become more evident than ever before. Pure sociology slowly has been raised to the rank of an auxiliary science of political economy, as was visibly documented by the founding of sociological associations in which economists have taken a leading part.

The concepts of social life, here submitted, although entirely new in their formulation, could not strike the economists as altogether strange. They were prepared for them by the contrast, with which they were familiar, between household economy (*oikos*) and money economy and some related concepts. The two leaders in German social science, Schmoller and Wagner, have both concerned themselves with this treatise, although from very different methodological viewpoints. Rationalism and the rational mechanization of production, indeed of the "world," increasingly have been recognized as the distinguishing traits of the whole modern epoch, and they have been expounded as such in several important investigations.

4

NORMAL CONCEPTS

EDITORS' NOTE. *This chapter makes it evident that Max Weber's elaboration of the ideal type as a conceptual image of essential reality has been anticipated by Toennies, both in his work on Hobbes and in passages from* Gemeinschaft und Gesellschaft *that commonly receive only a fleeting glance from the reader, if indeed they are read at all. In addition, Toennies' contention that thinking in "normal concepts," or ideal-typical thinking, is already contained in the writings of Hobbes makes it imperative to go beyond the classical economists and the Scottish moralists—not to mention Auguste Comte—in the search for the roots of sociological reasoning as we know it today.*

Two passages from Toennies' highly significant book on the life and work of Thomas Hobbes are followed by two passages from Gemeinschaft und Gesellschaft. *If seen together, they will make Toennies' position entirely clear.*

An additional piece about "Hobbes and the Zoon Politikon" *develops the concept of* Gesellschaft *out of the philosophy of Hobbes; the paper on "The Concept of* Gemeinschaft" *may be considered a companion piece.*

The Formation of Modern Theory

THE REAL significance of the philosophical disputes at the beginning of the modern epoch is the passing of the Christian world view and the rise of a new one, which seeks its basis in sci-

Translated from *Thomas Hobbes, Leben und Lehre*, 3d ed. (Stuttgart: Frommann Verlag, 1925), pp. 86–90. Statements on pp. 87–88 have been slightly abbreviated. Subtitles supplied by the editors.

entific understanding, instead of in faith, but for that very reason finds itself in opposition to all opinions that are held to be natural, traditional, and sacred.

The general character of the social change underlying these conflicts can be grasped by three criteria. The first is that the direction of aims and activities is one from the internal to the external. The second, closely related to the first, is a transition from relative rest to increased motion in greater freedom. And third, the whole spirit of the age and its outstanding thought is a progress from practice and art to theory and science.

For their relationship is that of motion to rest. Theory is motor power, destroying and building. Gradually developed out of practice yet remaining dependent on it, theory tends to become absolute and achieves a dominant position. Practice and art are firmly bound to tradition; with regard to them, thought is subject to authority and remains dogmatic, in agreement with the unlearned folk, to whom simplicity is second nature, the extant venerable, valid doctrine sacred. Theory and science search for what is new, think freely and critically, set themselves apart from common habits of thought, make everything equally an object of inquiry, fight persistence in the traditional ways, which turn as in a circle, and thus boldly progress in a straight line.

The transition from rounded restrictedness to the establishment of distant contacts, and thus, as it were, from the closed circular line to the infinite straight line, from the organic to the mechanical motion, characterizes the nature of the general economic development in this modern period. It provides for enlarged areas of commerce; subjects their inhabitants to the same laws, the same system of weights and measures, the same currency; makes the state, that is, the absolute government, the sole judge and master, who executes the administration of its own legislation as though by mechanical force. Like economic development, the state acts against folkways and all traditional authorities, hence also against the Church, whenever it keeps in line with its own motive power and its own conception. The state promotes the monetary economy, which it needs for its financial requirements and the augmentation of its power; the state, therefore, promotes not only commerce and manufacture but the sciences, which open up the treasures of the earth and set free the productivity of labor. To improve weapons technology and tooling for the construction of bridges, fortresses, and roads is the immediate aim of the state as the master of the armed establishment. As the highest judicial authority, it is clearly the concern of the state to act so that legislation be uniform, plain, and lucid, jurisdiction rapid and secure, and law and administration of justice commensurate to actual circumstances, that is, conceived rationally; its concern is to protect the life, property, and honor of everyone against everyone.

These effects of political action are fully analogous to the general social implications of the new development. Within both the political and the social systems arise the unprejudiced, even unscrupulous, rational-willed individual members of society, who aspire to power and make use of every available means for their own ends. As they are made, so they act: individual men, groups, states get more sharply differentiated, engage in competition, learn how to calculate more recklessly their own gain. It is between and beside these social actors that now steps the thinker, enlightened and spreading enlightenment. His activity, too, is one of sharp and clear distinction and combination, in its purest form calculation (arithmetic), and mathematics generally. He, too, turns from the internal to the external, from contemplation of his own self, his salvation, and his faith toward the external world, which no longer is a mere expedient but becomes a truly real object of understanding and knowledge. What the thinker perceives in the external world is no longer a state of rest as its natural condition because it was the godly and blessed condition of fulfillment: what he perceives now is nothing but motion. He analyzes the curve by a set of straight lines that are moving and of varied direction, just as he endeavors to analyze all data by their single component elements, so that what was obscure is rendered lucid, and what was confused can be sorted out. He no longer asks the purpose of things but inquires into the effective cause of all changes in location. He eliminates the variations that are due to differences in language and creed, and tries as much as possible to re-create all phenomena by their common factors. Thus he construes the mutual rights of individuals, who by origin are equal, as spheres of power established by common consent; he construes the state as the personification of this common will, which, at the same time, is an individual will.

What we here mark off conceptually is never found complete and pure in reality. But here, as elsewhere, we will have to understand reality in a first approximation and with the greatest clarity through ideally conceived schemata. The next step is to inquire into the transitions, and then into the constraints and complications.

The transitions are as fluid and varied as application and extension of rational thought are natural and necessary. Not until this method is freely used and constantly improved to reach fullest mastery are the relevant contrasts revealed.

The Logic of the Social Sciences

"I know (said Hobbes in the dedicatory letter of *De Corpore*) that that part of philosophy, wherein are considered lines and figures, has been delivered to us notably improved by the ancients; and withal a most perfect pattern of the logic by which they were enabled to find out and demonstrate such excellent theorems as they have done. . . ." Despite this acknowledgment, one cannot deny that the logic of Hobbes has some original traits. That famous dispute that arose over the logic of Aristotle: whether the universals, that is to say, concepts, or more exactly their objects, exist in the things or only in our thinking about them, is dismissed briefly. The most rigorous nominalism is to his way of thinking self-evident. Things exist naturally as single objects. We collect them, by giving them names according to their common criteria. We connect names in statements, and a statement is true whenever two names are in fact names of the same thing. Whether they are such depends on man's will, first of all on the will, or intention, of the speaker. But when many use the same name or (which comes to the same) the same language, they must be agreed about the use of names. This is particularly necessary in science, for science consists in exactly true statements. Every science must therefore start with definitions, that is, fixing the names to be used, which is an essentially arbitrary action. One may quarrel about the serviceability of a definition; its truth cannot be called in question. It is true and right for him who has made it and who, to be sure, is presumed to know what it is that he defines. If he decides and declares: this be A, that be named B, he must know the this and that,

Translated from *Thomas Hobbes, Leben und Lehre*, 3d ed. (Stuttgart: Frommann Verlag, 1925), pp. 111–14.

In an amending note to the 3d ed. Toennies elaborated on the text translated here. The first part of this note reads as follows: "The most important advance in Hobbes' theory of knowedge was that (1) his (nominalist) opinion that truth rested entirely on the combination of names and that names were arbitrary and by agreement, led him forth to (2) the insight that demonstrable truth exists only as regards those objects that we ourselves construe and create, and that in the definition of the names of such objects their origin and cause must be expressed."

whether by sense perception, or by a mere notion, or, finally, solely by a consciously conceived fiction; in one way or another he must have it before him in his mind. Hence also he who wants to converse with him.

This granted, the way the definitive names have been designed does not matter. They are nothing more than appointed signs, their value does not lie in them but in their being appointed, that is, in a clearly conscious and, as it were, contractual agreement. A thinker may settle for such signs only for himself, for his own use, just as much as several persons may settle for them for common use. But whoever wishes to be instructed must accept the definitions given him by his teacher, and he is at liberty only to examine the consistency of the conclusions, that is, of the connections between definitions and the statements derived from them.

"Thinking is computation"—all mental operations can be reduced to addition and subtraction. The nature of thought activity is not different from the combination and dissolution of images as they occur, when an object at first is recognized at a distance in vague outline, then on approach more distinctly, or, conversely, when it gradually loses its characteristic features as it disappears from view. The former is essentially the same as addition, the latter the same as subtraction.

It is a matter of regret that our philosopher, from these sound points of departure, did not penetrate more deeply into the nature of the thought process.

But in order to know something, it is necessary not only to be familiar with a true statement but to comprehend its content, that is, to recall what the names signify, to relate them to an object as well as to the impression one has of that object, since the name, if it is to make sense, must signify that impression. Scientific knowledge, for which these criteria are essential, is therefore in the last analysis based on experience and recall, just as in common knowledge with regard to facts, of which an animal also is capable. As the animal, so the human being learns by experience, which means to imagine a past event and to expect a future event. The human being, however, in doing so has the support of the system of names or language. Language is fixation in memory.

Science is, differently from all knowledge of facts, knowledge of the cause or of the origin of facts. Science, in the specific sense of a priori demonstrability, then, is possible only of the objects we understand and know for certain. If their causation is not contained in the definitions themselves, it cannot be extracted by a derivative statement. Known to us in this specific way, then, is only the origin of those objects that we make ourselves, "whose generation depends on the discretion of man himself." Objects of this kind are geometric figures, because the causes of their properties are contained in the lines drawn by us. Such objects also are right and wrong, equity and injury, "because we ourselves have created their principles, that is, laws and contracts" (*De Hom*, chap. X, 4, 5).

This is the final solution by Hobbes of a problem that deeply concerned him for a long time. He does not penetrate into the last depths of the theory of knowledge. And even at this final point he is still wrestling to give his ideas a different shape from the solution he came up with. What he was really after was the idea that pure science is possible only of pure objects of thought (*Gedankendinge*)—abstract objects and ideally conceived (*ideelle*), events—therefore also of a "body politic," which is not subject to sense perception but whose type we construct. All such objects of thought, pure and simple, are made by us, by sheer ratiocination. And those, of which we assume that they belong to the external and physical world, can in that reality be represented in a more or less perfect fashion. But what we can always do is to measure the facts of reality by those ideas of ours, even when they exist, like the state, only in our thoughts.

If such pure science is restricted to geometry and politics, as in that last-mentioned procedure, it is indeed relatively easily possible to explain the relationship, although this is somewhat more difficult in the field of politics than in geometry. But what remains problematic, because it no more than approaches the causation of real processes, is what Hobbes also demonstrates a priori in his system, namely kinematics, or the theory of motion. A discussion of this problem must be postponed to the chapter on physics.

Normal Concepts and Deviations Therefrom

The concepts of the forms and configurations of will, by and for themselves, are nothing but artifacts of thought, tools devised to facilitate the comprehension of reality. The highly variegated quality of human willing is made comparable by relating it —under the dual aspect of real and imaginary will—to these normal concepts as common denominators.

As free and arbitrary products of thought, normal concepts are mutually exclusive: in a purely formal way nothing pertaining to arbitrary will must be thought into essential will, nothing of essential will into arbitrary will. It is entirely different if these concepts are considered empirically. In this case, they are nothing else but names comprising and denoting a multiplicity of observations or ideas; their content will decrease with the range of the phenomena covered. In this case, observation and deliberation will show that no essential will can ever occur without the arbitrary will by means of which it is expressed and no arbitrary will without the essential will on which it is based. But the strict distinction between normal concepts enables us to discern the existing tendencies toward the one or the other. They exist and take effect alongside each other, they further and augment each other, but, on the other hand, to the extent that each aspires to power and control, they will necessarily collide with each other, contradict and oppose each other. For their content, expressed in norms and rules of behavior, is comparable. Consequently, if arbitrary will desires to order and define everything in accordance with end, purpose or utility, it must overcome the given, traditional, deeply rooted rules insofar as they cannot be adapted to those ends and purposes; or must subordinate them, if that is possible. Therefore, the more decisive arbitrary will or purposeful thinking becomes and the more it concentrates on the knowledge, acquisition, and application of means, to that extent will the emotional and thought complexes which make out the individual

Translated from *Gemeinschaft und Gesellschaft*, new ed. (Darmstadt, 1963), pp. 133–34 (Loomis, pp. 141–42). The translation, on the whole, follows the one by Loomis, but deviates from it in a number of instances.

character of essential will be exposed to the danger of withering away. And not only this, but there also exists a direct antagonism because essential will restrains arbitrary will, resists its freedom of expression and its possible dominance, whereas arbitrary will strives first to free itself from essential will and then attempts to dissolve, destroy, and dominate it. These relations become evident most easily if we take neutral empirical concepts to investigate such tendencies: concepts of human nature and psychological disposition which is conceived as corresponding to and underlying actual and, under certain conditions, regular behavior. Such general disposition may be more favorable either to essential or to arbitrary will. Elements of both may meet and blend in such a general disposition, and one or another may determine its character to a lesser or larger degree.

The Imagination of Types

It is form, not matter, that is enduring. In this regard, the forms of social structure and the forms of essential will are of the same kind; neither can be perceived by the senses or conceived in material categories. The form, as a whole, is always constituted by its elements, which in relation to the form are of material character and maintain and propagate themselves through this very relationship. Thus, for a whole (as enduring form) each of its parts will always be a transitory modification of itself, expressing the nature of the whole in a more or less complete manner. The part could be considered a means to the end of sustaining the whole if at the same time and while it lasted it were not, indeed, an end in itself. At any rate, the parts are similar insofar as they participate in the life of the whole, but different and manifold insofar as each one expresses itself and has a specific function. The same relation exists between a genus (*Realbegriff*) and the groups and individuals that belong to it. This is also true of the relation between individuals and every actual group encompassing them, which must be conceived as being in the process of becoming or declining or in transition to a higher form, always active, alive and changing.

Consequently, what we are taking our departure from is the *essentia* of man, not an abstraction, but the concretely imagined concept of humanity as a whole as the most generally existing reality of this kind. The next steps lead to the *essentia* of race, ethnic group, tribe, and smaller organized groupings and finally to the individual who, as it were, is the centerpiece of these many concentric circles. The more narrowing the lines of the circles which bridge the gap to him, the better is the individual understood. The intuitive and entirely mental recognition of such a whole can be facilitated and more readily grasped by the senses through the imagination (*Vorstellung*) of types each of which must be con-

Translated from *Gemeinschaft und Gesellschaft* (Darmstadt, 1963), pp. 173–74 (Loomis, pp. 171–73). Translation adapted from Loomis, but deviating occasionally. Subtitle supplied.

ceived as comprising the characteristic traits of all the specific manifestations that belong to them prior to their differentiation. Thus, the types are more nearly perfect than the specific manifestations because they embody also those forces and latent capacities which have withered away through lack of use. But, on the other hand, they are more imperfect because they lack the specific qualities which have been developed in reality. For the theory, the concrete but nevertheless constructed image of such a typical entity and its description represents the intellectual idea of the real essence of this meta-empirical whole. In actual life, however, the fullness of the spirit as well as the force of such a whole, can impart itself to its parts only through the natural gathering of the real living bodies in all their initial and actual concreteness; but it may also be conceived as embodied by selected representatives, or even by a single individual who stands for the will and existence of the collectivity.

Hobbes and the Zoon Politikon

The problem. In my monograph on Hobbes I drew attention to several points suggesting the gradual development of his famous political theory, as presented in the three consecutive works: *The Elements of Law Natural and Politic,*[1] *De Cive* (or *The Citizen*), and *Leviathan.*[2] Long before that, my *Notes on the Philosophy of Hobbes* had outlined certain aspects, which I still maintain are essential in the development of Hobbes' thinking. But on neither occasion did I examine the basis of the system of natural law, of which Otto v. Gierke[3] said that it was destined to shatter the traditional natural law doctrine. This explosive element is wrapped in the often repeated thesis that the natural condition of man was a state of war between men; Hobbes calls this, with an expression he did not invent but rendered classic, the war of all against all, while until then (as Gierke puts it) the traditional idea was that of an original community in peace and law. This traditional view fitted well with the thesis of the ancient philosopher that by nature man was an organism designed for the *polis,* that he was a *zoon politikon.* In the *Elements of Law* Hobbes did not mention this theorem. The first chapter of the second edition of *De Cive* (1646), however, which otherwise reproduces the argument of chapter 14 of the *Elements,* has in its second section a paragraph inserted, where Hobbes sets out to refute the doctrine of the *zoon politikon.*[4]

Translated from "Hobbes und das *Zoon Politikon,*" *Zeitschrift fuer Voelkerrecht* 12 (1923) : 471–88; slightly abridged. This paper appeared two years before Toennies issued the third edition of his monograph on Hobbes. References to the monograph have been changed to the third edition. The quotations Toennies selected and translated from Hobbes' writings are given in the original, although in modern spelling and punctuation.

1   Ed. F. Toennies, 1889, reprinted 1969, Frank Cass, London.—EDS.
2   Page references in the following are to the Cambridge University Press edition by Waller, reprinted 1935.—EDS.
3   Otto v. Gierke, *Johannes Althusius,* third ed., p. 300.
4   "The greatest part of those men who have written aught concerning commonwealths, either suppose, or require us, or beg of us to believe, that man is a creature born fit for society. The Greeks call him *zoon politikon.*"

In the first annotation he says: "Since we see actually a constituted society among men, and none living out of it; since we discern all desirous of congress and mutual correspondence: it may seem an amazing kind of stupidity to lay in the very threshold of this doctrine such a stumbling block before the readers, as to deny man to be born fit for society," Hobbes says. The annotation was, as one may infer as probable, called for by the fact that some of his readers had expressed in strong terms their astonishment at this paradox. Hobbes, it appears, was prepared in defense of his theory to make one important concession. It was true, he admitted, that no human being could live in solitude, nor an infant even begin to enjoy living without the aid of others, "wherefore I deny not that men, even nature compelling, desire to come together." Political societies, however—and the operative word is "political" —are not a mere matter of getting together but they are alliances, and to establish an alliance, trust and a compact are needed. Children and uneducated persons, Hobbes goes on, are unable to recognize the nature of these; those who have no experience of the damage that results from the absence of society do not know its usefulness. The ones, who do not understand what society is, cannot enter it; the others, who do not know what it is good for, do not care. "Yet have they, infants as well as those of riper years, a human nature; wherefore man is made fit for society not by nature, but by education. Furthermore, although man were born in such a condition as to desire it, it follows not that he therefore were born fit to enter it; for it is one thing to desire, another to be in capacity for what we desire; for even they, who through their pride will not stoop to equal conditions without which there can be no society, do yet desire it."

Critical evaluation. Hobbes has often been praised for the rigorous consistency in his thinking. Indeed the energy with which he knows how to pursue an argument is admirable. But how brittle at certain points those lines of thought are by which he undertook to establish that remarkable political theory of his, I have shown in my early paper of 1880.[5] In the interpretation to which my own

5   Notes on the philosophy of Hobbes I–IV, in *Vierteljahrsschrift fuer wissenschaftliche Philosophie*, 1879–80.

studies have led me, the original conception of the theory was as follows.

In the state of nature man is determined by his emotions, he is frightened of others; for various reasons men conflict with each other, and a state of war is the outcome. In the civil state it is the reasonableness of the possessor of political power which compels people to be amenable, and a state of peace is the outcome. A political power can arise out of the state of nature only in this way, that human beings, through the experience of the state of war, arrive at the insight that to end this terrible state they must create that thing called the State: its essential nature being the complete and unconditional possession and exercise of power, whether by a single or a collective person.

This fundamental idea, which ever so often recurs in his writings, is as it were pushed over by the new theory of the human mind, which Hobbes derived from his scientific and mathematical studies, more particularly from the mechanistic physiology he had learned from William Harvey. The gist of this theory is that the human will is exclusively determined by emotions, and that this determination is a necessary one: human will is emotionally egotistic, and cannot but be egotistical. Greed and fear are the dominant motives. This theory leads Hobbes to the conclusion that only out of fear, that is to say mutual fear, can society be produced. Greed will only move man to subdue and to dominate others. Mutual fear, and mutual distrust as its motive power, were also attributed to the state of nature, and therefore belonged to the general state of enmity. That, according to his own principles, it was a paradox to derive from the same source not only sociability but political power cannot have escaped the author of this theory, and it was presumably this contradiction to which some of his readers drew his attention.

In the second annotation to *De Cive* he tried to meet their objection that the effect of mutual fear must be that human beings could not even bear to look at each other face to face. He explains that by fear he means foresight or prudence, which most often leads to the attempt to cover oneself with weapons and other means of defense—"whence it happens that daring to come forth, they know each other's spirits; but then, if they fight, civil society arises from victory, if they agree, from their agreement."

This line of reasoning betrays Hobbes' perplexity. In the text to which this annotation relates, a power that quite obviously refers to the state as a fruit of victory had been clearly distinguished from the society (domination versus society): for domination, men would strive with all their greed if they were not kept in check by fear. We note that the philosopher, who places such a high value on definition, fails here to define what he means by society. Does he mean the same thing when he talks of society as such (in the text) as when he talks of civil society (in the annotation)? And is the latter, or are both, to be thought of as equivalent to the state (*civitas*)? Or, are only the "great and lasting societies" the same as the state?

The circumstantial argument. Just as Hobbes found it necessary to answer the objections about the *zoon politikon*, so it is probable that the passage in the text itself which criticized the Aristotelian concept was designed to meet an objection that had been raised in writing or in conversation, whether an objection against his English treatise (*The Elements*), known only by a few handwritten copies, or raised when he developed in conversation his theorem of the war of all against all. With such an objection he might have dealt in the following way, which would have been in line with the rest of his political theory, namely:

If your understanding of the *zoon politikon* is that it means that man cannot live without his fellowmen, one needs the other for his aid, for company, for intercourse, and for communication, then I agree wholeheartedly. The only reservation I, Hobbes, would have to make is that love and goodwill are only to a small part man's motives; it is far more his selfish motives on which the urge to be sociable and to live in society is based. But the selfish motives—and it is they that are second nature to man—lead far more often to quarrel and conflict, or even to open fighting and to war, than to harmony, obedience, and peace. Moreover, the peaceful relationships, for example, between husband and wife, parents and children, are often torn by antagonism, a domineering attitude, and revolt; in the state of nature there is no guarantee that they may last, none of permanent peace, hence no security against hostile attacks, although a sensible person who does not want to quarrel with himself must long for peace and security. ("Whosoever therefore holds that it had been best to have continued in that state, in which all things were lawful for all men, he contradicts himself." *De Cive* I 13.) This need is not satisfied by contracts, where everyone remains independent of everyone else, and which everyone may renounce whenever it seems to be to his advantage. It is not sufficient that, motivated by mutual fear, men come to hold the view that it is better to abandon the general state of war or to alleviate it by seeking allies by force or persuasion. Nor can one maintain oneself permanently by tyranny, which those who are being tyrannized will always try to escape. This need can be satisfied only by setting up a commonwealth, to whose established authorities, recognized by all as legal, those belonging together ("all") voluntarily and cognizant of its common benefits consider themselves subject. Such a commonwealth, by its very constitution, is a work of art. The civil state, which thereby is created, is an artificial state. Perhaps it can never be achieved in perfection, and it can be achieved only by cultivated people, who by restraint (*disciplina* was the term used in that first annotation) or by education (this is the term used in the English translation of that annotation) have learned to understand what is to their true advantage, and to take thought of the future. ("They therefore who could not agree concerning a present, do agree concerning a future good, which indeed is a work of reason; for things present are obvious to the sense, things to come to our reason only." *De Cive* III 31.)

As is suggested by the quotations I have given here, and as will be noted by the attentive reader, most pieces of this line of thought are really there as fragments, but in the text and the annotations they have not been properly joined. They somehow remain lopsided. Why is this? Because the final piece is missing, that is, the clear and complete distinction of a commonwealth, not just from any society or from sociability at large but as much from the "great and lasting societies," from alliances, from all forms of social life, which are possible also in the state of nature, and actually occur in it, and which as such belong to the state of nature. Again we must ask, Why?

The development of the political theory. In my book-length study of Hobbes I could show how the abstract-rationalist character of the theory was achieved only gradually in the author's thought.[6] While at the early stages he was still concerned with the basis of empirical states of governments, the definitive formation of the theory grew out of the clear insight that his problem was the abstract idea of the rational state, however far the actual so-called states did or did not measure up to the idea. I also proved that this line of thought did not reach its culmination until *Leviathan,* although even in that work there remain traces of the initial aim at a descriptive explanation of states as they are in reality. Nevertheless, it is only in *Leviathan* that the idea of the state became the main theme. In the first work, *The Elements,* it was the idea of law, in the second, *De Cive,* the idea of the citizen that was his theme. I tried to demonstrate that the progress in Hobbes' thinking was closely linked to the emphasis on the state as a person. In *De Cive,* Hobbes moves in that direction, but the theory becomes dominant only in *Leviathan.* It is there that he fully works out the proposition that the essence of "person" consists in representation (that is, of the words and actions of one or a number of persons, or of those of any other being to whom they can be ascribed, whether as something real or fictional). A natural person is the one that represents only himself, while any other person, being fictitious or artificial, represent the purposes and interests of others. In my paper of 1880 I had made it clear that the concept of the state as a work of art occurs as a dominant concept in *Leviathan,* and that it was in this work that Hobbes compared this political theory of his to architectural principles.

The question of whether man is or is not by nature social was in this context irrelevant. There is no more mention of the *zoon politikon,* and the whole discussion about the exclusively egotistical nature of man, with which it is connected, has been dropped.

---

[6]   Op. cit., 3d ed. [1925], p. 244.

True, he repeats: human beings derive no pleasure but a great deal of grief from being in each other's company when there is no power to keep them in awe. But alongside the causes of conflict in human nature—competition, distrust, vanity—he now discovers as many emotions that induce men to peace; they are fear of death, a desire for the things needed for a pleasant life, the hope of achieving these things by industry. The problem he had formerly approached from the outside, that is, of the possibility as well as the historicity of a change from a state of nature or war to the civil state of peace, thus disappears almost completely. The problem has now been internalized. The war of all against all is always latently there wherever competition, distrust, and vanity predominate; but at the same time these motives are being counteracted by other motives, and these will weigh heavier in the balance once the perfect state in keeping with the new doctrine and its rules has been achieved. Until that happens, the situation remains fraught with faults and the ever present danger of relapse. A series of the relevant passages I put together in my monograph[7] bear out this conception.

To appreciate fully this progress in the idea, it is of interest to compare the statements Hobbes makes about the war of all against all in the three consecutive versions of the theory. The emphasis on the internalized principle is perhaps strongest in one of his late writings (1674),[8] where he declared: "Most grateful, all men will agree, they must be to those who first induced them to get together (*consociarent*) and make contracts to the effect that they obey one supreme power for the sake of keeping the peace (*inter se paciscerentur*). But I would owe the next-greatest thanks to those who can persuade them not to violate their undertakings." A certain wavering is, however, discernible in his work between trust in an established supreme power, whatever its origin, on the one hand, and the stronger trust in better insight and in the effects of scientific understanding, on the other hand. Absolute power re-

---

[7]   Op. cit., pp. 244–48, p. 306, with reference to "Notes on the Philosophy of Hobbes," III, op. cit. pp. 428–56.

[8]   *Principia et problemata aliquot geometrica*, Latin Works ed. Molesworth, vol. V, p. 202.

mains decisive, but to be valid it must be based on common consent, as the expression of an enlightented view—today, one might say, of public opinion.

Argument from experience and abstract idea. The idea that the war of all against all does not reflect chiefly, much less exclusively, the position prior to the civil state, but also or even essentially the position within the civil, orderly, peaceful state is being sounded as early as *De Cive*. Not, however, in the text of that work but in the preface to the reader, which Hobbes wrote later. There he sets down, "in the first place for a principle," by experience known to all men: that the dispositions of men are naturally such that, unless they are restrained through fear of some coercive power, every man will distrust and fear the other; therefore, as by natural right he may, so by necessity he will be forced to, make use of the strength he has toward the preservation of himself:

Perhaps, you will object [Hobbes continues] that there are some who deny this; truly so it happens that very many do deny it. But shall I therefore seem to contradict myself because I affirm that the same men confess and deny the same thing? In trust I do not, but they do whose actions disavow what their words approve of. We see all countries, though they be at peace with their neighbors, yet guarding their frontiers with military installations, their towns with walls and gates, and keeping constant watches. To what purpose is all this, if there be no fear of the neighboring power? We see even in well-governed states, where there are laws and punishments appointed for offenders, yet individual men travel not without being armed for defence, nor do they sleep without shutting not only their doors against their fellow citizens, but also their trunks and coffers against those who share their abode or are their servants. Obviously, individual men as well as governments (states) who act in this fashion confess that they mutually distrust and fear each other. But in a controversy they attempt to deny it, which means that out of a desire to contradict others they end up by contradicting themselves.[9]

In a different context, in the middle of the chapter "Of the Natural Condition of Mankind," *Leviathan* (I 13) reproduces this thought. Here the inference, deduced from the passions, is being

[9]   P. 11/12 ed. Lamprecht.—EDS.

confirmed by experience. "Let him therefore consider with himself, when taking a journey, he arms himself, and seeks to go well
accompanied; when going to sleep, he locks his doors, when even
in his house, he locks his chests; and this when he knows there be
laws and public officers, armed, to revenge all injuries that shall be
done him: what opinion he has of his fellow subjects, when he
rides armed; of his fellow citizens, when he locks his doors; and
of his children and servants, when he locks his chests. Does he not
there as much accuse mankind by his actions, as I do by my
words?" Immediately following this, Hobbes concedes that "there
never was such a time, nor condition of war as this; and I believe
it was never generally so, over all the world: but there are many
places where they live so now." Renewed mention of the "savage
people in many places in America" ("except the government of
small families, the concord whereof depends on natural lust") is
followed by a sentence that is pregnant with conceptual significance; it reads, "Howsoever, it may be perceived what manner of
life there would be, where there were no common power to fear, by
the manner of life into which men that have formerly lived under
a peaceful government usually degenerate during a civil war."
The same idea occurs in the 1656 polemic about free will with the
Bishop Bramhall, where he says, "There are therefore almost at
all times multitudes of lawless men."[10]

Finally, Hobbes refers again as decisive ("though there had
never been any time, wherein particular men were in a condition of
war one against another" [*Leviathan, ibid.*] "since the creation
there never was a time in which mankind was totally without society" [Bramhall polemic]) to the example of the relations between different countries, or, more precisely, "kings and persons
of sovereign authority, because of their independency, are in continual jealousies, and in the state and posture of gladiators; having
their weapons pointing, and their eyes fixed on one another, that
is their forts, garrisons and guns upon the frontiers of their king-
doms; and continual spies upon their neighbors; which is a posture
of war." Curious the remark he adds: "But because they uphold

---

[10]   *The Questions concerning liberty, necessity and chance*, etc., No.
XIV, English Works ed. Molesworth, vol. V, p. 184.

thereby the industry of their subjects, there does not follow from it that misery which accompanies the liberty of particular men."[11]

Hobbes wrote in the years when the Thirty Years' War on the European continent was drawing to its end, and at that time, no less than today, there would seem to have been good reason to describe the misery of nations in analogy to that of individuals in a state of anarchy. In the seventeenth century, however, permanent armed forces were only in their beginnings. On the same plane as the analogy between the situation of individuals and that of countries is the viewpoint of international law as an applied general natural law, resting as it does on a rational concept of equality, with peace as its aim. Thus as early as in the last line of *The Elements*,[12] again in *De Cive* at greater length,[13] and in *Leviathan*.[14]

The old contrast superseded. There are other indications that Hobbes came to recognize his theory for what it was, that is, a strictly hypothetical scheme, or an ideal construct, invented for the comparison with the antistate.

One of his French correspondents acknowledged, under the date of January 4, 1657, the reply he had received to his own draft thesis; he wrote, "I find that you do not quite do justice to the state of nature by the illustration of the soldiers who serve on different sides, and that of the masons who work under different architects."[15] I would explain this as follows. Hobbes wanted to indicate by these illustrations that wherever people are not subject to the same regimen, and do not live under the same constitution, there is in fact something analogous to the state of natur⟨ —they do not want any dealings with each other, they remain strangers

11   *Leviathan* I 13, op. cit., p. 85.
12   ["For that which is the law of nature between men and men, before the constitution of the commonwealth, is the law of nations between sovereign and sovereign, after."] *Elements* II 10.10, p. 151, ed. Toennies.
13   *De Cive* XIV 4, p. 158.
14   *Leviathan* II 30, p. 257.
15   From these letters—Hobbes's own letters seem to have been lost, at least, they have as yet not been traced—I made some extracts in 1878 at the Hardwicke hunting lodge in Devonshire where Hobbes died on December 4, 1679. They are kept with some other remains of his in a file "The Hobbes Papers."

to each other, and are potentially opposed to each other. Whether the examples he gave were a happy choice, I would doubt with his French correspondent. It is possible that Hobbes replied once more, and tried to make his meaning clearer. He may in such a letter even have reverted to the question of the *Zoon Politikon*.[16] That he did eventually come up with a different view, as far as the Aristotelian formula is concerned, seems to me cannot be doubted. Such insight was bound to come to him the more he grew conscious of "the state as a work of art"—this, two centuries later, was going to be theme and title of the first part of Jakob Burckhardt's great work on *The Civilization of the Renaissance in Italy*—and it was this very conception to which he was led when he reexamined, in *De Cive*, his own introductory disquisition. Admittedly, the thesis of the ancient Greek philosopher, according to which the *polis* existed *physei*, and man was *physei* a being that was made teleologically for the *polis* (this being the true meaning of the famous sentence), cannot apparently be reconciled with the idea of a work-of-art state. I say "apparently," for the truth of the matter is that the remarks in *Leviathan* I quoted earlier show how Hobbes had indeed widened the conception by combining in his own theory the empirically descriptive study of existing countries as imperfect and faulty edifices with the pure theory of the topic as such and the rules of a consistent political architecture.

The result of this was that he could entertain as a possibility a progressive approximation of the real to the ideal—"Time and industry produce every day new knowledge . . . long after men have begun to constitute commonwealths, imperfect and apt to relapse into disorder, there may principles of reason be found out, by industrious meditation, to make their constitution (excepting by external violence) everlasting."[17] Compare with this the re-

---

16 Of the numerous letters he wrote to France some may quite possibly still be preserved in provincial libraries. I have searched the libraries in Paris, and not without success, see my "Seventeen Letters to Samuel Sorbière" etc. in *Archiv fuer Geschichte der Philosophie*, vol. III, 1898, pp. 58–71 [and the reprint by G. C. Robertson in *Mind*, vol. XV, pp. 440–47].
17 *Leviathan* II, chapter 30, p. 244, which I quoted in full in my monograph, 3d ed., p. 232.

mark that he was "at the point of believing this my labour as use-less as the commonwealth of Plato," yet recovered some hope "that at one time or another this writing of mine may fall into the hands of a sovereign, who will . . . convert this truth of speculation into the utility of practice."[18]

In a general sense, Hobbes could have said that the ancient antithesis of things existing *physei* and of things existing *nomo* or *thesei* was not absolutely valid; it was valid, in that the thinking about things existing *nomo* or *thesei* was a construction, that is, an abstract concept. But in reality art and the exercise of art belong to human nature, which by its very capacity for abstract thought dis-tinguishes itself from animal nature.[19] In the political theory itself, however, this view was not decisively followed up by Hobbes. The original conception proved too strong, as is particularly evident in his discussion about social animals (bees and ants), which occurs in all three versions. Each time Hobbes insisted, apart from other circumstances that distinguish human beings and counteract their natural harmony, that in the last analysis the agreement among those animals was natural but among men "by covenant only, which is artificial."[20] Had Hobbes at this point added words to the effect that the artifact based on reason is for man, because he is capable of reasoning, as natural as is instinctive or emotionally conditioned social behavior for certain animals, he would have ex-pressed only what fully accords with his whole way of thinking.

More clearly than in the discussion about social animals, this way of thinking comes to the fore in the last of Hobbes' principal works, *De Homine* (1658). Here he lists the most important ad-vantages man reaps from being endowed with speech. They are: first, the ability to count (which is considered at some length); second, the ability to advise and instruct; and third,

That we can give orders and understand orders, is a benefit of speech, and a very great one at that. Without this, there would be no society

---

18   Op. cit., II, chapter 31 [p. 268, Cambridge ed.—EDS.].
19   "We speak of art as distinguished from nature, but art itself is natural to man," as Adam Ferguson declared in *An Essay on the History of Civil Society*, 1767. [ed. Duncan Forbes, Edinburgh 1966, p. 6.—EDS.]
20   *Leviathan* II, chapter 17, p. 118.

among men, no peace, and consequently no high culture; but savageness, first, then solitude, and caves for dwelling-places. For although some animals have got some states (*politiae*) of their own sort, these are not adequate for the good life; they do not therefore deserve being considered here, and they are contrived by animals that are defenceless and have no great needs; man is not among their number, and as swords and shields, the weapons of man, are superior to those of animals, their horns, teeth and claws, so is man superior to bears, wolves and snakes. They are not greedy beyond their immediate hunger and savage only when provoked, but man surpasses them in his greed and savageness, he is famished even to the point where he strives to still his future hunger. From which it will be easily understood how much we owe to speech. By means of speech we socialize and, reaching agreement by means of contract, live securely, happily and in a refined manner; in other words, we are able to live because we will it so.[21]

But, this line of thought continues, speech is also afflicted by evil consequences. It is due to speech that man can err more and worse than other animals. Furthermore, he can lie and arouse enmity in the minds of his fellowmen to the conditions of society and peace; animal societies are not exposed to this. In addition, man can repeat words he has not understood, assuming he is saying something when in fact he says nothing. Finally, he can deceive himself with words, which again the beast cannot do. "Therefore, by speech does man become not better, only more powerful."[22]

Individualism. No trace whatever can be found in Hobbes of an idea which is more appropriate for us today than his view of the original state of life, or the state of nature hidden beneath civilization: the idea, that is, that the modern, urbanized, *Gesellschaft*-like civilization, of which he knew only the beginnings, represents a concealed war of all against all. Yet this is in fact the real substance of his theme, even if in abstract expression and in form of a model, which can claim to be conceptually as accurate as the statement that our planet is a sphere. "Individualism" has often been described as the very nature of our age, and hardly ever in such depth of historical insight as in Burckhardt's *Civilization of the Renaissance in Italy*. It is this individualism that as an eternal truth

[21]   *De Homine* X 3, Latin Works ed. Molesworth, vol. II, p. 91.
[22]   Ibid.

was made the foundation of Hobbes' system of political philosophy. The generally observable conflict among individuals is indeed the consequence of their unconditional self-affirmation. Our more recent times, with their unfettered economic competition, their class struggles, their contests between political parties, and their civil wars, have more and more revealed that Medusa's head (to borrow an expression of Marx)[23] that hides itself under the veil of the presumably highest achievements of civilization, such as the triumphant progress of technology, of worldwide communications, and of science.

[23]   Preface to the first edition of *Das Kapital*.

The Concept of Gemeinschaft

For a long time it has been accepted as an achievement of German scientific endeavor that it supplemented the concept of the state, which from of old had occupied the central place in the philosophy of law, by that of society. The essential merit for this is ascribed to Hegel, who, in his lectures on *The Philosophy of Right*, places "civil society" as the second link—the antithesis—between the family and the state, making these three combined phenomena, which reach consummation, of course, in the third, the realization of right (or law) as the moral order (*Sittlichkeit*). In attaching to society the adjective "civil," he takes up an expression which had become current in the French and English literature of the eighteenth century—for instance, through Ferguson's *Essay on the History of Civil Society* (1767)—although no attempt had yet been made to render this expression as a concept. Hegel had an eminent successor in Lorenz Stein, who (for the first time in 1849) expounded "the concept of society and the principles of its transformation" as an opening chapter to the *History of the Social Movement in France since 1789*. He wanted to show in this work that the constitution and administration of a state are subject to the static elements and dynamic movements of the social order. The economic order, he said, becomes, by means of the division of labor, a social order, comprising man and his activities; and the social order, in turn, through the family, becomes a lasting order of the generations. Within the social order, moreover, the community of men is the organic unity of their lives; "and this organic unity of human life is human society." Stein goes on to argue that the content of the life of the human "community" (*Gemeinschaft*) must be a continuous struggle between state and society, the state, being, to him, the "community" of men asserting itself, as if it were a personality, in will and action. The principle of the state rests with its task of developing

---

Translated from "Der Begriff der Gemeinschaft," *Soziologische Studien und Kritiken* 2 (1925) : 266–76; the latter part of this paper, about one fourth of the whole, has been omitted.

itself and, for the sake of that self-development, to strive with its highest power for the progress, wealth, vigor, and intelligence of all individuals encompassed by it. The principle of society, on the other hand, is interest, hence the subjection of individuals by other individuals, that is, the fulfillment of the individual by means of the dependence from it of the other individual.

This theory, which Stein applied and unfolded ingeniously, won its most important follower in Rudolf Gneist, whose influence helped to shape the constitutional and administrative law of Prussia and of the new German Reich. In his treatise on the *Rechtsstaat,* Gneist sets out by acknowledging that the contemporary world, with its deep antagonisms, can be understood only on the ground of *Gesellschaft.* "Science, too," he says, "is compelled to acknowledge that the abstract 'I' from which the older natural law constructed the state is not a part of the real world; that in reality every people is divided and articulated according to the possession and acquisition of the external and spiritual goods which mankind is ordained to acquire and enjoy—an articulation which I comprise, in this treatise, in the concept of "society" (*Gesellschaft*)." And, in a note, Gneist makes reference to "Stein's masterly explication," which, he adds, was of decisive importance for his own treatment of English constitutional history.

If the concepts "state" and "society" are placed side by side, the first observation to which the juxtaposition gives rise is that while the latter term merely denotes a collectivity of men interrelated in manifold ways, the term state, whatever its other connotations, indicates at any rate an association—a union or, as is customary to say nowadays, an organization—to which so and so many persons belong who, to begin with, live next to each other in a "state territory." Against the theory of modern natural law according to which the state proceeded, like another association (*"Sozietaet"*), from the will of the individuals, the historical school of jurisprudence had revolted by declaring that the state was something that had grown, something organic, something original in its core, and not at all brought into existence by contract. This polemic against the natural law theory resulted from a misunderstanding of that doctrine and, at the same time, from a conservative (or restorative) intention to impede the activity of the state that arose from the French Revolution as well as from the princely absolutism that had preceded it and whose avocation and fitness for legislation and codification were denied by the outstanding founder of the historical school (Savigny).

Nevertheless, it must be granted and understood that another construction of the state, as well as of other associations, is possible than that which represents it as a means for the common ends of a great many individual persons; even if it were thought of as a means, it must not necessarily be thought of as an isolated, mechanical means, but may also be an end, so indissolubly intertwined with the common ends of a multitude of individuals that it in fact expresses them by and in itself. For an association may, by its "members," not only be called but also conceived of as a "corporation," essentially independent from the members, as parts, and—while its component parts change, and through that very change—maintaining itself as a living entity or organism. And just as in the case of an association, a mere relationship of two or more men will appear one way if these men are thought of as essentially strange to each other but meeting in their wishes and interests and entering into an exchange relationship for mutual advantage—and another way if it is thought that there is something that they have in common to begin with from which mutual services result as a consequence. The thing they have in common may be, for instance, common descent; but also a common end such as the founding of a common household, that is, if the latter is thought of not as an object of wishes that are incidentally coinciding but as a common incumbency, a duty, and a necessity. In the same manner, all social values which the individual shares either by unreservedly feeling and thinking them as belonging to him or by a mere relationship of high valuation may be thought of in two different ways: either as objective or, in the perfect case, sacred values which exist and persist independently from the evaluating participant although the participant shares in their enjoyment as a companion (*Genosse*); or as caused by the individuals who severally recognize and posit the value. In the first case, the common value is to be conceived of as an indivisible totality or at least one which, if divided, flows back again into one whole. In the second case, the common value is to be conceived of as composed of the contributions of individuals, always remaining divisible, a mere quantity of means intended for a more or less limited end.

I thought it necessary to state that all social relationships, social values, and social unions and associations, insofar as they exist for their subjects—the social men—are created, posited, or instituted by the will of the latter, and that it is this psychological conditioning which constitutes their essence because, in this manner, they are seen, as it were, from within. This stands in contrast to Stein's definition of the concept of society, or *Gesellschaft*, ("the organic labor in human life"), which remains stuck to the outside of things. Moreover, community, or *Gemeinschaft*, with Stein, is merely an expression meaning that "the whole exists for the sake of the parts." Consequently, he calls society (*Gesellschaft*) and the state "the two great elements of *Gemeinschaft*." (*System der Staatswissenschaft*, vol. 2.)

In contradistinction to this usage, the foremost principle for the subdivision of the social entities must be found in the differing quality of the human will which is contained in them and, indeed, is the maxim of their existence. This becomes more evident if the noun "will," which is a *perfectum*, is replaced by the verb "to affirm," which is in the present mode, so that we may speak of the affirmation of social relationships, social values, and social associations. The sharpest contrast, then, arises if affirmation of a social entity for its own sake is distinguished from an affirmation of such an entity because of an end, or purpose, which is extraneous to it. I call a will of the first kind *essential will*, and a will of the second kind *arbitrary will*. Evidently, this view differs strongly from a theory which is sometimes encountered and which distinguishes "involuntary" from willed or voluntary unions, associations, and so on, and as the former regards, by a definition which is merely external, those which did not originate from a specific decision of the individuals concerned and therefore can be said to be "without will," as, for instance, the family into which one is born. In fact, however, it may be supposed to be the normal case that a man affirms his family with all his heart, so that he posits it by his

essential will, precisely as he posits by his arbitrary will a commercial company, which has the limited purpose of maintaining
the value of an investment and deriving the highest possible profit
from it.

Further, this view in no way coincides with that which conceives of "spontaneous organizations" as originating from feeling
and instinct. In the first place, I do not emphasize the genetic aspect, but a lasting inner relationship. For instance, a marriage—
to consider a very individual relationship—may be entered into
very enthusiastically, for its own sake, and yet after a short time
be maintained and affirmed by both spouses simply with a view to
"what people say," for the sake of social respectability, as a means
to maintain one's position and the position of one's children in
society: in other words, as a *marriage de convenance*. Second, my
synthetic concepts of essential will and arbitrary will do not correspond to the distinction of instinctual and volitional actions, as
these terms are used by Wundt and others. Essential will definitely
comprises what psychologists would call volitional actions inasfar
as they affirm means and ends as an organic whole, that is, as a
belonging together. The concept of arbitrary will arises, as it
were, only when and to the extent that means and ends become
separated (become alienated from each other), to the point even
of becoming outright antagonistic to each other. A perfect arbitrary
will affirms a relationship, even in spite of a definite aversion to it
—that is, exclusively for the sake of the desired end. For instance,
a hike in the mountains, the aim of which is to reach a high sum-
mit, I will affirm and welcome as a whole thing, despite great difficulties and labors. But I will consent to a train trip from Eutin to
Berlin—especially under the conditions obtaining in 1919—only
for the sake of its aim and end. I will make this decision reluctantly insofar as I am thinking of the trip itself, which is envisaged
merely as the unavoidable means for reaching my goal. As a rule,
some of the pleasurable connotations of the end will be communicated to the means, just as the displeasure caused by the actor to
others reflects back to the actor himself; but the more cold reasoning strives to reach the end, seeking it unconditionally, the more
will the reasoning human being become indifferent against unin-

tended consequences and incidental phenomena connected with its pursuit—both in concrete reality and in anticipatory thought; he will become indifferent to his own immediate displeasure and even more so to the displeasure caused to others, and to the compassion which may stir in him. All these relationships are conceived of still more generally, if the more general concepts of affirmation and negation are applied. For precisely as the person motivated by arbitrary will disregards inner displeasures, so will he disregard other forms of inner negation; for instance, he will use words which he cannot truly affirm or which he even knowingly negates; in other words, he will deliberately tell an untruth calculated to deceive others.

On the other hand, volitional acts, including words, remain within the meaning of the concept of essential will, if these words are spoken in full conviction, even though they may at the same time be used with a view to gaining some end. Likewise, a relationship which is affirmed through love or affection, or because it has become dear through custom and habit or in the line of duty, remains within the concept of *Gemeinschaft* (community) even though it may at the same time be thought of and appreciated in full recognition of its usefulness to me, the affirmer.

The concept of community in this subjective sense must be strictly distinguished from the concept, or, rather, notion, which common speech intends in combinations such as folk or ethnic community, community of speech, community of work (*Volksgemeinschaft, Sprachgemeinschaft, Werkgemeinschaft*) and so forth. Here, reference is only to the objective fact of a unity based on common traits and activities and other external phenomena. Stein took his misconception of community from this common usage. To be sure, bridges exist between this external (objective) and the internal, or intimate, (subjective) concept of community which I am using and which, likewise, has affinity to common usage. All forms of external community among men comprise the possibility, even the probability, of an internal, or intimate, community (communion), and may thus be conceived of as a potential *Gemeinschaft* of those united in it. Thus, the more language rises into consciousness as an element constituting a bond of minds and as a value which is held in common, the more will a linguistic community, instead of being a mere external fact, become a significant and unifying relationship. The same is true of the community of descent, which is closely akin to, though not fully identical with, the community of language; true, that is, of the folk community or the nation. In this sense, with which I agree, it was said that on August 4, 1914, the German people became a community. It is somewhat different with a religious community, which, to be sure, can be considered merely in its external shape or form but which, essentially at least, intends and ought to be an intimate community or communion. For it is its very essence that men who pray to, and conceive of, the same God feel bound to each other and that they wish to be bound to each other by a common consciousness. This is especially so if they conceive of themselves as members of a mystical body, the Church, and still more so if they believe that they partake of and receive into themselves the divine head of the Church by participating in a "communion," whereby they enter into a suprasensual-sensual bond with that divine head, and hence with each other.

I proposed three kinds of internal, or intimate, community, distinguished by the familiar terms kinship, neighborhood, friendship. The first two of these frequently and simultaneously designate merely external facts or things, which, indeed, they often are.[24] One can say that the idea of community (*Gemeinschaft*) attains fulfillment in friendship, in contrast to the counterconcept of hostility, even though it should be noted that no type of inner community excludes hostile feelings and conduct of those associated in it as factual phenomenon. A relationship, for instance, a marriage, may in the consciousness of those associated in it exist as an essential community and yet often be disturbed by such feelings or conduct. To be sure, they corrode the community and may dissolve it internally, although it may continue to exist externally, even though confirmed by the will and consent of those associated in it. It has then become a societal (*Gesellschaft*-like) relationship in the sense mentioned above. In order to supplement what we

24   Also, friendship, so called, in the superficial sense of acquaintance, would have to be considered as a predominantly external relationship.— EDS.

have said of communal relationships with names of true comunal unions, I am adding here the terms family, local community (*Gemeinde*), and fellowship (*Genossenschaft*).

Parallel with these divisions and permeating them there is, finally, a distinction by which I discern, as both foundation and expression of *Gemeinschaft*, being together (*Zusammenwesen*), living together (*Zusammenwohnen*), and working, or acting, together (*Zusammenwirken*). If, in contrast to linguistic usage, being (*Wesen*) is here used as a verb, this is done in order to express that through the combination with the term together what is called being becomes an activity, a psychological process. Being together means belonging together raised to consciousness, living together means the affirmation of spatial proximity as precondition of manifold interactions, and working together means these interactions themselves, as emanating from a common spirit and an essential will. Being together, so to speak, is the vegetative heart and soul of *Gemeinschaft*—the very existence of *Gemeinschaft* rests in the consciousness of belonging together and the affirmation of the condition of mutual dependence which is posed by that affirmation. Living together may be called the animal soul of *Gemeinschaft*; for it is the condition of its active life, of a shared feeling of pleasure and pain, of a shared enjoyment of the commonly possessed goods, by which one is surrounded, and by the cooperation in teamwork as well as in divided labor. Working together may be conceived of as the rational or human soul of *Gemeinschaft*. It is a higher, more conscious cooperation in the unity of spirit and purpose, including, therefore, a striving for common or shared ideals, as invisible goods that are knowable only to thought. Regarding being together it is descent (blood), regarding living together it is soil (land), regarding working together it is occupation (*Beruf*) that is the substance, as it were, by which the wills of men, which otherwise are far apart from and even antagonistic to each other, are essentially united.

With respect to being together, the deepest contrast among human beings, especially with respect to its psychological consequences, is the biological difference of sex; as a consequence, men and women always part with each other while at the same time they are attracted to each other; the principle of what is eternally female (*das Ewig-Weibliche*),[25] or the principle of motherliness, is the root of all being together. Men depart more readily and farther from the natural foundation of essential will and *Gemeinschaft*. Correspondingly, women persist more readily in the forms of understanding, custom, and faith, which are the simplest forms of communal will; men find it easier to pass on to those of contract, statute, doctrine as the simple forms of societal will. As men and women live together, so is the same kind of interdependence required for all forms of communal will. This last observation also applies to the discussion that follows.

The deepest contrast with respect to living together is that indicated by the concepts of country and city. This contrast is akin to, and of a similar kind as, the aforementioned one. The countryside, not unlike women, abides in the forms of understanding, custom, and faith, while the city develops the forms of contract, statute, and doctrine. But the city remains surrounded by and, in a way, dependent upon the country, as the male does upon the female. The city emancipates itself from the countryside the more pronouncedly the more it becomes a metropolis (*Grosstadt*).

Again, a similar deep contrast is discernible with regard to working together. This is most plainly indicated by the traits of poverty and wealth. In the present context, however, I want to relate it particularly to the spiritual-moral area, in which it appears as the contrast of the uneducated mass of the common people and their educated rulers. The common people (to use this term for brevity) remain more faithful to understanding, custom, and faith, and are caught in or bound to these forms; those that are educated are more dependent upon contract, statute, doctrine, and these forms, in turn, require education as a necessary condition more than the former do. But also the relation of the essential dependence of the educated strata upon the common people resembles the dependence of city upon country and of men upon women.

As the sexes depend upon living together in a nexus of kin relations, through marriage and the family, so stand country and city, the mass of the people and the ruling class, in mutual de-

25   The expression is taken from the last act of Goethe's *Faust*.—Eds.

pendence upon each other. Especially, country and city need to live in peaceable neighborliness; the mass of the people and the ruling class, in addition, must live in a kind of friendship and companionship of mutual trust. Intensive forms of communal living together resemble a companionship in a common struggle.

In all these relationships, there are many other important differentiations besides those mentioned, partly paralleling them, partly mingling with them.

In being together, there is not only the contrast of the sexes but also, in a less pronounced way, that of the ages. In this respect there is a certain duality of young and old, especially regarding children, or sexually immature, and adults, or sexually mature persons.

In living together, there is the differentiation not only of city and country but already of the more densely populated countryside and a widely dispersed population; consequently, of the rural folks of the plains from that of the mountains, of that of the fertile marshes (*Marschen*) from that of the high and dry land and the heath (*Geest* and *Heide*).[26] Likewise, the big city stands in contrast to the small country town, and so does the big city, or metropolis, to country and small towns taken together; and even more so contrasts the capital city to the provincial towns and cities, and the cosmopolitan megalopolis to all other towns and cities. Furthermore, whole regions and areas differ in the same respect, and so do, under the influence of different geographic and cultural conditions, entire ethnic groups. All these differences partly are parallel to and partly overlap the differences between country and city.

In working together, there is—comparable to the differentiation between the mass of the people and the ruling class—the differentiation of a variety of occupational groupings within the people and of estates (*Staende*) within the ruling stratum. As to the people, we have the distinction of menial laborers and traders, and within the laboring classes there is the distinction of agricultural and industrial labor (the crafts). As to the ruling stratum, there are

26   These terms refer to ecological regions in Schleswig-Holstein.— EDS.

different dominant estates, especially the ecclesiastic and the secular estate. Within the secular estate, finally, there is an older substratum, essentially tied to landed estates, and a younger substratum, essentially powerful through the disposition over capital.

II. Elaboration of Concepts

EDITORS' NOTE. *Between the years 1899 and 1924 Toennies clarified the concepts which he had first formulated in* Gemeinschaft und Gesellschaft. *The earliest of these pieces,* Prelude to Sociology, *is nearest in time and content to the book that made its author famous. The second, a paper read before a gathering of the Gehe Foundation in 1907, presents the most mature formulation of Toennies' basic ideas. The earlier St. Louis Exposition paper of 1904,* The Present Problems of Social Structure, *bears a certain resemblance to it, yet differs because it was written in response to a specific assignment. Inasmuch as the paper addresses itself to an American audience, Toennies is intent to draw attention to the then prevailing differences between Germany and the English-speaking countries with regard to the theoretical approach to social studies; his references to Spencer and Morgan are particularly noteworthy.*

Part II concludes with the paper The Divisions of Sociology *(the Naples paper) of 1924. This paper foreshadows the major work that Toennies published in his later years,* Introduction to Sociology *(1931).*

5

A PRELUDE TO SOCIOLOGY

THE UNITY of a number of human beings, like every unity, can be conceived in two ways. Either it exists prior to the multiplicity of individualities which is derived from it, or the multiplicity is earlier and unity, or union, is its creation. In observable nature, the first case marks the essence of an organism, the second denotes the inorganic aggregate as well as the mechanical artifact. In the first case, unity is a reality, it is the thing in and of itself; in the second case, unity is of an ideal nature, that is, conditioned by human thought; and thought, in turn, whether on the basis of sensual perception or not, arrives at the image and finally at the concept of the totality which we call unity. Inasmuch as, moreover, totality, or a whole, is composed of its parts, a unity can, and perhaps must, be thought of as the creation of the parts; this remains true even in the event that the composition of the parts has been forced ino being by human will. The cooperation of the parts in the same direction and in uniform motion in the latter case is the purpose and in the former, at least, the consequence of the composition of the whole. This direction or motion, then, already something immaterial, is the common element, it is part and parcel of objective reality, and basic for thought.

The same contrast is repeated when unities, or totalities, are considered which as such are in no way initially given for the per-

Translated from "Zur Einleitung in die Soziologie," *Soziologische Studien und Kritiken* 1 (1925) : 65–74; the last paragraph has been omitted, and the notes have been abridged.

ception of the senses (because they are nothing but a multiplicity of similar objects) and therefore require a particular energy of thought to be recognized and thereby to gain a quasi-objective existence. Such is the nature of the general (*universale*), which relates to particular and individual things as a whole does to its parts. It is in this sphere that the famous controversy between realism and nominalism took place, the complete disappearance of which (as a result of the total victory of nominalism) is in the highest degree characteristic of the scientific, and especially the mathematical-physical or mechanical orientation of all modern philosophy. Yet, the truth of realism deserves to be restored. To be sure, it would seem that this truth has lost its last refuge on account of the critique of the concept of species in the theory of evolution, but actually it receives new life from a deeper biological view: for insight into the origin of the species is no detriment to its existence, as it is not detrimental to that of any higher or local group; and in its growth and its acquisition of new abiltiies and loss of those that are no more serviceable, as well as in its progressive differentiation, each species shows that it is alive and active; no less than any individual organism that maintains its essence despite changing parts and by means of the change of its parts.

This treatise pursues the same cardinal antinomy in different, although already indicated, areas. The social unity of men can be understood only psychologically. As a material thing, it must be conceived of in analogy to the individual will, which, however, can borrow its own substantial essence only from the analogy to a material object. On the other hand, even the enduring form of the organic body is something substantial which is accessible only to thought and belongs to psychic as well as physical reality.

At any rate, the social will, or body, is a whole whose parts are human individuals, that is, beings endowed with reason. But this whole, too, either exists prior to the parts or is composed of them. All forms of one kind I call *Gemeinschaft*, all those of the other kind *Gesellschaft*. The germinal forms of *Gemeinschaft* are motherly love, sexual love, brotherly and sisterly love. The elementary fact of *Gesellschaft* is the act of exchange, which presents itself in its purest form if it is thought of as performed by individuals who are alien to each other, have nothing in common with each other, and confront each other in an essentially antagonistic and even hostile manner. Both kinds of unions are universal, and both in a twofold sense. Concerning *Gemeinschaft:* (A) by means of the unity of the species, all men are "brothers" and united through a common ancestor (Adam). However, this idea gains real importance only as restricted to certain peoples or groups of peoples and in connection with religious ideas; (B) the real and most intimate communal relationships are secured as general and necessary by the nature of man. Concerning *Gesellschaft:* (a) as anybody can be anybody's enemy, so can anybody trade with anybody and enter into a contract with him; (b) for this reason an association which, developing from this principle, negates hostility must finally embrace and have as its subjects all men. It is evident that the ideas (A) and (b) converge, while those of (B) and (a) repel each other.

The conceptual constructions are entirely separate and mutually independent. The theory of *Gemeinschaft* is, in the main, a genetic classification of its forms, of which in an ascending series the types of household, village, and town are most noteworthy. The scientific value of this classification is not diminished by the fact that it has been the basis of the social-philosophical discussions of the sages of ancient Greece while it has been neglected in recent times. Indeed, however intricate or confused the political forms of life may be, the above mentioned social, chiefly economic, units are everywhere clearly discernible. They are natural units, or living organisms in a very specific sense, which will be indicated presently. Their becoming and their decline are the real content of cultural history.

The theory of *Gesellschaft*, on the other hand, is purely a matter of thought (*ein reines Gedankending*), a conceptual construction, connected exclusively with the fact and the necessity of existence upon this earth. But as this concept strives toward realization, it finds itself limited by historical conditions. Its first enactment is in the city, dominated, as it is, by the exchange of merchandise whose subjects are free individuals; separated from the material matrix of communal life and thought, they pursue their own ends.

Then follow associations of cities, and of cities and regions, finally enlarged in ever widening circles to *territories*. The process of *Gesellschaft*, entailed in the principle of exchange, primarily denotes the predominance of men who conduct exchange for its own sake and on the basis of their particular skill; that is, the predominance of the commercial class, whose power consists in money as a generalized means of purchase. Further, labor itself—as industry —becomes a branch of commerce, which in industry can most purely free its basic concept, the self-utilization of money, from all accidental conditions (purchase of labor, incorporation of labor in commodities, sale of commodities according to their value). Here we are confronted by the "social question," that is, a condition which demands the resolution of an enigmatic contradiction. In *Gesellschaft*, all individuals are equal insofar as they are capable of engaging in exchange and entering into contracts: that is its concept. The trading, lending, enterprising individuals, as capitalists, are the masters and active subjects of *Gesellschaft*, using the working "hands" as their tools. This is the reality of *Gesellschaft*, inasfar as it develops in the direction indicated; the question as to whether, to what extent, where, and when *Gesellschaft*, and especially this specific condition in *Gesellschaft*, actually exists, must be left to a more specific investigation and analysis.

The content and intent of this theorem can be understood in its entirety only by means of its historical and polemic relations and references. In the book *Gemeinschaft und Gesellschaft* (1887) these relations and references had to be assumed as being present in the reader's mind, so that the book's doctrinal character could be preserved. But there is some reason to suspect that among those who found it worth reading only few actually were sufficiently conversant with the present as well as the past state of doctrines in the philosophy of law and society to be able to notice what was new and contrasting in it. The author therefore believes that he should indicate these points more explicitly than he has done in the preface to *Gemeinschaft und Gesellschaft*.

More recent authors, in their dependence on Hegel, under whose influence all the springs of tradition had been buried, considered it a miraculous achievement on their part to have established the concept of society beside that of the state. Actually this concept of society is nothing but a new version of the old concept of the state of nature (*status naturalis*), which always had been thought of as persisting underneath the political state. The term civil society, too, was not at all unfamiliar in the three principal European countries during the last quarter of the eighteenth century; it was well known that it was civil society that had rebelled against the state in the great revolution and attempted to create a new state. Both the name and the thing subsequently passed to the socialists as heirs of the revolution. To them we owe a combination of the otherwise separate arguments of natural law and political economy, along with an improved historical understanding which is gaining more and more adherents everywhere. The efforts of Lorenz von Stein, which have decisively influenced thinking in the political and social sciences (*Staatswissenschaften*) in Germany, ought to be evaluated in the same sense. However, Stein's theory is best understood as a renewal and basically correct interpretation of the blunt principles of Thomas Hobbes. To wit: Society (*Gesellschaft*), or mankind in its natural state, is characterized by cleavage and hostility; it is the purpose of the state to introduce peace and order in society as well as to restore against the lack of freedom (of the person) and the inequality (of property) which result from the intrinsic movement of society, the ideally conceived equality and liberty. That every empirical state is shaped by society and its social classes, that it emanates from them, and that even that kind of society which is contradictory to the principle of the state uses, and necessarily must use, the state as its instrument —these are conclusions in which (so far as Stein is concerned) the moral postulate of a reform of society comes to terms with the insight into the actual conditions of the present age.

On the other hand, in spite of the fact that his concepts point in all directions, Stein lacks the simple basic schemata and constructions that are required in the theory of law. For it is evident that society and the state fall under the comprehensive concept of an organized group and must be understood according to the general or particular ends which they pursue. The main error, however, rests with the consideration that society and the state are treated as *empirical facts*, supposed to be uniformly present throughout the entire range of our historical knowledge. From the empirical standpoint one can rightly rebel against these concepts, as was done in earnest by the historical school and the theories underlying the politics of the Restoration period. Both influences remain powerful today. Society, whether taken in its proper sense or in a restricted sense encompassing only free and propertied persons, presumably indicates a multitude of individuals, dispersed over an area of some size, engaged in peaceful intercourse, and enforcing the observation of certain rules. Experience simply says: there is no such society. We observe that people are united in households, villages, and towns, in guilds and religious congregations, in countries and empires, ordered by age and sex, and either by achieved or acquired status or occupation; we do not see the mechanical unity which a universal association, wherein all differences between individuals are abolished, would present. What we do see is an interconnected arrangement of organic units whose origin in an ultimate unit, like a people or ethnic (racial) group, does not need to be clearly and concretely recognizable as long as that origin remains alive as a postulate of reason. Analogously, one can argue against the corresponding definition of the state, although here the *name* in its generalized meaning is maintained. To be sure, the opposition to the rational concept of the state is implicit in the attempts to explain the essence of the state as an organism and consequently in the fervent criticism which supposedly has put the contract theory out of commission; yet the contract theory is naturally appropriate to the reality which we may call the modern state, that is, a structure of thoroughgoing artificiality and marked by a high degree of scientific consciousness.

It is therefore with good reason that the seemingly victorious organic theory of the state recently has been attacked again and that attempts have been made to overthrow it on the grounds that it is useless for the purposes of the jurist. That it doubtless is, not in every sense, but surely in the individualistic sense which is fundamental to all scientific jurisprudence. For the individualistic point of view, the state must be conceived of as a *person* that exists only in thought or fiction and must be construed in analogy to the *individual* persons whom we know empirically. In Roman jurisprudence, to be sure, there was no thought of a construction of the *res publica*. This is explainable from historical causes. For there was still alive the idea of the urban commonwealth (which, indeed, survived far into the period of the Holy Roman Empire); this commonwealth, in the sum total of its families and through the protection of its gods, appeared as a living, even as an eternal, entity. In contrast, the states and governmental structures of the modern age, although to a moderate extent first developed in free cities and frequently modeled after the example of the Roman empire, arose chiefly from the power of princes, primarily of the Italian city tyrants. This power was absolute, arbitrarily legislating, law destroying and law giving, and elevated high above all subjected wills, customs, and convictions. The important theories of the state of the seventeenth and eighteenth centuries, on the one hand, have arisen from the intention to justify this power; neither as personal power in private law nor as divine power in the Church, which (because it would have meant that the state was conditioned by the Church) would have neutralized the absoluteness of state power, but as general and necessary power in public law; and, on the other hand, from the will to condition and to limit the power of the state.

Certainly, even here the state always remains specifically different from all private associations. It is the *only* person in public law—a confederate state therefore being anomalous—because this quality must be derived from the will and the rights of private persons which exist only *once;* one must think of the general will to defend oneself and to use force to this end and of the monopoly of using force legitimately, which is the essential characteristic of the state. Now, inasfar as it is the simple idea of society (*Gesellschaft*) that it should make possible peaceful intercourse among men, the state is nothing but society itself, setting itself up as a single fictitious person over against the natural, individual persons.

At first glance, my theory appears as a combination of the conflicting organic and mechanical, or historical and rational, theories. But my initial intention was merely to affirm both of these as *possible:* and, indeed, they prove their possibility by their existence. None of these theories is new, but my way of relating and explicating them is new because I juxtapose them without meaning to say that one of them is false and staking an exclusive claim to be right for the other.[1] Does this mean that each is correct in its own way, that each of them contains a fraction of the truth, while the whole truth would have to be sought for in a higher mediating view? I expressed myself otherwise in the preface to the first edition of *G. & G.* where I speak of the doctrine of natural law and the individualistically conceived political economy as the separate disciplines which together express empirically the construct of *Gesellschaft:* "The present theory attempts to absorb these theories and to keep them in a state of dependence." This implies that the "organic" view is the original and comprehensive and, to that extent, the correct theory. Indeed, that is my opinion; consider that I have said that "the strength of *Gemeinschaft* persists, although with diminishing vigor, even in the period of *Gesellschaft* and remains the reality of social life" (p. 252; Loomis, p. 232). The concept of *Gesellschaft*, then, signifies the normal and regular process of decline of all forms of *Gemeinschaft*. This is its truth, and the term *Gesellschaft* is indispensable for the expression of that truth. For this reason it would have to be coined if it had not been formed previously, even if this formation occurred without the awareness of its necessity and real significance. In his treatment of the process of *Gesellschaft,* the author had *modern* society in mind; appropriately he took advantage of the exposure of its "economic law of development" by Karl Marx, as those familiar with the subject will readily recognize and as is expressly noted in the preface to the first edition of *G. & G.*[2]

1   It is the weakness of the historical school, both in the philosophy of law and in economics, to have arrived at neither a psychological derivation of its social concepts nor a sociological foundation of its psychological concepts. Wherever it attempted to do this, it relapsed into theological or mythological obfuscation.

2   I am saying this with some pride because to acknowledge or even to stress Marx's importance for theoretical sociology was quite unheard of in 1887. Accordingly, a reviewer (Albert Schaeffle—Eds.) in the *Zeitschrift fuer die gesamte Staatswissenschaft* (Tuebingen, 1892, p. 559) noted in my book " a not so very weak ingredient of Marxomania." The

It further follows from my presentation that the "organic" theory will receive its own proper delimitation only if it is understood psychologically. A quasi-organic character can be imparted to a union of men only by the sensation, emotion, and will of those associated with it: by means of this foundation my theorem is clearly set off from other current "organic" doctrines which do not perceive that by their biological analogies they confine themselves to biology, albeit an expanded one, thus missing the specific characteristics of sociological facts. However, the lasting importance and the general scientific value of the position of natural law lie in its opposition to all supernatural explanations and its recognition of the own thought and will of men as the *ratio essendi* of the social structures (*Gebilde*) within which they are moving; natural law fails, however, in that it presents *rational will*, which sharply separates means and ends, as the *only* type of human will, hence comprehends all social relations but as means to individual ends that coincide merely accidentally.

This is precisely why I thought it necessary to draft a theory of the human will, complementary and parallel to social theory. I define as essential will that which corresponds to the concept of *Gemeinschaft* and is basic and essential to it, while by arbitrary will I mean that which corresponds to the concept of *Gesellschaft* and is essential to it, that is, basic to its ideally conceived reality (*ideelle Wirklichkeit*). I conceive of both types as referring to *thinking man* and consequently I call thought the decisive trait of human will generally. But while essential will is will involving thought, arbitrary will is will existing as thought only. The characteristic common to them is a thinking (conscious) affirmation

---

observation is not so much denunciatory as superficial. On the other hand, a much earlier review by G. Schmoller (*Jahrbuch*, 1888, pp. 727 ff.) says simply and correctly: "Resonances of Marx characterize these discussions" (about the theory of society). But even Schmoller's fair review does not perceive the relation of my theory to the very real and particular problems which are ever-present in the history of thought. I agree with Schmoller entirely, however, when he says that "only those readers will be able to appreciate the book fully who are familiar with the philosophical, historical and socio-political literature on which it is based."

or negation of the object—that is, of a material object or an activity. Affirmation and negation of an object are always reducible to affirmation and negation of an activity. Affirmation is the will to preserve (*conservandi*) the object or to conquer, posit, or possess it—and therefore also the will to create or bring about, to form, or to make it; negation, then, is the will to destroy or remove the object, to dissolve it or to deprive it of its essential properties.

Thinking itself is an activity, involving either affirmation or negation, combination or separation, union or disunion. The thinking affirmation or negation of one object is affirmation or negation with reference to another object, meaning that the objects are brought into relationship to each other; the ideas (thought images, or representations) of the objects are associated with each other. The association of ideas is a likeness of the association of men. It is most significant and important for us as the association of means and ends. The end is what is properly and ultimately wanted. With the idea of the end is that of the means necessarily connected. The question then is: do means and end include or do they exclude each other? If they include each other, they belong to an essential unity, to a whole which is prior to the parts and which dissolves into these by a process of spontaneous differentation. Such an essential unity is found in every creative idea and what is akin to it.

In that case the end is the fulfillment; the means leading to it are the object itself in the stage of development. Product and action condition and include each other. The activities are affirmed because the product is affirmed, and vice versa; the joy of affirmation, and hence the willing, is directed toward the *whole*. The most perfect realization of this idea is found in artistic activity. On the other hand, if the ideas of end and means exclude or negate each other, a unity must be constructed out of them. This is most distinctly the case whenever the end is an event that is not in my power but the means an event that is in my power. In that case, means and end confront each other as if they were strangers and of a different kind; and inasmuch as the one event is a movement which meets an impediment in the movement or position of the other, so that they obstruct each other, it can be said that their confrontation is essentially hostile. Their interaction consists in mutual mechanical coercion; to desire the end becomes the cause of the willing of the means—which is supposed not to be wanted spontaneously—so that the willing of the means becomes the cause that achieves the end. In the first case, the thought-of (ideal) event B is the cause of the real event A; in the second case, the real event A is the cause that leads on to the realization of event B. For instance, the relation of means and end is most distinctly expressed in exchange; at the same time, exchange personifies, as it were, the antagonistic character of such willing. The alien object is negated because it is alien, that is, because it belongs to somebody else; it is affirmed as possibly one's own. One's own object, on the other hand, is affirmed, its loss negated; but its relinquishment and transmission from one's own possession into that of another person are affirmed, not as an end, but as means to an end. The concept of arbitrary will appears in still greater perfection whenever the act of exchange is part of a combination of several such acts, as in trade, speculation, capitalistic production, in short, in every effort that aims at surplus value or net profit.

It is in the nature of the development of human thought that the type arbitrary will ascends to predominance over the type essential will. For if sensual perception already consists in comparison, so much more is this the case with the varieties of exact comparison, that is, the highly rational activities of measuring, weighing, and calculating, on which the arbitrary will is based. I therefore spoke of it as a form of thought more characteristic of men in contrast to women, of the aged in contrast to the young, and of the educated classes in contrast to the common people.

This contrast of the kinds of will, which my book works out in a variety of ways, hitherto has been utilized unsystematically in linguistics, poetry, biography, and history. I gave it a theoretical foundation for the first time. My treatment disregards ethical implications, however closely such implications may touch upon its content. Harald Hoeffding, who has examined my book most carefully, emphasizes "the calm objectivity with which it observes the phenomena of human life." At the same time, he underscores its "unique combination of sociology and psychology."[3] My only exception to the Danish philosopher's critique is that he makes too much of what he calls the author's "social pessimism." My pessimism refers to the future of the present civilization, not to the future of civilization itself.

My sole purpose was to point out the change which occurs in the relationship of man to man and of man to things, therefore also in the human will, when particular ideas come to be sharply distinguished from each other, that is, when they become entirely individual in character. It must be understood that they are never distinguished in perception, always in thought; never in reality, always in abstraction.

[3]   *Mindre Arbeider* (Copenhagen, 1899), pp. 142–57.

6

THE NATURE OF SOCIOLOGY

THE FACTS of human social life are the subject of scientific observation and knowledge at three levels.

As a rule, these three approaches are not being kept separate, and it is certainly not possible to do so absolutely. But neither are they being distinguished epistemologically, that is, properly understood conceptually, and yet this is not only possible but is a necessary requirement.

For one must distinguish (a) the biological, (b) the psychological, and (c) the strictly sociological view of the facts of human social life. The difference between the biological and the psychological views of the facts of social life is not difficult to comprehend.

Translated from the paper "Das Wesen der Soziologie" read before the Gehe Foundation, Dresden 1907; first published in *Neue Zeit- und Streitfragen* IV, vol. 13, no. 9; reprinted in *Soziologische Studien und Kritiken* I, pp. 350–68. Slightly abridged. Subtitles are supplied by the editors. The reference in footnote 2 is to the Naples paper (1924): cf. "The Divisions of Sociology," chap. 8 this volume.

In a note to the Gehe Foundation paper Toennies comments on the partial similarity of this paper and the paper presented at the Congress of Arts and Science—Universal Exposition, St. Louis 1904; cf. "The Present Problems of Social Structure," chap. 7 this volume. In Toennies' opinion the Gehe Foundation paper partly enlarges and partly modifies the St. Louis paper. Both papers are meant to affirm the theorems first elaborated in *Gemeinschaft und Gesellschaft* (1887) and also to refer critically to the position of Otto von Gierke, especially to his paper "Das Wesen der menschlichen Verbände" (Leipzig 1902). The St. Louis paper follows this paper.

We are entirely accustomed to looking at all organic beings, including man, as having a physis and a psyche; they are two sides of the same thing. Consequently human social life, or the living together, of men as well of other organisms is the object both of natural and of spiritual analysis—if one may say so. Symbiosis among lower organisms is almost exclusively understood as being a natural event, namely, a fact of mutual nourishment, assistance, and so forth; naturalists are not intensively, or not at all, concerned with the emotional life of animals and plants. This has something to do with the fact that cognitive functions for a long time have been regarded primarily as a thing of the intellect and, even more so, the human mind as the normal mind—modes of thinking which are being shed but slowly and with considerable difficulty. Of late, however, a voluntaristic view is coming more and more to the fore, according to which drives and emotions are considered the universal heritage of organic beings, including elementary organisms and plants; the mind is then not a thing that somehow, in a puzzling way, is "connected" with the body; rather, it is the essence of the organism itself inasmuch as the organism exists by and of itself and not merely in the perceptions of other minds.

We can of course observe the life of human beings, and consequently their social life, from the "outside," but it is only from the "inside" that we can understand it; that is to say, we must interpret it on the basis of self-knowledge, which teaches us that as a matter of necessity human beings are determined by certain passionate urges, by strong emotions that accompany the stimulation and the restraint of such urges; and that human beings use their sense perceptions and, as a reservoir of their sense perceptions, their intelligence as guides, as scouts, as warners, so that they may discern even from afar and in advance what is friendly or hostile, what is favorable or dangerous. Thus, it is also complexes of feelings and emotions that hold together human beings, and lead them to one another—that "bind" them to each other, and hence "connect" them. For they are not connected by an external physical cord, as are, for example, two prisoners, who, with their wrists chained, are being moved together. It is only metaphorically speaking that there are psychological bonds, ties of love and friendship, unions

(*Verbindungen*) and associations (*Verbaende*) among human beings.

We know that the social and benevolent motives and thoughts are continually in contradiction and conflict with those of an opposite nature; that love and hate, trust and distrust, gratitude and vindictiveness cross one another; but also that fear and hope and, based on these emotions, human interests and intentions encounter each other, either in harmony or in disharmony, so that feelings as well as designs partly connect, partly divide human beings, singly as well as in groups of all kinds.

The psychological view of human social life regards attraction and repulsion, aid and combat, peaceful association and warlike conflict by themselves as equally important and relevant. The biological view is concerned with all such differences only because of the effect they have on increasing or reducing, stimulating or preventing life. The sociological view, as distinct from both, is essentially and in the first instance concerned with those facts that I call facts of reciprocal affirmation. Sociology investigates these specific and restricted social facts, analyzes their motives, and, in doing so, I maintain, must give particular attention to the difference whether reciprocal affirmation is based more on motives in feeling, or more on motives in reasoning; it must trace the process, which in this differentiation I design as the development from natural, or essential, will to rational, or arbitrary, will.

Essential will is volition as it has become, arbitrary will is volition as it is made. Man is by nature inclined toward affirmation of man, and therefore to union with him—not only through "instincts" (although instincts produce the strongest drives) but as much through "nobler" feelings and a reasonable consciousness. Out of the inclination arises volition (*Wollen*) and unequivocal affirmation, which recognizes the value of the object affirmed, and accordingly acts toward its full and durable affirmation. In the diverse forms this affirmation can take, the object is always affirmed directly or, as we say, as an end, that is, for its own sake. This does not, however, exclude its being affirmed at one and the same time also for another end, so long as the two ends remain in harmony and are reciprocally affirmative. Thus, the rider likes his horse; he does so because it is useful and it adds to his enjoyment; but he likes it, too, because he is immediately delighted with it; it gives him pleasure.

On the other hand, the idea of the end, the external purpose, may grow so strong that it causes affirmation of a means despite complete indifference toward its quality, therefore without arousing any pleasure; finally, notwithstanding a decided dislike. The dislike is being overcome, one forces himself to do, to take, to give something, although he does not care for it; he makes up his mind to do it because it appears to be the sensible (*vernuenftig*) thing to do. It is quite correct, and has often enough been discussed, that over a wide range an association and mixture of ideas may take place, by virtue of which the indifferent, even the loathsome, just because it is useful, may become acceptable and therefore I would say also be affirmed by essential will. Here is the location of that most important formation of essential will, which I indicate by the well-known term of habit, and which I relate to memory. This, however, is a secondary phenomenon, and there remains open a wide area, in which that association is not achieved but the original relation persists. The result is that even a single element which is affirmed by arbitrary will grows into a highly complex product or system—that is to say, a mechanism consisting in arbitrarily willed actions that are imagined and aforethought. Yet the nature of arbitrary will, as the nature of volition of any kind, is not restricted to action. It extends to anything that can be thought of as a means to human ends, and consequently may even extend to the whole nonself as the stuff for the desires, the aspirations, the interests of the self.

In the relation of one man to others, it is the arbitrary will, as understood here, that is relevant to the sociologist, whenever it can be thought of as reciprocally effective. In a unilateral way, it tends to treat the other as a thing or, as I prefer to say and did say, as stuff, while in the reciprocal relation, such tendencies are being balanced insofar as the other person is seen and accepted as a person, that is, as a subject endowed with arbitrary will. Consequently, one person may represent to another a mere means to his ends yet not be subjugated to these ends, in such a way that they remain free agents in relation to one another and are therefore capable of entering into a free relationship of reciprocal affirmation.

Even well-known sociologists are repeating ad nauseam the old thesis that man is by nature a social animal. But it is no more valid than the opposite thesis that, being by nature egotistic, or asocial, he becomes social as he makes reasoned judgments about his own well-understood interests; that he behaves socially only according to circumstances, that is, when and inasmuch as he thinks it will be to his advantage to come to terms and seek a working arrangement with his opponent—for to a degree, at least potentially, everyone is everyone's opponent.

I maintain that each of these opposite theses holds good, that each in its own area is valid and applicable, that they complement each other. The former is basic for the concept of *Gemeinschaft*, the latter for the concept of *Gesellschaft*.

This theorem of mine has often been understood to mean, and has so been interpreted, that these kinds were being distinguished in the same way the botanist distinguishes trees and grasses or the zoologist vertebrates and invertebrates. This is not my meaning. My method is comparable to that of the chemist rather than that of the descriptive natural sciences. It is a matter of isolation (*Scheidung*) rather than distinction (*Unterscheidung*). The point is to decompose the phenomenon of the social relation into its elements, and conceptually to set free these elements, whether or not their pure formation occurs in real life.

Social Relations

To conceptualize the social relationship is the first and fundamental scientific theme that essentially belongs to sociology.

We cannot discuss this theme without reference to those relationships that as legal relationships are the subject matter of a pure theory of civil law or of natural law in the old and true sense of the term.

The concept of social relationship is wider than that of the legal relationship. The legal relationship is a special category of the social relationship.

The really fundamental difference is to be found in the causes of the legal relationship. The first main cause of the relationship in private or civil law is *contract*, which is the prototype of a legal transaction with the object of doing something that has an effect in law. (Obligations arising from tort, that is, *ex delicto*, I would not count among immediate legal relationships). The other main cause is the natural condition, or status, of man, which today is of formal significance only in close family relationships. Not by contract but by status are we father or son, brother or sister, head of state or citizen, and on the basis of status have we certain subjective rights, or legal duties, with correlative subjective rights of others.

It is of the very nature of the legal relationship that the law, or the legal system, endows it with rights established by it and imposes duties originating in it. But entirely in analogy with the legal, we conceive of moral relationships, and talk of moral obligations and morally justified claims. Only on first appearance, however, is this concept as clear and straightforward as that of legal relationship. The truth of the matter is that, with regard to anything called moral, we never know without a specific indication whether this means something required by the mores, or by custom, or by positive morality as an accepted moral code which is closely related to custom, or, finally, by a generally accepted theological or philosophical system of ethics. This division produces at least three different species, or certain shadings, of moral relationships, even though most of them are subject equally to all three authorities and though, as a rule, all three agree about the norms that determine these relationships. Yet one has not far to seek for examples where those regulators, as they may be termed, diverge widely.

What in a specific sense of relationship is called an affair or a liaison between persons of different sex is being denied by custom and, as it were, passed over in silence. The legal system also ignores the "immoral" relationship. The accepted moral code, if independent from custom, at least puts up with it, provided that neither person is married, but derives scarcely any moral rights and duties from it—especially to the male partner who belongs to an upper social stratum it accords a degree of freedom and impudence which is indeed its—the accepted morality's—own disgrace. Theological ethics prefers to treat these things in the same way as custom. But a free and independent philosophical ethics will realize that the "immoral" relationship, though on principle ranking beneath the connubial and reprehensible when adulterous, may in special circumstances be equivalent to marriage in its moral nature and may in fact occasionally be superior in its moral value to many marital unions. But such ethics would, in all such cases, make exacting and serious demands in respect to the duties that arise from such a relationship, particularly for the male partner who belongs to a privileged social class—duties toward the woman, even when he discovers that she is not "worthy" of him, but most certainly duties toward their common offspring.

In whatever way one defines a moral relationship, it remains analogous to a legal relationship, in that an authority—if only, as in philosophical ethics, the autonomy of our practical reason— connects an "ought," or obligation (*ein Sollen*), with the relationship or derives such an obligation from it. Moral and legal relationships, therefore, are the subject matter of normative disciplines. But to conceptualize social relationships is the foremost task of a purely theoretical science of sociology. It differs from the natural sciences by virtue of the fact that its objects can neither be made visible by either telescope or microscope nor be perceived by the other senses. Only thought is capable of discerning them. They are a product of thought because they are abstracted from real life situations, that is, from the facts of social interaction. If we contemplate that at least the germs of a social relationship lie in all peaceful (or, as I have put it earlier, positive) conduct among human beings, and that conscious restraint from hostility represents such a germ, we have before the mind's eye the entire variety of sociological subject matter. The limitation to peaceful conduct, however, does not mean that forms of hostile conduct are irrelevant to the sociologist. They are, to be sure, as relevant to him as unorganized matter is relevant to the biologist or the physical states of matter are relevant to the chemist. It is the objects of research that are different in each.

It needs only a brief reflection to notice that social relationships to a large degree coincide with legal relationships, and that both those that coincide and those outside that field present in more than one sense a moral aspect. But even rights and obligations concern the sociologists first and foremost only insofar as they are actually perceived and thought of as such by the persons connected by these relations. And yet this way of looking at it is secondary in comparison with the study of real life conduct, in which the facts of social relationships are embedded.

Social Will

The second main theme of sociology, to which we now turn, is the field of social will and its products, for volition apart from the social context is a matter of psychology. In any social relationship there is present, albeit potentially, an element of social will, but its scope is far greater. The scope of social will is the whole of the environmental conditioning of social interaction. Custom and common law, religion and legislation, accepted usage (*Konvention*) and public opinion, style and fashion—all of them are expressions of different formations of social will. A simple and unambiguous instance of social will is a resolution passed commonly by a number of persons. The immediate content of a common resolution is that we intend to act in a certain way. Its content may be, too, that we want such and such to happen, something to be or become actual. And this occurrence or actualization may relate to others' acting or refraining from acting in some way. At this point we must take note of an important difference in what is meant by volition. The language constantly mixes up willing in the proper sense, which relates to one's doing something, with mere wishing. That something should happen, which is not the result of my own action, I can only wish. But to wish for something is very much like willing it, if I am determined to make it happen indirectly, more so if I am determined to force it into being, and still more so if I am capable of doing this. Wishing, then, merges into commanding.

Commands may emanate from single persons, or from several persons who have taken a common resolution. But they conform to the nature of social volition only, if the several persons are willing, hence enforcing their commands, and especially if they are capable of doing so. In circumstances such as these it does not matter, to begin with, for what reason the "others" obey, whether they are in a social relationship with those who command or whether they are subjected enemies or slaves. But the others can be these persons themselves as individuals, whose united volition forms the social volition which manifests itself as command. This is the most important case for sociological consideration: that human beings give themselves commands which they themselves obey—in commanding they perform a social action, in obeying they act as individuals.

Though most transparent when social volition takes the form of a resolution, social volition is no less important in its other formations. As I represent resolution as the type of rational volition, so do I represent habit as the type of irrational volition. That taking a resolution has both social and individual implications is self-evident; but it is no less manifest in the case of habit. As individual, man follows his habits; they control him, and he is often the "slave" of habit. In the same manner, people in the mass, though still individually, depend on habits with a social content, which we learn to discern as usage, custom, or common law; their extent and force increase as we delve in our researches into the life of the common people.

But how about habit—in what way is habit a social will? There appear to be two main reasons why this is not realized and accepted as the plausible explanation. The first has to do with the fact that self-reflection teaches us to understand volition as something that arises from reasoning, something that, as it were, is made, and being of our own making contrasts as something bright and lucid with our dark and unintended desires and urges. I do not mean to suggest that the concept of volition be fashioned in such a manner that it comprises impulses and stirrings of the psyche, including those that remain unconscious. I would keep closer to linguistic meaning, and stress the perfect tense of volition in a linguistic sense —to will means literally to *have* made up one's mind, to *have* decided about something, and to *be* resolved. And how alive, even how necessary, this element in our concept is, language shows by creating variations of the word "to will," once this has worn off and become threadbare as an ordinary verb: such as "to be willing," "to be determined," "to be disposed," all of which are merely a refresher of the original sense, and can have no other function. It is this original sense that I extend in one direction, by drawing into my concept of volition also the being-used-to or being-in-the-habit-of, since it shares with the being-determined its essential criterion; namely the compelling destination toward an action, which is based on one's own inclination and one's own wish as the autonomous factor.

This leads directly to the second reason, which I think explains the failure to appreciate the point I have made, namely, the fact that reasoning must rely on linguistic usage, even when this is lax, indistinct, ambivalent. Language does indeed not discriminate between habit as an objective or, as one might put it, external fact and habit as a subjective, psychic or "internal" fact. The former usage, as external fact, contains nothing but the frequent repetition and regularity of acting and happening. But the latter conveys what we express when we say that habit is ingrown and has become our second nature and when we speak of the immeasurable influence that the habits of every person have on how he acts as well as on what he wishes and what he thinks, on his emotions and on his opinions. In the same way, we talk, without being aware of the difference of folk habits, of usages, of customs. They are indeed of interest as sheer facts of environment, as substantive processes; but in a quite different manner, and for the sociologist, they are far more immediately relevant as authoritative expressions of the folk spirit (*Volksgeist*), that is, as social will. In this latter meaning, custom has always been compared with law. Both of them possess validity, that is to say, they are of an ideal nature, they are a product of thought, demanding something that ought to be, and it needs a will to say that something ought to be.

Custom and formal law differ chiefly by their reasons. Custom states: because this is how it has always been, how it has always been done, practiced, considered proper. The formal law states: because this is what the legislator commands, and he commands it because he considers it correct and appropriate, and because he

wishes to achieve something by the command. Opposition and conflict between custom and law manifest themselves mostly in the contest between common law, on the one hand, and statute law, on the
other. No reminder is needed of the fact that formal statute law
originates in resolution, in particular resolutions passed by assemblies.

So much about the contrast between resolution and habit; but
the forms of the social as well as the individual will extend much
further than that. An object of the greatest importance for sociological research is the religious creed, which is so closely connected
with custom. Divine beings are not merely imagined and assumed
beings, but as such they are, and are chiefly, beings that have been
willed. The social will that posits them reveals itself not only by the
faith in their existence, their power, their wrath, and their benevolence but even more so in the reverence devoted to them, in the
temples and altars built to them, in sacrifices, and in all kinds of
worship. They are creatures of folk imagery, and how else can
something be made unless it is made by creative volition? They
are, however, not only objects but, by virtue of that very fact, and
thanks to the profusion and the ardor of the folk spirit, which, as
it were, are being infused into them, they are subjects and bearers
of the social will. As a rule they are being thought of as the zealous
guardians of custom, chiefly because, and particularly so in the
savage mind, they sternly insist on the observances, on receiving
what is their due, in the image of despots and warlords. But they
are also being thought of as legislators, or as inspiring the legislator. Though habits and titles are immutably valid, yet the god
may change and renew them; his representatives on earth, in the
name of god, whether they be called high priest or king, pope or
emperor, may engage in free explanation and interpretative transformation of tradition, sacred though it be held in its substance.
We owe valuable comments on these matters to Sir Henry Maine, a
legal scholar who was able to think sociologically. But he, too, was
unable to advance to the important insight that it is only different
manifestations of social volition that are expressed in common law
and sacred rights, on the one hand, and in freely conceived and
planned legislation leaning on scientific theories, on the other.

For our unreflected awareness that which is, the actual reality, is indissolubly tied up with what is valid, and everything that is valid has its validity either for an individual alone through his individual will or for a number of individuals through their social will. The latter by far outweighs the former in significance. I recently published an essay I wrote nine years ago,[1] in which I have applied this truth to the meaning of words in common language and compared it to the validity of currency notes and coins. It is equally applicable to weights and measures, to chronology and epochs, to written signs and other symbols, to currently held views and opinions, particularly moral standards, to manners and etiquette—in short, to everything conventional. To appreciate what is conventional, and what is its scope, means to understand at least one major facet of the nature and the power of social volition.

We know, of course, that only in a few and relatively insignificant cases what is given validity by convention rests on an actual agreement that is like a contract. We say and assume, however, that there are many things so constituted *as though* they had been settled upon by agreement, and it is this feature that can best be indicated by the term "conventional." The term also connotes, in a minor key, something rigid and stiff, something artificial, therefore something frosty and cold. This connotation is a pointer to a highly significant difference in social volition whenever it establishes current values. The difference has its origin in a process from the internal toward externalization, from the organic to the mechanical agent, from essential will to arbitrary will—a process that takes place in the social as much as in the individual will. For custom and religion persist through that genuine warmth in emotion and imagination, that youthful naïve freshness, but also the innocence and childish folly of the common people's mind, or the folk spirit (*Volksgeist*). In the course of cultural development these motives are continually modified by matured experience, by increased knowledge, and by a more pronounced deliberateness in the pursuit of external ends. If they are, therefore, in part transformed and converted, in part challenged and abandoned, the im-

---

1   "Philosophical Terminology," *Mind* VIII N.S. pp. 289–332, 467–91 and IX N.S. pp. 46–61; *Philosophische Terminologie in psychologisch-soziologischer Ansicht* (Leipzig, 1906).

pulses of the process are particularly due to the influence of individual persons who distinguish themselves by intellectual freedom and a daring character.

The contradictions and conflicts between religion and science, between superstition and enlightenment are, no less than those between folk custom and the state police, between common law and statute law, the contradictions and conflicts between different and, indeed, opposed species or directions of social volition. The contradictions appear to indicate merely differences in thought and opinion; however, thoughts and opinions are backed up not only by the interests of classes and political parties but by different value systems called forth by changed circumstances; and in these value systems a more or less general volition crystallizes.

Social Unions

Of the scope and the implications of the problems located here, not much more than a faint idea can be conveyed in this outline. But the nature of sociology completes itself in its third main theme, where sociology breaks away even more decidedly than in the first two from biology and psychology, to enter a domain entirely its own. The third theme concerns the unions and associations among men, their fellowships and societies, communities and congregations, to name but a few of the general terms of those units, in the varieties of which pluralities of human individuals represent themselves. What is their essential nature? Are they something real or unreal? In what sense can they be the objects of scientific study? How are entities such as a race, a people, a nation, a tribe, a clan, a family, which also signify units in and above the pluralities, related to these categories? How are related to them the concepts of the state and of the church, which have gained such tremendous weight in all social life and its history? What are all these structures?

First of all, one must attend here to a significant difference, on which my whole exposition is based, that is, the difference between the various approaches to the study of human social life. For some of the units I have mentioned can be studied biologically, since their unity rests on natural facts of procreation and birth, descent and hereditary characteristics, while at the same time they are imbued with a psychological valuation as units that are carriers of social ideas. To inquire into their reality would mean to renew the old controversy between realism and nominalism; this has been settled in modern science with hardly an exception in favor of nominalism, which holds that only what we call single things are real. To discuss this matter here falls outside my plan for this paper. But, since it all too often has been completely disregarded or badly neglected, I must emphatically underline the distinction between such biological and at best psychological universals and groups, on the one hand, and the actual social wholes or, preferably, social bodies, on the other. Only with these are we concerned here and now, although there is every reason to keep in mind the former, when occasion arises, and to heed certain points of contact between the two fundamentally different genera.

A social union has, in the first instance and immediately, something like an existence only through the united, therefore, social will of the persons that belong to it, as and when they posit the union in their minds. As a rule this truth is being expressed by the statement that a social union is a fiction. This expression, however, is regularly applied only in jurisprudence. The jurist talks of corporate persons that exist besides natural persons or individuals, and he explains them as a fiction created for specific purposes by the law or the legislator. The sociologist is interested in a much wider range of human units, and it does not matter at first whether or not they have been recognized in a legal system as bearers of rights and obligations, just as it was of no significance to us whether or not a social relationship also appears in the form of a legal relationship. Trade unions and workingmen's federations have not yet (1907) been endowed with the legal status of a corporate person; even less so political parties or associations. Does this mean that they do not exist? Are they not extremely important formations in our present-day social environment? Whereby, then, do they exist?

They do exist, (1) and chiefly, through the will of their members who have established such an association or, like its founders, assume and affirm it by their performance. They furthermore exist (2) through being taken notice of and given recognition on the part of other individuals and associations, especially their equals; and (3), for the spectator and theorist, as he takes note of these modes of existence, and distinguishes them from other modes of existence. But obviously the first *ratio essendi* is the fundamental one, and the others depend on it. We know that any group of persons can call into being an association, if they will it in common and can agree on it, and in doing so they perform an act of pretense or fiction. For at first it is in their imagination only, in their idea, but dependent on their volition, that the association exists; and they have a common purpose the association is meant to serve.

The association can achieve this purpose by its mere existence, that is, by being construed—and as it is being construed, it receives a name—but as a rule it must be capable of a will of its own, it must be capable of being represented, and the agreement, which legally is called the articles of association, must settle how the representative will is to be formed: thus the association is given its constitution. This simple, logically lucid instance is known to all of us by experience. The question arises whether this concept of association can provide the standard for measuring all species of human units. What has, in the context of this question, made the greatest stir is the question whether even the state, or the government, can and ought to be conceived of as an association. This is the problem of the social contract.

The Age of Enlightenment unanimously believed, and, what is more, was convinced it knew and had clearly and unmistakably understood, that the state was based on contracts. The nineteenth century, which in its main currents of thought was an age of restoration, destroyed this belief and this certainty; yet it produced in its turn no generally accepted political theory. Initially it was history that was being appealed to, and the historical school of law staked its claim against natural law. States, it was claimed, had in reality originated everywhere, or only with insignificant exceptions, in ways other than by contracts, and until this day this plausible truth has been echoed vividly enough. Against it, one may refer to Kant, who had made it abundantly clear that what the contract theory was about was the idea of the thing but not the question of the historic origin. To everyone who knows natural law theory and the philosophy at its root, this is downright self-evident. Yet, it is retorted, the origin, the development, the historical being-as-it-has-become, are all that counts; they are the only instrument with which to grasp the nature of the thing. Whose nature? Well, the state's. And what precisely is the sort of thing the state is? Well, something that has developed, that is to say, a living thing, an organism.

At this point, the resistance against the natural law concept of the state joins up with a school of thought that, by now precariously surviving among natural scientists, has been eagerly embraced by modern sociology. Among the sociologists, however, the chief interest lies with "society" or "the social body" rather than with the state. Whatever its particular shape, this view is opposed to the individualistic view of social life. I do not defend this individualistic view. But I do maintain that the subsumption under the concept of organism, whether of society at large or of the state, contains a tangle of misconceptions, and I refer back to what I have already strongly underlined, that is, the difference between objects of research in biology and sociology. I do maintain that conceptualistic realism (as defined more recently) should, as far as organic beings are concerned, not be dismissed as easily as, curiously enough, this is being done by those selfsame natural scientists, to whom the application of the concept of organism to social formations seems to be the most natural and most evident thing under the sun. I accept as valid, in fact, I set great store by, the insight that a people, a race, a family as biological phenomena exist as a reality in the exact meaning of the term, difficult though it may be to define that reality precisely. In other words, they must, and certainly may, be understood as real beings since we cannot but ascribe to them the essential criteria of life, such as in particular the self-preservation of the whole by the elimination of old and the reproduction of new parts. But all the more energetically I must emphasize the theory that social entities or unions and associations among men are of an essentially ideal (*ideell*) nature; that they are a product of thought in the sense that the very fact of their being entities entirely depends upon the minds of their members, of whom one can rightly state what Bishop Berkeley applied to the whole of the external world: *esse = percipi* (to be is to be perceived). For all that, I attribute to them, as much as the metaphysical idealist attributes to matter as such, a certain empirical reality: it is that social reality which is grounded in the ideas about them, hence in the minds of men. This is why I say that the sociological view of life follows, and depends on, the psychological view, as the psychological view follows and depends on the biological.

As social unions, so social relations and social will and the values posited by it exist only and insofar as they are perceived, felt, imagined, thought, known, and willed, primarily by individuals. Does there exist, then, such a thing as a folk mind, a natural consciousness, a common and united feeling and thinking? Whether some such thing does exist, except in the agreement among individuals and the harmony in their feelings and thoughts, is a problem that once more leads back to conceptualistic realism. The problem is a different one in relation to material things, a different one in relation to the mind (*Seele*). If it is accepted for organisms, it is hardly possible not to accept it with regard to the mind. For organisms, as live matter, as I have said earlier, *are* mind rather than merely connected with mind; the mind is located in the organism. The fact of the matter is that organisms must be understood as matter and mind at one and the same time. If, as I believe, thinking and willing exist as objective reality, then especially those formations of social will that are so close to it—social habit, social belief, custom, and religion—are something entirely different, depending on whether they are considered in this, their objective reality (which they possess by virtue of being subjective entities), or in their subjective, or as we now prefer to say, their social reality; therefore, as ideally constructed objective entities. However, this somewhat intricate point need not concern us here any further.

I repeat that, at any rate, as all unions among men, communities, fellowships, corporations, and so forth, so is the state something that is ideally constructed. The remaining question is, then, of what kind this ideational element is and how it can be conceptualized. With this question we return to the contrast in the concepts of essential will and arbitrary will, *Gemeinschaft* and *Gesellschaft*. The state can be experienced and thought of by its own subjects, its citizens, and its people, as essential purpose, therefore as being alike to an organism or a natural whole, which comprises all those who know themselves dependent on it and conditioned by it, whose members they are, and which by its very nature exists before they exist. Here is the seat of the connection with the biological view, the conceptualistic realism, and the theory of organism. For it goes without saying that in its psychological implications this view is easier and more likely to be adopted when any unions thus constructed are identical with natural wholes, or at least as similar as may be; if—to put it plainly—for example, the state possesses a close likeness to the family (considered as a social entity) and the family as a social entity is a reminder of the family as we know it from natural history.

This last condition is most nearly satisfied in a social union whose special basis is consanguinity and common descent. The family, in its two varieties of patriarchal or matriarchal domination (*Herrschaft*) and of fraternal-egalitarian fellowship (*Genossenschaft*), is therefore the type of *Gemeinschaft* based on essential will. But in its further development, particularly under the impact of urban civilization, this structure moves far away from its type and ceases to be like a family that carries its own purpose in itself in all its naturalness and inevitability; it comes to resemble more and more an association, which has an external purpose and is essentially a means to achieve the expressed or unexpressed, open or latent ends of its founders and members—from which we started as from the clearest and most rational social entity. The association is the type of *Gesellschaft*, which has sprung from free rational, or arbitrary, will, whether actually or in its intention. *Gemeinschaft*, I repeat, assimilates to the rational purpose—association. But against this must be held the possibility that *Gemeinschaft* may remain, and continue to develop as *Gemeinschaft*, if the corresponding way of thinking and its social will gains the support of new aids; if, for example, the whole or the commonwealth, though no longer and less and less like a natural union, or a quasi-organic whole, yet portrays itself as such an entity in emotion, imagination, and reflective thought, that is to say, if the common spirit wants to maintain it as such.

It is here in particular that the inestimable influence of religion on social life lies, and one might say even more specifically on political life. This influence is preserved despite the fact that gradually, with the scientific outlook advancing and faith, whether for this or any other reason, decaying, religion must content itself with a mere role, which it plays under the masks of its priests and other dignitaries. The idea remains the same: the commonwealth is being hallowed and raised above criticism; it is being thought of as a god, or the special emanation of a god, whether this godly loftiness and grace are effused over the person and the inherited rights of a sovereign or live forth in the tutelary genius of a city community. What matters is that, with the statute and the law also their originators, interpreters and transformers are being lifted to the supranatural glow of beings to whom reverence is owed. Consequently, the social union, whether called the state or by any other name, exercises that higher authority, or lays claim to it, over the individual subjects and citizens, which a creator claims over his creatures, a mother over her children, whom she has nourished at her bosom. But then it is fatal indeed if religious consciousness brings forth, as it were, from its own powers a community as a *Civitas Dei*, in opposition to the worldly commonwealth, which in turn is being stigmatized as temporal and profane, if not as *Civitas Diaboli*—the Church against the Empire, which now must borrow its godly attributes from the Church.

That the Church is of godly origin is self-evident to the faithful. But is the empire, or even the city community? With the deities of its citadel, the Hellenic *polis* was a place of pious faith and cult. The modern city could never quite gain such intrinsic exaltedness, notwithstanding the fact that in the last century three or four cities were misshaped in the caricature of a sovereign member of the German federal system. The old German empire, as is known, remained until its demise the Holy Roman Empire.

What we must try to understand is that for the actual nature of the state or of any other community, in particular one that is not specifically ecclesiastic, the decisive criterion is the economic relation of the whole to its parts, in other words, the rights of ownership. Can private property be construed—and is it in its chief functions such that it can legitimately be so construed—as independent, free in its own right, as though the people, some with their capital and their land, some with their naked bodies, had entered into the state, and concluded the social contract in the same manner in which the captain of industry or the lord of the manor contracts on the basis of formal equality with people offering their labor as a commodity? Or, is it true that one must construe the state as a guardian angel, who attends to the distribution of wealth according to the principles of merit and justice, and then grants the one an annual income of two to five million, the other an income of one hundred or two hundred dollars?

I cannot enter, at this stage, into a discussion of this problem. No simple answer is possible, but it will be understood that here I am touching on the problem of socialism. This problem can, as a matter of fact, be formulated thus: whether social volition and reflection in our time will prove strong enough to develop the modern state into a genuine community (*Gemeinschaft*) which extends to the mastery over private property—perhaps, instead of "to develop," one ought to say "to transform"; or, whether the tendencies of *Gesellschaft* will remain preponderant in this social volition and reflection.

With these comments on the three objects of knowledge—social relations, social will, social unions,[2] I hope I have succeeded in expressing exhaustively the essential nature of sociology.

To be sure, concerning social relations, the sociological approach remains closely connected with related approaches in biology and psychology. But concerning social volition and social un-

---

2   The triadic division of the objects of knowledge in pure sociology has more recently been re-formulated, so that social will is replaced by "collectives" (*"Samtschaften"*), which in the same manner as relations and corporations (unions) represent a species of social bonds. Social will, apart from its being treated in social psychology, is then subordinated to these species of social bond, as being conditioned by them.

ions, while connections with psychology are evident, the subject matter of sociology is of a particular nature, because it is conditioned by reason and thought; it is therefore meaningless to speak of "states" of bees and ants. The social life of animals can be approached biologically and psychologically, but one cannot in the least assume that their social relations, their common volition, and especially their unions are objects to them; and because this is so only with regard to humans, it can be stated that this *Trias* is the natural and necessary subject matter of a conceptual, that is, a theoretical or philosophical science of sociology.[3]

Sociology is confronted by the vast profusion of social, and that means also historical, life. Its task is to take hold of it through its categories, to stir it up, and to saturate itself with it, in order to ascertain what its patterns are, and at least to conjecture its wherefrom and whereto. For scientific knowledge about it can be achieved but only in dim outline. It ought to be added that history is not a separate science. The writing of history is a profound art, resting though it does on the search for truth, which must be undertaken in the scientific spirit. She has her own rules, her glorious tradition, her celebrated masters. It is not surprising that she refuses to accept new standards, let alone prescriptions, from an immature sociology. Applied sociology's task is not to compete with the writing of history. It is nothing but the philosophy of history, however little or much that may be thought to involve. But this should certainly be fashioned in such a way that the historian may learn from it, indeed, cannot help but learn from it. The main body of philosophy, in the course of the last few centuries, has been transforming itself more and more from a theological into a secular-scientific synopsis and synthesis. On this road the philosophy of history has so far remained farthest behind. The theological world view has sought and found its fulfillment in a philosophy of history. The scientific world view, likewise, must be consummated in the philosophy of history.

[3]   This paragraph is a summary of somewhat more extensive statements in the text.—EDS.

7

THE PRESENT PROBLEMS OF

SOCIAL STRUCTURE

THE PROBLEMS of social structure we find in a rather confused state at the present moment. In an earlier stage of sociological
thinking, considerable expectations were attached to the interpretation of social phenomena by means of biological analogies or
what was called the organic theory of society. These expectations
may now be said to have been disappointed. The organic theory
has almost universally been abandoned. Yet even its severest
critics are likely to admit that there is some truth in or behind it,
although they seem to be at a loss to explain properly what kind
of truth it is.

By a curious coincidence, the three most notable representatives of that doctrine—the Russian Paul von Lilienfeld, a man of
high social standing; the German Albert Schaeffle, with a reputation as a political economist; and the Englishman Herbert Spencer, whose fame needs not to be emphasized—all departed from
life in the year 1903, the two latter in the month of December; all
in advanced old age. To these three men sociology owes a debt of
gratitude, because, after Comte, they were the first—at least in
Europe—to formulate a theory of social life in large outline. From

From "The Present Concept of Social Structure," *American Journal of
Sociology* 10, no. 5 (March 1905) : 569–88. The paper was read at the
Congress of Arts and Science, St. Louis, September 1904. It appears that
Toennies was invited to the Congress by its two Vice-Presidents, Hugo
Muensterberg, Professor of Psychology, Harvard University, and Albion
Small, Professor of Sociology, University of Chicago. The other speakers
in the section "Social Structure," where Toennies delivered his paper,
were Gustav Ratzenhofer and Lester F. Ward.

all, but especially from Schaeffle and Spencer, we receive, and shall continue to receive, constant and fertile impulses or suggestions. But I feel safe in predicting that it will soon be universally acknowledged that the foundations of their theories were not laid firmly enough for permanently supporting those boldly planned structures of thought.

For a long time past I have cherished the opinion that these authors, as well as nearly all their successors and critics, are hampered by a fundamental lack of clearness as to the subject of their inquiries—a subject which they are in the habit of designating by the very indefinite name of "a society," or, as Schaeffle puts it, "*the* social body." Confusion of ideas invariably proceeds from a defect of analytical reasoning; that is to say, of proper distinction.

I believe and assert that three distinct conceptions, the common object of which is social life in its broadest sense, are not sufficiently, or not at all, kept apart nor even recognized as being distinct, namely, the biological, the psychological, and the sociological in what I call the exclusive sense, the subject of only this third conception being entirely new, as compared with the subjects of other sciences or departments of philosophy. It seems to me to be our fundamental task as philosophical sociologists to deduce from this last conception, and others implied in it, a system of social structure which shall contain the different notions of collective entities in their mutual dependence and connection; and I firmly trust that out of such a system will be gained a better and more profound insight into the evolution of society at large, and into its historical phases, as the life of these collective entities. It is therefore in the struggles, first, between any of these groups and the individuals composing it; second, between their different forms and kinds—for instance, the struggles between Church and empire; between Church and cities; between Church and state; between cities and other corporations; between the sovereign state and feudal communities, and consequently established orders or estates; between single states and a federal state—it is in these and similar struggles, presupposing the *existence* of those collective entities, that the growth and decay of higher civilizations exhibit themselves most markedly.

I

When we speak of a house, a village, or a city, the idea immediately arising in our minds is that of a visible building; or of larger and smaller groups of buildings; but soon we also recollect the visible contents of these buildings, such as rooms and cellars and their furniture; or, when groups of buildings are concerned, the roads and streets between them. The words "house," "village," and "city" are, however, used in a different sense when we have in mind the particular contents of buildings which we call their inhabitants, especially their human occupants. Very often, at least in many languages, people are not only conceived of as the inhabitants of, but as identical with, the buildings. We say, for instance, "the entire house," "the whole village"—meaning a lot of people the idea of whom is closely connected with the idea of their usual dwelling place. We think of them as being one with their common habitation. Nevertheless it is still a visible union of individuals which we have in mind. This visible union, however, changes into an invisible one when it is conceived of as lasting through several generations. Now the house will become identified with a family or perhaps with a clan. In the same manner, a village community or a township will be imagined as a collective being, which—although not in all, yet in certain important, respects—remains the same in essence, notwithstanding a shifting of matter; that is to say, an incessant elimination of waste portions—men who die—and a constant accretion of fresh elements—children, who are born. Here the analogy with the essential characteristics of an organism is obvious. Vegetable and animal organisms likewise are only represented by such elements as are visible at any time, and the law of life consists in this, that the remaining portions always predominate over the eliminated and the reproduced ones, and that the latter by and by move and fill up the vacant spaces, while the relations of parts—for example, the cooperation of cells as tissues, or of tissues as organs—do not undergo a substantial change. Thus such an application of biological notions to the *social life* of mankind—as the organicist theories or methods set out to do

—is not to be rejected on principle. We may, in fact, look upon any community of this kind—maintaining itself by renewing[1] its parts—as being a living whole or unity. This view is the more plausible if the renewal itself is merely biological, as indeed is the case in the human family, and, as we think, to a still greater extent —because a family soon disperses itself—in certain larger groups; a tribe, a nation, or a race; although there is involved in this view the question whether there is a sameness of nature—or, as we usually say, of blood—guaranteed, as it should be, by inbreeding (German: *Inzucht*).[2] Indeed, this self-conservation of a group is the less to be expected, the smaller the group; and it is well known among breeders that it is necessary for the life of a herd not to continue too long selecting sires of the same breed, but from time to time to refresh the blood by going beyond the limits of a narrow parentage and by crossing the race by mixtures with a different stock.

At any rate, this is what I should call a purely *biological* aspect of collective human life, insofar as their conception is restricted to the mere existence of a human group, which, so to speak, is self-active in its maintenance of life.

This aspect, however, does not suffice when we consider social units of a local character, which also continue their existence, partly in the same, but partly in a different, manner. With reference to them, we do not think exclusively of a natural *Stoffwechsel*, as it is effected by births and deaths of the individuals composing the body, but we also consider the moving to and fro of living men, women, and children, the ratio of which, like the ratio of births and deaths, may cause an increase or a decrease of the whole mass, and *must* cause one or the other if they do not balance. In consequence of this, we also have less reason to expect a biological identity of the stock of inhabitants at different times than a lasting connection between a part of space (the place), or rather a piece

1   The original has "receiving," obviously a misreading of Toennies' manuscript.—Eds.
2   The original has "in-and-in breeding of parents." That T. does not mean inbreeding in the pathological sense is clear from the subsequent sentence.—Eds.

of the soil, and a certain group of men who dwell in that place and have intercourse with each other, although the place itself grows with the number of its inhabitants, and although even among these inhabitants there may be, for instance, not one direct descendant of those who occupied the place say, a hundred years ago. We may, it is true, take it to be the rule that at least a certain nucleus of direct descendants keeps alive through many generations—a rule so much more certain if it is a large place, a whole region, or even a country that we have in mind. Still, we shall not hold this to be a *conditio sine qua non* for acknowledging the village or the city to be the same; it being in this respect much more relevant that the nucleus of the place, of the "settlement," has endured and has preserved itself through the ages. Now, since place and region, air and climate, have a very considerable effect upon the intelligence and sentiment of the inhabitants, and since a considerable change may not justly be expected with respect to this, except when the minds as well as the external conditions of the newcomers are totally different from those of the older strata, we may consider the identity of a place, insofar as it is founded upon the social connection of men with a part of the soil, as a *psychological* identity, and call this aspect of social life a psychological aspect. There can be no doubt that this psychological aspect is in great part dependent upon the biological aspect and is, as a rule, closely interwoven with it. Yet it needs but little reflection to recognize that both are also to a certain extent separate and independent of each other. The subject matter of a social psychology is different from the subject matter of a social biology, though there exist a great many points of contact between them, and though both, apart from the foundations here given to them, may be applied to animal as well as to human societies.

II

Neither of the above-mentioned conceptions of a continuous unity or whole implies that the essential characteristic of the unity is perceived and recognized by those who belong to it, much less that it is perceived by others, by outsiders. And this is the third idea, by far the most important one for the present consideration—the idea of what I propose to designate by the name of a *corporation*, including under it all social units whatever, insofar as they have this trait in common—that the mode of existence of the unity or whole itself is founded upon the consciousness of its existence, and consequently that it perpetuates itself by the conception of its reality being transmitted from one generation to the next one; which will not happen unless it is done on purpose by teaching, and generally in the form of tradition. This evidently presupposes human reason and human will, marking off sharply this third genus from any kind of animal subhuman society.

We are now going to give closer attention to this conception. For the most part, though not always, it is the conception of a unity different from the aggregate of members; the idea of a psychical or moral *body*, capable of willing and of acting like a single human being; the idea of a self or person. This person, of course, is an artifical or fictitious one. It represents indeed, as the former two conceptions did, a unity persisting through the change of its parts, but this unity and identity persisting in the multitude are neither biological nor directly and properly psychological, but must, in distinction from these, be considered as specifically *sociological;* that is to say, while the second is the social consciousness or social mind itself, this is the product of it, and can be understood only by looking into the human soul, and by perceiving thoughts and wills which not only have a common drift and tendency but are creators of a common work.

The idea, however, of a body capable of willing and acting is, as said above, not always, and not necessarily, implied in the idea of a sociological unit. This is a conception preceding it, as protoplasm precedes individual bodies; namely, the general idea of a society (or a community, if this important distinction is adverted to), which is not essentially different from our second idea of a psychological unit, except in this one respect, accessory to it, that the idea of this unit be present somehow in the minds of the people who feel or know themselves as belonging to it. This conception is of far-reaching significance, being the basis of all conceptions of a social, as contrasted with a political, corporation. It therefore comprises especially those spheres of social life which are more or less independent of political organization, among which the economic activity of men is the most important, including, as it does, domestic life as well as the most remote international relations between those who are connected exclusively by the ties of commercial interest. But practically it is of little consequence whether this general idea be considered as psychological or as sociological, unless we precisely contemplate men who consciously maintain their own conception of their own social existence, in distinction from other ideas relating to it, chiefly when it is put in contrast to the idea of a political corporation, and the political corporation of highest import is concerned—the state. And it was exactly in these its shifting relations to the state that the idea of society proper—though without recognition of its subjective character—was evolved about fifty years ago by some German theorists—notably Lorenz Stein, Rudolph Gneist, and Robert Mohl—who were more or less strongly under the sway of Hegelian philosophy, seeing that Hegel in his *Rechtsphilosophie* develops his idea of human corporate existence under the threefold heading of (1) the family as "thesis," (2) civil society as "antithesis," and (3) the state as "synthesis" of the two former.

But, though I myself lay considerable stress upon this general notion of society, in juxtaposition and opposition to the state or political society, I still regard it as more indispensable to a theory of social structure to inquire into the nature and causes of what may be called, from the present point of view, genuine corporations; that is, those conceived of as being capable of willing and acting like a single individual endowed with reason and self-consciousness. The question arises how a "moral person" may be considered as possessing this power.

Evidently this is an impossibility, unless one single individual or several together are willing and acting *in the name of* that fictitious being. And in order justly to be taken for the volitions and acts of an individual distinct from their own individualities, those volitions and acts must be distinguishable by certain definite marks from the rest of their willing and acting, which they do in their own name; they must be differentiated formally. There must be a tacit or an open understanding, a sort of covenant or convention, that only volitions and acts so differentiated shall be considered as volitions and acts of the said moral person whom one or those several individuals are supposed to represent. By the way, this question of marks and signs, consensual or conventional, by which a thing, physical or moral, not only is recognized as such but by which its value (or what it is *good for*) is differentiated from its existence (or what it *is*), pervades all social life and mind, and may be called the secret of it. It is clear that certain signs may easily be fixed or invented whereby the volitions and acts of a single individual may be differentiated from the rest as being representative. But how if there are more than one, who only occasionally have one will and act together, and who cannot be supposed to agree in their feelings as soon as they are required to represent their moral person? It is well known that these must be "constituted" as an *assembly* or as a whole capable by its constitution to deliberate and, what is more, to resolve and act. It must be settled by their own or by the will of another person (1) under what conditions, and with respect to what subject matters, their resolutions shall be considered as representing declarations of will of their own body; and (2) under what conditions, and with respect to what subject matters, declarations of will of this body shall be valid as declarations of will of the moral person they represent.

It is therefore the *constitution* of a multitude into a unity which we propose as a fourth mode, and as a necessary consequence of the third one, unless the moral person be represented exclusively by a single man or woman as a natural person. The many constitute themselves or are constituted as a body, which is, as far as it may be, similar to a natural person in such relations as are essential precisely for the notion of a person. Consequently, this body also is a unity, but a unity conceived a priori as being destined for a definite purpose, namely, the representation of a moral person— the third or sociological kind of unity. And it is different from that third notion only by this very relation, which evidently cannot be inherent in that person himself. That, in consequence of this relation, it has a visible existence apart from its own idea, while the moral person represented is nothing beyond his own idea. We may distinguish, therefore, between five modes of existence in a moral person represented by a body: (1) the ideal existence in the minds of its members; (2) the ideal existence of the body constituted, which represents the moral person, being as well in the minds of the natural persons who compose that body as in the minds of members of the corporation generally; (3) the visible existence of this body, being the assembly of natural persons, willing and acting under certain forms; (4) the intelligible existence of this assembly, being conditioned by a knowledge, on the part of those who externally or theoretically perceive it, of its constitution and its meaning; (5) the intelligible existence of the moral person or the body represented, being conditioned of a knowledge of the relation between this corporation and the body representing it, implying the structure of the former in the first, and of the latter in the second instance.

The visible existence of an assembly means that members are visible as being assembled, but the assembly as a body can be recognized only by a reflecting spectator who knows what those forms mean, who "realizes" their significance, who *thinks* the assembly. Of course, a corporation also, apart from its representation, can be perceived only mentally, by outsiders as well as by its own members, and these are different perceptions (distinguished here as ideal and intelligible existence): members perceiving it directly as a product of their own will, and therefore in a way as their property (a thing which they own); and outsiders perceiving it only indirectly, by knowing the person or body that represents it; this being an external perception only, unless it be supplemented by a knowledge of its peculiar mode of being, that is, of its constitution and of the relations which members bear to the whole, and the whole to its members.

But it is, above all, in this respect that great differences exist between different kinds of corporations. The first question is whether individuals feel and think themselves as founders or authors or at least as representative ideal authors of their own corporation. Let us take an obvious example. Suppose a man and a woman contract a marriage (we waive here all questions of church or state regulations for making the marriage tie public). They are said to found a family. Now, the children springing from this union and growing up in this family cannot justly feel and think themselves as the creators or authors of it as long as they are dependent upon their parents. However, they partake of it more and more consciously, and some day they may take upon themselves the representation of this whole internally and externally, in place of their father and mother. They may learn to feel and to think of themselves as bearers of the personality of this ideal being, playing, so to speak, the parts of the authors and founders, whom they also may survive and will survive in the normal course of human events; and they may continue the identity of the family beyond the death of their parents. They may maintain the continuity of this identical family, even when new families have sprung from it which may or may not regard themselves as members of the original one. The proposition that it exists still is true at least for those who will its truth and who act upon this principle; nay, it is by their thought and will that they are creating it anew as it was made originally by the wills of the first two persons. A different question is whether the existence of this corporation will be recognized and acknowledged by others who may stand in relation to its members or may simply be impartial theoretical spectators.

But, further, there is this fundamental difference in the relation of individuals to that ideal entity which they think and will, whether they be its real or merely its representative authors, namely: (1) they may look upon the corporation, which they have created really or ideally, as upon a thing existing for its own sake, as an end in itself, although it be at the same time a means for other ends; or (2) they may conceive it clearly as a mere tool, as nothing but an instrument for their private ends, which they either naturally have in common or which accidentally meet in a certain point.

The first case appears in a stronger light if they consider the social entity as really existing, and especially if they consider their corporation as a living being; for a real thing, and especially a living thing, has always some properties of its own. The latter has even something like a will of its own; it cannot be conceived as being disposable, divisible, applicable, and adaptable at pleasure to any purpose, as a means to any end—this being the notion of pure matter, as it exists only in our imagination; and therefore a thing which has merely nominal existence would be really nothing but a mass of such imaginary matter, absolutely at one's disposal, offering no resistance, being stuff in itself, that is to say, potentially anything one may be able to make, to knead, to shape, or to construe out of it (of course real matter may and will more or less approach to this idea). On the other hand, to think of an ideal thing as being ideal is not the same as to think of it as imaginary matter; but if one aims at a certain object, if one follows out one's designs, one is constrained by a psychological necessity to break resistances and to subject things as well as [other] wills to one's own will; one tends to make them all alike, as "wax in one's hand," to remove or to oppress their own qualities and their own wills, so as to leave, as far as possible, nothing but a dead and unqualified heap of atoms, a something of which imaginary matter is the prototype. Of course, it is only as a tendency that this dissolving and revolutionary principle is always active, but its activity is manifest everywhere in social life, especially in modern society, and characterizes a considerable portion of the relations of individuals to each other and consequently to their corporations.

As long as men think and regard "society"—that is to say, their clan or their polis, their church or their commonwealth—as real and as truly existing; nay, when they even think of it as being alive, as a mystical body, a supernatural person, so long will they not feel themselves as its masters; they will not be likely to attempt using it as a mere tool, as a machine for promoting their own interests; they will look upon it rather with awe and humility than with a sense of their own interest and superiority. And, in consequence of feelings of this kind, they even forget their own authorship—which, as a rule, will indeed be an ideal one only; they will feel and think themselves not creators but creatures of their own corporations. This is the same process as that which shows itself in the development of men's regular behavior toward their gods, and the feeling and thinking just mentioned are always closely related to, or even essentially identical with, religious feeling and thinking. Like the gods themselves, to whom so regularly *la cité antique*, with its temples and sanctuaries, is dedicated, the city or corporation itself is supposed to be a supernatural eternal being, and consequently existing not only in a real but in an eminent sense.

But, of course, all feelings of this kind are but to a limited extent liable to retard the progress of a consciousness of individual interests, or, as it is commonly spoken of—with a taint of moral reproach—of selfishness. As a matter of fact, it is the natural ripening of consciousness and thinking itself which makes reflection prevail over sentiment, and which manifests itself, first and foremost, in reflection upon a man's own personal interest in the weighing and measuring of costs and results; but, second, also in a similar reflection upon some common interest of business which a person, from whatever motive, selfish or not, has made his own affair; and third, in that unbiased interest and in reflection upon the nature and causes of things and events, of man's happiness and social existence, which we call scientific or philosophical.

All reflection is, in the first instance, analytical. I have spoken already of the dissolving principle which lies in the pursuing of one's own personal affairs, of which the chase after profit is but the most characteristic form. But the same individualistic standpoint is the standpoint, or at least the prevailing tendency, of science also. It is *nominalism* which pervades science and opposes itself to all confused and obscure conceptions, closely connected as it is with a striving after distinctness and clearness and mathematical reasoning. This nominalism also penetrates into men's supposed collective realities (supernatural or not), declaring them to be void and unreal, except insofar as individual and real men have consented to make such an artificial being, to construct it, and to build it up mentally. Knowledge and criticism oppose themselves to faith and intuition, in this as in most other respects, and try to supplant them. To know how a church or a state is created means the downfall of that belief in its supernatural essence and existence which manifestly is so natural to human feeling and intellect. The spirit of science is at the same time the spirit of freedom and of individualistic self-assertion, in contradiction and in opposition to the laws and ties of custom—as well as of religion, so intimately connected and homologous with custom—which seem entirely unnatural and irrational to analytical reasoning. This reasoning always puts the questions: What is it good for? Does it conduce to the welfare of those whom it pretends to bind or to rule? Is it in consonance with right reason that men should impose upon themselves the despotism of those laws and of the beliefs sanctioning them?

The classical answer has been given in a startling fashion by one whom Comte called the father of revolutionary philosophy. There is, says Thomas Hobbes, a realm of darkness and misery, founded upon superstition and false philosophy, which is the Church; and there is, or there might be, a realm of light and happiness, founded upon the knowledge of what is right and wrong; that is to say, of the laws of nature, dictated by reason and by experience, to check hostile and warlike individual impulses by a collective will and power; this realm is the true state, that is to say, the idea and model of its purely rational structure, whether it may exist anywhere as yet or not. Hobbesianism is the most elaborate and most consistent system of the doctrine commonly known as that of natural law (*Naturrecht*), including, as it always did, a theory of the state. As a matter of fact, this doctrine has been abandoned almost entirely, especially in Germany, where it had been exerting a very considerable influence in the century which preceded the French Revolution, when even kings and absolutist statesmen were among its open adherents. It has been controverted and abandoned ever since the first quarter of the nineteenth century—a fact which stands in manifest connection with the great reaction and restoration in the political field following the storms of that revolution and of Bonapartist rule in Europe. There is hardly a liberal school left now which dares openly profess that much-derided theory of a "social compact." This, I believe, is somewhat different in the United States. As far as my knowledge goes, this theory—that is to say, an individualistic construction of society and of the state—is still the ordinary method employed in this country for a deduction of the normal relations between state or society, on the one hand, and individuals, on the other; for, as needs no emphasis, it is not the opinion of an original contract in the historical sense that is to be held in any way as a substantial element of the theory. And yet the obvious criticism of that pseudo-element has been the most powerful argument against the whole theory, which consequently has seldom met with an intelligent and just appreciation in these latter days. And it is in opposition to it that, apart from a revival of theological interpretations, the recent doctrine of society or state as an organism has become so popular for a time.

This doctrine, of course, was an old one. Not to speak of the ancients, in the so-called Middle Ages it has preceded the contract theory, as it has supplemented it in more modern times. It was, indeed, coupled with the theological conceptions and religious ideals so universally accepted in those days although it was not dependent upon them. The doctrine of St. Thomas [Aquinas] and of Dante, however, contains a theory of the universal state; that is to say, of the empire, not a theory of society, of which the conception had not yet been formed, as we may safely say that a consciousness of it did not exist. This traditional organicism—applied as well to the Church, the mystic body, of which Christ was the supposed head —has been transferred of late to "society," after it had regained fresh authority as a political doctrine. However, the conception of a "society," as distinguished from political or religious bodies, is much more vague and indefinite. Either it is to be taken in the first and second sense, which I have pointed out as a biological or a psychological aspect of collective life, in which case organic analogies hold, but the whole consideration is not properly sociological; or it may be taken in our third, or sociological, sense, in which case it implies much less than any corporation the idea of what may be called an organization. It is well known that a lively controversy has been aroused about the new organicist theory, as proposed by Mr. Spencer and others, chiefly among those sociologists who center in the Institut International of Paris, where the late lamented M. Tarde played so prominent a part. Tarde has been among the foremost combatants against the vague analogies of organicism; and I fully agree with most of his arguments as set forth in the third sociological congress of 1897. I even flatter myself on having anticipated some of them in an early paper of mine upon Mr. Spencer's sociological work; which paper, however, did not become known beyond the small public of the *Philosophische Monatshefte* (1888). I have especially, and to a greater degree than Tarde, insisted upon the radical difference between a physiological division of labor and that division which is a cardinal phenomenon of society. I said: If we justly call it a division of labor that England manufactures cotton and China produces tea, and that the two countries exchange their products, then there is not and has not been a common labor or function preceding this division and dividing itself, as in the case of an organism; no state of society being historically known where China and England were one whole, working in harmony upon the spinning wheel and upon the tea plant. This is far from being true; each had its own historical development until they met in the mutual want of barter; and even this consideration implies that the countries themselves may justly be said to entertain trade and commerce with each other, though this is hardly more than a *façon de parler* with respect to a country like China.

It may be objected that there is a better analogy if we think of a primitive household, where labor is indeed one and is shifting among members of the community, while at a later stage it splits up into several families, some cultivating the soil, some becoming warriors or priests or artisans and tradesmen. And in the same way a village community, even an independent township like the ancient or medieval city, and a whole territory of which a city is the center, may reasonably be conceived of as one real household, of which all single households form organic parts. They would thus be contrasted with modern society, which is more adequately conceived of as a mere aggregate of individual households, each pursuing its own interest, maybe at the cost of all the others. This is my own objection, and this view is contained in my own theory of *Gemeinschaft* and *Gesellschaft*, meaning the dualism of that primitive economic condition surviving in many respects down to our own days, on the one hand, and commercial or capitalistic society, of which the germs are traceable in any form of what, with an abstract term, may be called communism, on the other. It is the former sense that even modern political economy may be spoken of (as we style it in German) as "national" economy. But even if this be allowed, the organic analogy does not hold other than in a rather indefinite way. Where is the one "social body" which thus evolves its organs and members, being in its early stage like a single household or a village community, and growing to be a complex *ensemble* of manors and municipalities and great cities, some of which have their manufactures working for foreign export, some for inland consumption? Is it England that has taken a development of this kind? Or is it England and Wales? Or are Scotland and even poor conquered Ireland to be included?

The more we should try to follow out the admirable attempt which Herbert Spencer has made in this direction of employing the organicist view as a working hypothesis, the more we should become convinced that our real insight into the lines along which social evolution travels is more hampered than promoted by that method of biological analogies.

III

But did I not say there was truth in the biological conception of social life? Indeed I did, and I say so again, if social life is considered externally and if we speak of a group as a living whole, where life is understood in its genuine sense, that is to say, biologically. And from this point of view, as that famous term, "physiological division of labor," is borrowed from economic fact and theory, we may, vice versa, apply physiological terms to social life considered externally. We may speak of organs and functions in a nation or society, or even with respect to mankind at large. We may metaphorically call the civilized nations the "brain" of humanity, and we may say that the United States has become an independent lobe of the cortex in the course of the last forty years. In the same way it was only lately, I understand, that your President spoke of railways as the arteries through which the blood of trade is circulating. The force of this metaphor will, I believe, not be impaired by the fact that several theorists point in more than a figurative sense to money or credit as the social fluid into which all substances of commodities are changed and which nourishes again the social brain and social muscles; that is to say, men and women who perform mental and physical work; in consequence of which analogy banks, and their correspondence by letters and bills and checks, would, more than railways, resemble arteries and veins. Of course, it would be small trouble to adduce a number of similar ambiguities, which make sociological inquiries of this kind appear as a matter of rhetoric and poetry but not of science.

Is there no other, no philosophical, truth at least in the comparison of a corporation to a living body? If there is, it can, according to the present view, be only in this respect, that a corporation may be thought and felt as an organic whole, upon which the members think and feel themselves dependent in such a way that they consider their own individual existence as subservient to the life of the whole. The question whether a society *is* an organism must be kept apart from the question whether there are societies the relations of which to their members are so qualified as to imply thoughts and feelings of that kind on the part of their members. We are well aware that social systems, which have been called by some eminent authors "ancient society," truly exhibited this characteristic trait. Why is not modern society—and, above all, the modern state—an organism in this peculiar sense?

I believe, indeed, that there is strong reason for controverting the theory in its application to these collective beings as they actually are. We live, as everybody knows, in an individualistic age, and we seek each other's company, chiefly for the benefit that accrues from it; that is to say, in a comparatively small degree from motives of sentiment and to a comparatively great extent from conscious reflection. It is this which makes us regard the state also as an instrument fit for serving our particular interests or those we have in common with some or with all of our fellow citizens rather than as an organism, ideally preexistent to ourselves, living its own life, and being entitled to sacrifices of our life and property in its behalf. It is true that in extraordinary times we live up to this view, but then we do not speak so much of society and of the state as of the fatherland which puts forward its claim to what we call our patriotism. A feeling of brotherhood and fellowship, of which in ordinary times the traces are as sadly scarce among compatriots as among those who are strangers to each other, rises, in moments of public danger, from the bottoms of our souls in effervescent bubbles. The feeling, to be sure, is more of the nature of an emotion than of a lasting sentiment. Our normal relations toward our present societies and states must not be taken as being accommodated to this extraordinary standard. They are, howsoever men may boast of their patriotism, generally of a calm and calculating character. We look upon the state, represented as it is by its government, as upon a person who stands in contractual rather than in sentimental relations to ourselves. Certainly this view is more or less developed in different countries, under different circumstances, with different individuals. But it is the one that is endorsed by the most advanced and the most conscious members of modern societies, by those powerful individuals who feel themselves as masters of their own social relations. Societies and states are chiefly institutions for the peaceful acquisition, and for the protection, of property. It is therefore the owners of property to whom we must look when we are inquiring into the prevailing and growing conceptions of society and of the state. Now it cannot be doubted that they do not consider either society or the state as representing that early community which has always been supposed to be the original proprietor of the soil and of all its treasures, since this would imply that their own private property had only a derivative right —derived from the right and law of public property. It is just the opposite which they think and feel: the state has a derivative right of property by their allowance and their contributions; the state is supposed to act as their mandatary. And it is this view which corresponds to the facts. A modern state—it is by no means always the youngest states that are the most characteristic types of it— has little or no power over property.

I cannot refrain from quoting here, as I have done elsewhere, a few sentences of the eminent American sociologist Lewis Morgan, in which he sums up his reflections upon modern as contrasted with ancient society. "Since the advent of civilization the outgrowth of property has been so immense, its forms so diversified, its uses so expanding, and its management so intelligent in the interests of its owners, that it has become, on the part of the people, an unmanageable power. The human mind stands bewildered in the presence of its own creation." He thinks it is true that "the time will come when human *intelligence* will rise to the mastery over property, and will be able to *define* the relations of the state to the property it protects, as well as the obligations and the limits of the rights of its owners." He declares himself unwilling to accept "a mere property career" as the final destiny of mankind.

But this outlook into a future far distant—although it was written, I believe, before there were any of the giant trusts established and before anybody in these states seemed to realize the dangers of the enormous power of combined capital—does not touch immediately the present question. It is the actual and real relation of the state to individuals which best reflects itself in the lack of power over property, as pointed out by Mr. Morgan, or, in other words, in the subservient position which the governments hold, in all countries more or less, toward the wealth-possessing classes. I do not say—although maybe I think—that this ought to be different; *"je ne propose rien, j' expose."* It is merely as a theoretical question that I touch upon this point. But I am not prepared to deny that it is also the great practical problem of social structure to reconstruct the state upon a new and enlarged foundation; that is to say, to make it, by common and natural effort, a real and independent being, an end in itself, a common wealth (in two words) administered not so much for the benefit of either a minority or a majority, or even of the whole number of its citizens, as for its own perpetual interests, which should include the interests of an indefinite number of future generations—the interests of the race. It cannot be overlooked that there are at present many tendencies at work in this direction, but I believe they are in part more apparent than real. The problem, we should confess, is an overwhelming one; and I for one do not feel at all sure that this splendid and transcendent constitution of ours will overcome its difficulties; that there will be sufficient *moral* power even if intelligence should rise to a sufficient height for solving in a truly rational way the "social question" as a question of social structure.

To sum up the argument, I put it in the form of a few theses or propositions:

1. The object of sociological theory proper, in distinction from

either biological or psychological, though these be ever so closely connected with it, is the corporation, for the most part represented, as it is, by a constituted body.

2. Religious faith makes some of the most important corporations appear as real, organic, mystic, and even supernatural beings. Philosophical criticism is right in discovering and explaining that all are creations of man and that they have no existence except insofar as human intellect and human will are embodied in them.

3. But nominalism is not the last word of a scientific philosophy. The existence of a corporation is fictitious indeed, but still is sometimes more than nominal. The true criterion is whether it be *conceived* and felt as a mere tool or machine, without a life of its own, or as something organic, superior to its temporary members. The true nature, however, of this conception is legible only from facts.

4. As a matter of fact, modern society and the modern state are prevailingly of a nature to correspond to an individualistic and nominalistic conception and standpoint. This is distinctly perceptible in the relation of the public power to private property.

5. This relation, and the relation dependent upon it, may substantially change in the course of time. An organic commonwealth may spring into existence which, though not sanctioned by any religious idea, and not claiming any supernatural dignity, still, as a product of human reason and conscious will, may be considered to be real in a higher sense than those products, as long as they are conceived as mere instruments serving the interests and objects of private individuals.

8

THE DIVISIONS OF SOCIOLOGY

I DISTINGUISH, first of all, general and special sociology. General sociology is the generalized study of human living together. This comprises all relationships of men in space and time, independent of whether or not they know each other, or have any relationship to each other, or whether they have a full or limited knowledge, or no knowledge at all, of each other's existence, whether they accept or reject each other, whether they live in a primitive state (formerly called a state of nature), or whether they live together or against each other in a state of a more or less developed culture. The study includes *all* these very diversified forms. But it excludes all kinds of social engineering (*Kunstlehren*) related to any one of these relationships; it only wishes to be a science of what is; this includes, however, what was and what will be, to the extent that it may become knowable.

The entire complex can be approached more specifically, depending on whether (1) the biological or (2) the psychological aspects are considered and explored or, finally, (3) out of both of them a specifically sociological investigation emerges.

In this sense, social biology and social psychology have at-

Translated from "Einteilung der Soziologie," *Soziologische Studien und Kritiken* 2 (1926) : 431–42; first published in *Zeitschrift fuer die gesamte Staatswissenschaft*, vol. 79, book 1 (1925) and presented before the Fifth International Philosophical Congress in Naples, which took place 5–9 May 1924. This paper, known as the "Naples paper," may be considered as the principal systematic forerunner of the book-length *Introduction to Sociology* (1931).

tained a position which includes them into general sociology, from which, however, special sociology is to be strictly distinguished.

General Sociology

Social biology, corresponding to its name, may also be extended to include the symbioses of plants and the so-called animal societies, but may be considered as a part of general sociology only to the extent that it explores human living together. In this sense, it also is called social anthropology. The subject of this science is man as an animal creature that feeds itself and procreates, moves back and forth and settles down, and, in the pursuance of all this, changes the surface of the earth, cultivates the soil, builds houses and ships, invents utensils, instruments and tools; all these things and the labor which produces them are of interest for this approach only inasmuch as they are *objective facts* which are part of the living together, that is, the very existence of man, furthering or hampering it. Likewise, the living together itself must be considered as far as it means mutual aid or, to the contrary, mutual damage and destruction in the world of external phenomena. The living together in space and time—that is, human life as a process of living next to each other, following each other, with and for or in spite and in defiance of each other—is here a sum total of natural events, which are subject to the general natural laws of growth and decay. These laws would be no less effective, if the living together were not accompanied, and even guided, by feelings and ideas. Within the area of social anthropology, psychology may thus be altogether disregarded.

Social anthropology deals with the races of mankind and their subdivisions insofar as their existence in large measure implies a spatial distribution of the human species continuing over long periods of time and a corresponding inbreeding; but also insofar as interbreeding with discernible results occurs and as consequently people of either the same or of different races and their subdivisions cooperate or are in a state of conflict with each other. To this area belong the questions of improvement and degeneration of the race together with the whole struggle for existence of naturally related human groups, struggles against the resistance of nature, struggles against each other for living space and for power and domination (*Herrschaft*). Power and domination may also be considered merely external facts, particularly the external coercion exerted by some against others for the purpose of making them serviceable and operating them like raw or processed objects of nature. Social biology is found as a component in several independently pursued sciences and can be singled out from these. *Ethnography* describes ethnic groups (*Voelker*), particularly primitive peoples whose culture is underdeveloped as far as the means of external existence are concerned. Next to ethnography may be placed demography, that is, the description of civilized nations, which provides insight into their life more thoroughly by means of enumeration and tabulation. Ethnography becomes ethnology, and demography becomes demology, that is, special sciences of the causal relationships between the phenomena observed. Ethnology and demology transfer their generalized results to social biology, which, in turn, transfers their elements to the theory of population; the descriptive sections, ethnography and demography, can be summarized as "sociography," which corresponds to the original and genuine meaning of statistics and is to be utilized in social biology, social psychology, and special sociology. Sociography also includes whatever belongs to the science of political economy, under the heading of "descriptive economics."

Social psychology is the necessary complement to social biology, as psychology generally complements biology. Social psychology considers all the factors included in the biological approach to human existence from the inner, psychic, or subjective side. It makes us perceive how people are brought together, kept together, and drawn close to each other by manifold motives, but also, on the other hand, how they are disunited, become hostile and alienated from each other by equally manifold motives. In these considerations men are conceived as individual carriers of a will, each of whom has particular psychic experiences in relation to all others and confirms or negates them to a lesser or larger degree. In addition, social psychology deals with those psychic experiences which are shared by several people inasmuch as they feel and react in the same way and want one and the same thing collectively. It is on account of this difference that Hans L. Stoltenberg has distinguished between "sociopsychology" and "psychosociology."

We accept this distinction and recognize in psychosociology the transition to the third division of general sociology, that is, to special sociology or sociology proper. The border area which, at the same time, is the first half of a bridge, includes the theory of social will, inasmuch as it is conceived as the common will of several individuals, but not yet as the unified will of an entity based on a common will, or a social entity.

Psychosociology thus includes the theory of masses (mass psychology) and of groups to the extent to which they are considered as merely externally connected aggregates.

Special Sociology

I subdivide special sociology into: *pure sociology; applied sociology; empirical sociology.* The reason for this subdivision is methodological; pure sociology is constructive, applied sociology is deductive, and empirical sociology is inductive.

Pure Sociology

Within pure sociology, I distinguish the following subdivisions: the basic concepts of *Gemeinschaft* and *Gesellschaft;* the theory of social entities; the theory of social norms, dealing with the content of the will of social entities; the theory of social values, dealing with the objects in the possession of social entities; the theory of social structures or institutions (*Bezugsgebilde*), dealing with the objects of action of social entities. These subdivisions are based on the concept of social entity. Social entity is conceived of as that which is not directly experienced; it must be seen and comprehended through the medium of the common thought and will of those individuals who are part of such an entity and who designate it. Such an entity exists only by means of this common will and therefore must always be conceived of as dependent on it. But the place of individuals or natural persons can also be taken by corporations or fictitious persons.

Basic concepts of sociology. The theory of the common will and its forms is the last extension of psychosociology, and consequently belongs to the area of social psychology, but leads from there directly to pure sociology. Within pure sociology, right at the entrance to it, I put the concepts of *Gemeinschaft* and *Gesellschaft*. The meaning of these concepts is that all relations among people as well as the derived relations of social corporations with individuals and with each other, even the relations between men and their gods, which like social entities are products of their imagination—all these complexes of positive relations which constitute a bond among men—(*vinculum*) have a twofold origin: either man's essential will or his arbitrary will. I conceive here as essential will the forms of volition, that is, affirmation as well as negation, which have their roots in feeling (in natural inclination and in instinct). They are strengthened by exercise or by way of habit and fulfilled as belief or trust. Part of essential will is also the affirmative volition inasfar as it is a means to an end, but only as long as these means are experienced and conceived in essential unity with the purpose. At this point, however, the break occurs, if and inasmuch as end and means fall apart, that is, if and when a means, in total isolation, finally indeed in opposition to the purpose, nevertheless is affirmed and willed as expedient; this occurs even in spite of an aversion which must be overcome, for instance, resistance, disgust, or remorse. The unit of *these* forms of willing I call arbitrary will. I understand community (*Gemeinschaft*) as based on essential will, association (*Gesellschaft*) as based on arbitrary will. Throughout, these concepts are logical, not genetic, in character.

The theory of the types of social entities. Among social entities, I distinguish: social relations, social collectives, and social corporations.

A social relation is essentially different from a natural as well as a psychological relation among men.

The *natural* relation among men, first of all, is an object of biological knowledge, therefore also of social biology. Individuals of the human species are interrelated like the individuals of another species by the facts: (1) that one organism descends from another, most directly from the mother organism; (2) that male and female individuals need each other for the purpose of procreation and therefore are attracted to each other; (3) that they are more or less akin, therefore more or less similar to each other; so that for these natural reasons they remain spatially close and have easy contact with each other. Natural relations, therefore, differ widely, according to their content, strength, and meaning. One may consider all people as brothers and sisters, but one will do so the more, the closer they are related by descent; within such multitudes, one may think of each generation as the mother of the following and the daughter of the preceding generation. But this always would have only a biological, not a psychological or sociological, meaning.

The *psychological* relation between people consists in the objective fact that they feel attracted to, or repelled by, each other either (a) by inclination or disinclination, familiarity or strangeness, trust and a sense of obligation, or by mistrust and a sense of antagonism, or (b) by self-interest, calculation of advantage, awareness of the usefulness or harmfulness of the other for one's own purposes: that is, either by essential will or by arbitrary will. Consequently, one may say that people feel related to each other by the fact that they think of each other as belonging together as natural friends and comrades, or as hampering and excluding each other, as real or possible—more or less probably—antagonists and enemies. A psychological relation of the former kind may be conceived of as a positive, that of the latter kind as a negative relation.

A *social* relation evolves from a positive psychological relation to the extent that it is not only experienced, thought of, and known as such but also affirmed and willed as existing and permanent. Every social relation is more or less based on a natural relation inasmuch as this relation is, or becomes at the same time, a positive psychological relation. A good example is the archetype of a communal relationship: the relation of mother and child. According to its origin as a natural relation, it is in the beginning a one-sided psychological relation and as such not essentially different from the relation to a beloved object. Normally, the one-sided relation becomes a mutual one and is affirmed as such by both subjects and consciously conceived as permanent and real. It is this consciousness that marks man as man. The Oedipus myth and the tragedy originating from it movingly express the dreadful fate which derives from ignorance and error in this regard.

By the will to continuity and permanency as well as by the consciousness of its correctness, the social relation connecting man and woman is raised to the status of marriage. The German word *Ehe* denotes—if perhaps not in its origin, so in its meaning—unlimited continuation, that is, eternity (*Ewigkeit*). Religious ideas and legal prohibitions usually protect this will to a legitimate marriage; but this protection is not an essential part of marriage as a social relation. Considered purely sociologically—without regard to legal validity or prevailing moral ideas—common-law marriage (*Gewissensehe*), too, is a real marriage if the mutual firm will to the relation, that is, enduring faithfulness, prevails and proves itself in it; such a marriage may even surpass the average of legally valid marriages in its quality as true marriage.

It belongs to the essence of every social relation as a mutual relationship approved by both parts that each of the persons involved makes and asserts a claim to a certain—regular or occasional, more or less permanent—conduct of the other person or persons; in other words, that conduct is expected as originating from their free will and conforming to the wish and will (the self-interest) of those who expect it. This mutual attitude is demanded and dictated by the common and uniform will essential to a social relation which appears as the will of the relationship itself, because the relationship is conceived in terms of an entity. It is therefore the relationship which generates duties or obligations, which raises corresponding demands and consequently also negates and prohibits free actions contradicting these obligations. In societal (*Gesellschaft*-like) relations, rights and obligations differ from each other with rational distinctness. We know of totalities of internally connected relations: such a relation is the family as the epitome of relations which are communal (*Gemeinschaft*-like) in their essence. Societal relations may also be connected in this manner and form an indeterminate unit: for instance, a number of people interested in the same business, as far as they know each other in this role.

We are here confronted with the transition to the second concept of a social entity, that is, the concept of the *collective*. By collective, I understand a number of individuals who are so connected with each other by natural or positive psychological or social relations between themselves that they are thought of as a unit. Natural collectives are those units of a biological character in which men of every age, both sexes, and any conceivable residence are comprised: as race, people, tribe, or other genealogical complexes to which the individuals belong and by which they are conditioned inasmuch as they have inherited from their ancestors the characteristics, or qualities, peculiar to such blood-related collective totalities. These collectives are psychic in nature, inasmuch as those qualities are psychic and manifest themselves in psychic phenomena. However, there also exist psychic collectives that are essentially determined not by natural but by psychic attributes, namely, by the abilities and achievements of its members. Such are linguistic and religious collectives, vocational groups, and the like, all of them considered quite externally as objective facts, as territorial census and statistical enumeration count them without thinking of drawing any conclusions regarding inner cohesion and social relationships. I call these and others *social* collectives if they are willed and affirmed by the people belonging to them more or less clearly and consciously and either emotionally or rationally: they are thus supported more by essential or more by arbitrary will and correspond either more to the category of *community* or more to the category of *association*. I subdivide social collectives into (1) those which are essentially economic and caused by economically determined social facts; (2) those which are essentially politically determined; (3) those which are essentially mentally and morally determined. Examples are: (1) Estates and classes; (2) the nation, civil society; (3) Christendom, the republic of letters, artistic or philosophical schools of thought, and so forth.

The social entity reaches fulfillment in the concept of the *corporation* and the social body. In this form, the concept is exclusively sociological: the social entity now is no longer conceived merely as such, but as a *person,* that is to say, it is conceived, like the gods, as a rational being; it thinks, consults, and decides; it has a will and asserts that will. Here we encounter *Gemeinschaften* and *Gesellschaften,* unions and associations of all kinds and, again: (1) in the economic, that is, the general social area; (2) in the political area; and (3) in the mental and moral area. The most important examples are, (1) the clan, the village community, the guild as communal (*Gemeinschaft*-like) bodies; the joint-stock companies, cartels and trusts as associational (*Gesellschaft*-like) bodies; (2) commonwealths (*Gemeinwesen*) and leagues (*Buende*) as communal groupings, states (in the modern sense) and political organizations as associational groupings; (3) religious communities, religious orders, churches according to the category of *Gemeinschaft,* and associations formed for religious or other moral purposes according to the category of *Gesellschaft.*

The essential and basic reason for the existence of social relations, collectives, and corporations is always the will of the natural or collective persons of which they are composed. In the second place, however, they gain existence through external recognition, which as such follows their formation, by other natural or collective persons; but such approval may also be the cause, that is, the condition, of their existence, which in this case appears as "made" and preceding the naturally evolving existence. But the actual life of social relationships rests exclusively with this natural existence which evolves through the wills of the participating individuals. Finally, every social entity attains a third form of existence, the quasi-objective one, in the mind of the observer and the thinker who both knows and acknowledges it.

Corporations in particular may also be established and organized by an exterior will, be it an individual will or a collective will. They are then subsumed under the general concept of the institution (*Anstalt*): they are founded. Collective will can establish the foundation either directly—by a resolution (a decree)—or indirectly: by a charter, that is, within the whole complex of a stipulation about the rules of cooperation in a social body.

The difference and the contrast of *Gemeinschaft* and *Gesellschaft* are also evident in social bodies. But these concepts in all their manifestations must be interpreted in such a way that transitions from one form to the other appear possible and under certain conditions probable.

The theory of social norms. The next and third area of pure sociology is the theory of social norms. Social norms are general precepts and prohibitions imposed by a social entity (relation, collective, or corporation) concerning the subjects or members, that is, primarily individuals, which is to say, all precepts restricting the freedom of their conduct and binding their will. They are of great variety and of very different extension and intensity. They restrict relations, collectives, and corporations as well as individuals.

I distinguish between: norms of order; norms of law; norms of morality.

The social forms of will on which norms as the contents of volition are based are:

The communal (*Gemeinschaft*-like) form of will, which I call: (a) concord (the totality of all common willing which because it is based on communal relationships seems to be self-evident as both natural and necessary); (b) custom (basis: communal habit); (c) religion (basis: the communal belief in supernatural ruling and norm-giving powers).

The societal (*Gesellschaft*-like) forms of will, which I call— (a) convention (the totality of all willing which is conceived as a means for common purposes, by expressed or tacit agreement); (b) legislation (a common will which demands a certain action or abstinence from action as necessary in the sense that a will to compel, to coerce, or to impose a punishment is connected with it); (c) public opinion (a common will which exercises critical judgment for the sake of a common interest and thereby affects "private" forms of conduct and action in either a restraining or furthering manner).

Order, law, and morality have been distinguished according to the following viewpoints. (1) Order is the most general complex of norms. It is based predominantly on concord or convention, more or less on either form of social volition. (2) Law is the complex of norms which according to their idea, that is, the will, on which they are based, are to be interpreted and applied by judicial verdict. This complex develops more or less through custom (common law) or through formal purposively conceived legislation (statute law). (3) Morality is a complex of norms, the interpretation and application of which is conceived as the competence of an ideal judge, be it a god or an abstract entity, reason, or conscience, or of mankind or any ideal entity; as, for instance, humanitarianism. These norms are formed and more or less confirmed either by religion or by public opinion. In both forms they react upon the general social and particularly the political domain.

All forms and contents of the social will are in a variety of ways interrelated and interwoven with each other. All social relations, collectives, and corporations exist, in the first place, in the first-named complex of norms: they have an orderly existence; secondarily, they have a legal existence; and, finally, a moral existence. One or the other kind of existence finds in them its stronger or weaker expression, depending upon their more communal or more associational character. It is the special task of the theory of social norms to describe and analyze this diversity.

The theory of social values. The fourth main section of pure sociology comprises the theory of social values. Social values are: the objects of social volition, (1) inasmuch as this willing aims at the objects themselves, confirms and appreciates them, wants to keep them, or acquires them; (2) inasmuch as it feels and knows itself in command of them, in other words, as it possesses them. The concept of social value reaches perfection in a more or less absolute desire to keep in possession, depending on the degree and kind of appreciation. I subdivide social values into:

(1) Economic values. To these belong all material objects in common possession. Human individuals are included, inasfar as they are conceived as such objects, be it as things, like slaves, or as persons, like children. I can merely mention here the significance of the social property of land and other immobilia but also of movable things and the problems connected with it; the values of mineral resources; and material values which at the same time have an ideal significance.

(2) Political values. These are partly material, partly ideal

values. To the former belong: the territory of a country or of a town, even though such territory may not be conceived of as common property; the means of defense and attack available to a political community, the houses of assembly, the instruments and documents of political life. Political values of ideal significance are partly the same, partly the institutions, constitutions, laws, and rights, inasmuch as the national community affirms them and wishes to preserve them, at least in their basic substance.

(3) Ideal and spiritual values. These are: (a) *persons* who are generally esteemed and honored; included are persons who are alive or have lived as well as persons who are imaginary, that is, men as well as gods, deified heroes, saints, and the like; (b) *objects,* such as works of art, of the performing as well as the visual arts, and also of science, which are felt and thought of as common property, in particular cases as national property. Common language, native customs and habits, religion in its specific cultural manifestations, all of these in their capacity as such goods or social values may be objects of passionate love and devotion; (c) the social signs—a very varied and significant group of ideal social values. The nature of a sign is not so much its material existence as its meaning and validity. Its value consists precisely in its validity.

I subdivide social signs into:

(a) Signs standing for social values. To these belongs language as a system of signs for the ideal value of mutual understanding and the capability to communicate; further, writing, including printing, as a sign of signs. Finally, all the so-called value symbols are included here, the most important of which is money: as symbols of material values they belong to these, quite aside from the fact that at the same time they *are* material values—like hard cash or *specie.*

(b) Purposive signs, for the will that something should be or should be done. They are differentiated according to the norms which indicate what ought to be. Consequently, we have signs of valid order, valid law, valid morality; these include signals— agreed upon or imposed, acoustic or optic—as well as judicial decrees and laws, for which particular forms and formalities are signs of their legal validity; finally, there are corresponding signs for morally valid concepts and rules.

(c) Symbols. These are signs expressed in words, actions, or objects, denoting in a more specific sense relations, situations, or norms which are understood either as existing, that is, having validity, or as desirable, that is, signs which ought to have validity. Signs, like ideally conceived values generally, can be determined and conditioned to a larger or lesser degree by essential or by arbitrary will; their meaning, to a larger or lesser degree, can be communal or associational.

The theory of social structures or institutions (Bezugsgebilde). As the fifth and last area of pure sociology, I describe social structures, or institutions, that is, the systems of activities in which the social will of every kind is manifested. Such structures, or institutions, have: (a) economic, (b) political, (c) spiritual-moral character. Subdivisions are: (a) domestic economy, city economy, regional economy, national economy, world economy; (b) all kinds of human communities (commonwealths), legal systems, defense systems, constitutions; (c) all systems of religion, the arts, philosophy, the sciences, instruction, and education.

All social structures, or institutions (*Bezugsgebilde*) may also be conceived of as social values, and several already were mentioned as such above. But in the present context they have a different meaning: that of parts of a living culture which is being fostered and promoted or inhibited and corrupted and whose state conditions and keeps dependent all other manifestations of social life, that is, all other objects of pure sociology.[1]

---

[1]   The last two sections of this paper, dealing with the divisions of applied and empirical sociology, are omitted. Formulations comparable to those contained in these sections may be found in the following chapters in this volume: "Social Structures or Institutions: Effectiveness of Factors"; "Statistics and Sociography"; "The Individual and the World in the Modern Age."—Eds.

III. Pure Sociology

EDITORS' NOTE. *In his book* Einfuehrung in die Soziologie[1] *Toennies deals only with special sociology and, here again, only with pure sociology. He omits what he designates as general sociology, that is, physical anthropology, demography and social psychology, and within special sociology he presents only the sketchiest outline of applied and empirical sociology. He considers statements in pure sociology as conceptual, that is, as static rather than dynamic in character although he cannot help introducing a dynamic element whenever he refers to concrete examples to illustrate a concept. The entire work is divided into six "books." The first book defines essential and arbitrary will as well as* Gemeinschaft *and* Gesellschaft *as basic concepts. The second book deals with social entities or configurations, namely, social relations, collectives, and corporations. The third book deals with social values, namely, economic, political, and ethical values. The fourth book deals with social norms, namely, order, law, and morality. The fifth book deals with social structures or institutions and its principal "factors," namely economics, politics, and spirit (=* Geist *= culture in a narrower sense). The sixth book, which has the character of an appendix, outlines the fields of applied (= historical) and empirical sociology.*

The excerpts are from books II, III, IV, and V.

[1]   1st ed., 1931. Chapters 9–15, this volume, are translated from the 2d ed. (Stuttgart: Ferdinand Enke, 1965).

9

SOCIAL ENTITIES OR

CONFIGURATIONS:

GENERAL CHARACTERIZATION

Social Relations and Social Collectives

PURE SOCIOLOGY, in the first place, is the theory of social entities or configurations. The concepts of social entities are presented most perfectly through corporations, that is, through associations which signify for the consciousness of their own members a unit capable of willing and acting, in other words, a person comparable to an individual human being. However, I distinguish separately from these as conceptual steps: (1) social relations, (2) social collectives. Both are to be conceived as basically similar to corporations, namely, insofar as they move, influence, determine, and, in an extreme case, force individual wills.

Social relations in their simplest form are dualistic, but they can be extended and, as a unit of several pair relationships, become a social circle. Relations exist through a common will of two or more persons to give each other mutual aid or other support, the least that can be done being mutual toleration or refraining from hostility. But for their carriers or subjects they are not units capable of will or action. I relate all kinds of social relations to the rational and ideal type of "alliance," especially because this concept is mainly applied to relations between such important corporations as states; for states, or governments, are the most extreme types of social configurations which, as persons capable of willing and acting, are, and ought to be, controlled exclusively through arbitrary will, and therefore represent the essence of the

---

Translated from *Einfuehrung in die Soziologie*, book 2, chap. 1, pp. 19–34 (§5). Subheadings are adapted from the table of contents.

egotistical volition in pure type. This type can serve as the measure for all kinds of relationships.

Alliance As a Rational and Ideal Type of Social Relations

The alliance—whether between natural or artificial (fictitious) persons—is concluded by means of a contract, that is, through an agreement of wills, principally of two such persons. This agreement has a definite purpose which always implies mutual aid. Immanent in the alliance is the tendency toward unified action which, in cases where the alliance is one between states, becomes evident in times of war as common attack or common defense.

A contract, or treaty, presupposes the formal equality of the contracting persons, insofar as they acknowledge or respect one another, as in the same manner capable of being useful or harmful to each other, although possibly in varying degree. It always implies a mutual promise which, reduced to its rational core, is nothing but a statement about future action or the lack of it; one as much as the other is meant by this statement to be made probable to a higher degree than would otherwise be the case. The will thereby expressed with reference to future action or the lack of it may be a more or less determined will; the opponent, that is, the contracting party to whom a promise is made, receives and interprets the statement as the sign of a more or less determined will, that is, he deems the first to be bound by his declaration of intention; this means that he may be inclined to act in accordance with the promise, both through his own determined will and through the will of him to whom the promise was made: such conduct is thus made doubly probable, insofar as the willing of two persons is twice as probable as the willing of one.

The formal equality of the parties to the contract (*Paziszenten*) signifies equal liberty of decision prior to the contract. If this condition is fulfilled completely, both parties will be equally bound by the alliance. In reality, this condition can never be fulfilled to perfection.

Social relations, as rationally (typically) represented by the alliance, exist in various shapes; some of these are not based on contracts at all or, if they are, spring more from essential than from arbitrary will. As naturally grown relations, those based on essential will are recognizable more easily in natural than in artificial persons. They are based mainly on natural—biological—relationships between human beings because of which human beings (not unlike many species of other living creatures) are driven toward mutual aid, be it through mutual attraction (sex drive, love, maternal and paternal instinct, pleasure in playing and living together) or through habit or through the sentiment and the thought of moral necessity or duty. This sentiment derives from habit or liking while thought changes into a growing awareness of self-interest, thus representing the transition toward a relationship based on arbitrary will.

Social relations of the kind mentioned—*Gemeinschaft*-like relations—do not presuppose formal equality or equal liberty of the persons involved; rather, they exist in part because of natural inequalities—of sex, age, physical, and moral forces within the actual conditions of life. But in part, they approach the ideal or rational type of alliance through equality or sufficient similarity of these conditions of life, such as sameness of sex, approximate sameness of age, similarity of physical and moral powers expressed in temperament, character, and especially in the way of thinking. But in these cases, too, mutual attraction, habituation, and the consciousness of mutual obligation are the psychological prerequisites of such social relationships. These, therefore, usually have their origin in the feeling and consciousness of interdependence, on account of kinship, spatial, or other common conditions of life: good and evil, hopes and fears. I perceive this fact in verbal form as being together (*Zusammenwesen*); the special phenomena evolving from proximity, as dwelling together (*Zusammenwohnen*); finally, those deriving chiefly from common conditions of life, as acting together (*Zusammenwirken*). Here the transition toward the rational configuration of the alliance is clearly evident. But this acting together (*Zusammenwirken*) is also the basis and form of the most spiritual relationship which may be understood as friendship, just as being together (*Zusammenwesen*) may be understood as blood relationship, and dwelling together (*Zusammenwohnen*) as neighborliness.

Social Collectives

All those phenomena which I will designate as collectives (*Samtschaften*) may be referred to the concept of "party" as ideal type. Party is here understood as the group one joins, the object one seizes, the viewpoint one chooses—all this insofar as it is done in the realization that it may be of advantage for one's own ends. Consequently, the party or "side" is a collective based on arbitrary will which is consciously "joined" ("taken") as a means for achieving more or less definite ends. It is a concept to which reality rarely corresponds perfectly. But it approaches it more nearly than other concepts of collectives in which the individual may find himself, and where he realizes far less that he has chosen such collectives of his own free will and for the purpose of furthering his own interests than is the case with regard to the party. Surely, one is justified in thinking of the party, especially the political party, that it is embraced or joined in this spirit. Indeed, as a rule, the advantages expected from the existence and the activities of a party are the motivation by the strength of which the party is formed and held together. That is so, even if often a strong conviction is upheld that the party's aims represent the absolute good and just and that the party holds a monopoly on truth. The subconscious and the conscious are often intermingled; and that which is explainable only through subjective attitudes strengthened by habit, tradition, and indoctrination appears as the plain truth, self-evident and of itself necessary. This is valid for the party's way of thinking, its prejudices and principles, and implicitly for the party itself and for one's adherence to it. In this regard, all collectives are similar to the party, insofar as their members approve of them, affirm them, and regard them to be of value.

In the same way in which every party finds itself in opposition to other parties, often hardening into open and bitter enmity, every other collective to a larger or lesser degree is aware of being the negation of one or several other similar collectives, of which one may surmise or know that their members have a comparable awareness and self-confidence. In this sense, the self-consciousness of a social estate (*Stand*) asserts itself against the self-consciousness of another estate, or estates, the self-consciousness of a social class against the self-consciousness of another class, or classes. The same is true of the self-consciousness of the common folk against the ruling class and vice versa, and the self-consciousness of an entire people against another people, or peoples. In this sense especially the "nation" has come about as a collectivity, confronting other nations in exclusion, negation, and even challenge, so that all this is regarded as the hallmark of a proper sense of nationality, a true national consciousness. "Nationality" asserts itself even more sharply against another or several other nationalities if, against its own will, it is politically tied to such a superordinated nationality. In all these cases and in many others—we may remember the relations of religious persuasions toward one another—the collective is a party or shows the tendency of becoming a party; but as a rule, it is far removed from the ideal type of party established here, which may be chosen by the arbitrary will as a tool for its own ends.

However, these collectives are more likely to be formed in combination with deep-seated feelings, such as love for one's kind, for one's native country, for one's language and customs, pride in one's ancestors, in possessions, especially in landed property and wealth. But it may also be combined with sentiments which spring from the lack of such privileges and goods, and these again may develop feelings of solidarity and comradeship, perhaps focused and expressed in a common love and admiration of the leader of a party, a common faith, and a common hope. It is natural for faith to be faith in the validity of one's own cause, the correctness, even sanctity, of one's own opinions, the justification, even necessity, of one's own striving. Religious faith in one's own god or gods, in their protection and aid, especially in battle, is only the elevated and transfigured expression of that personal faith. Hope is as natural and general as the faith of a party or another collective: the hope of every fighter for victory, that is, the hope to defeat his enemies and the pleasant consequences ensuing therefrom, be they the enjoyment of triumph or purely material advantages. Here, then, the approximation to the ideal type of the party described above becomes apparent, that is, when opposition between parties or collectives of some kind develops into conflict or war: the party is embraced because, by so doing, advantages are presumed to be gained. This happens in spite of complete indifference as to the value of the object, that is, the case of the conflict. For example, people without any political conviction, without even any consideration of interests of estate or class which might be concealed behind apparently independent convictions, join a party only because they expect it to be victorious and, knowing that the spoils belong to the victor, hope to snatch some of them. The same applies in wars between nations and states, if an initially neutral state decides, after a period of waiting, to support the country with the best chances to be the winner.

Social Corporations

The concept of association (*Verein*) represents most clearly the rational and ideal type of all organized groups (*Verbaende*) or social corporations (*Koerperschaften*) insofar as they are autogenous, meaning that they exist through the will of their members. For this concept the specific purpose which the association is meant to serve is not an essential element: only the form is relevant. We conceive of an association as coming into being through the combined wills of several individuals who meet for the purpose of initiating this association. They are unanimous in this will, therefore also in the will to establish a constitution, a system of rules for the association. Consequently, they regard the consensus of a section of the assembled as the expression of the will of all and let it be valid as such. Those assembled consider themselves as forming a unit for this purpose, as "an assembly competent to pass valid resolutions." The form by which the competence is achieved is the majority principle which results from simple, practical considerations.

Similarly, the typical constitution of an association comes into being. Provided there is a quorum, the membership meeting is established as the organ of the association, representing the will of all members. With this meeting rest the decisions about the affairs of the association, its will is considered to be the will of the association; the meeting is "sovereign," insofar as it intends and believes to be determined exclusively by its own will. But the membership meeting is only of ideal duration; its artificial body cannot remain assembled uninterruptedly in one place; its members disperse for shorter or longer periods. Thus it cannot easily and efficiently conduct the business of an association, because this requires a persevering and constant will. This task is normally transferred to a single person or to a small standing committee that can get together without difficulty: the board of directors of the association. Within this board, usually one single person or several persons in turn take the chair, that is, are in charge of the proceedings as required by the regulations for each meeting and for each committee. If the general meeting reserves final decisions to itself, it thereby restricts the powers of the board from the start and makes it "responsible" for carrying out the decisions that have been taken. But it is also conceivable that an association is founded by a narrow circle that can meet relatively easily, reserving all decisions for itself and creating an extended circle of members only to entitle them as individuals to share in the purposes and privileges of the association, without allowing the whole body to be an organ of the association. Even a single individual, a natural person, could, in this sense, gather around him a group of other persons who under him—the "head"—assist or offer him their services, just as he does to them, without their acquiring thereby any corporative competence of will and action. But in that case, the form of an association would be completely abolished; nevertheless, the group thus formed could be effective in the manner of a corporation, whose will would then be represented by the head, that is, a single natural person or persons; likewise where a small circle of people forms the association, the will of all, including the associate members, is represented through a small executive committee. In these two cases, however, a corporation can live only if and as long as its passive members recognize the permanent representation of their will and of the interests they have invested in the corporation, in the executive committee, or in the individual head.

Viewed from the abstract scheme of the association, this agreement of the passive members—who may constitute the large majority—may be thought of as a voluntary surrender of all activity and the transfer of the representation of their interests to the executive committee or to the head. Such a transfer can also be thought of and exist in extensive and highly important areas in such a way that the members of an association transfer to a smaller body the determination and the decision concerning common affairs but reserve for themselves the right to regulate the composition of this body through their own will; whether they elect members of this small corporation in smaller subdivisions or elect them at large. They might even reserve the right, in certain circumstances, to have a voice as a unit—after the constituent original assembly—in order to repeal decisions of the small corporation and perhaps also to alter regulations about its composition. It follows that the constitution of the association may contain, apart from such regulations about the powers of a small corporation—whether they include the final decision in every case or not—further rules about other powers of other corporations founded for the purposes of the association or of individual natural persons, each of whom has conferred upon himself, in accordance with such rules, duties which he is supposed to discharge in the name of the association.

If we take the abstract scheme of the formation of an association as the yardstick for all original autogenous corporations, we will soon notice that the more the corporation bears a *Gemeinschaft*-like character, the more remote from this scheme are their formation and their structure. This *Gemeinschaft*-like, or communal, character is either authoritarian (*herrschaftlich*), or cooperative (*genossenschaftlich*), or a combination of both types. In each case, it can be structured in such a way that its forms resemble the variation of the rational scheme which was distinguished from the normal scheme, because there is a passive membership who believe their will to be contained in the will of a single person or of a corporative group of active members. But the reason for the cohesion of a *Gemeinschaft*-like corporation, the motivating element of its union, is essentially different: it exists *before* the individuals and their purposes, not as in the ideal type of association (*Gesell-*

schaft), *after* the individuals and their purposes, and arising only from their getting together. It is based on essential will, not on arbitrary will. Therefore, the members of a *Gemeinschaft*-like union are persons who feel and know that they belong together on the ground of the natural closeness of their minds. This closeness may be temporal, namely that of descent, kinship or blood, or spatial, namely that of the place in which they live, be it a house, a home town, or an entire country, or, finally, the spiritual closeness of a communal way of thinking, namely that of a common and unifying faith, common desire, volition, and hope, all of which lead to a common reverence for human beings and gods, alive or dead. Of this kind are organized groups (*Verbaende*) in the field of religion or any other common persuasion and all such groups based on being, dwelling, or acting (working) together or on several or all three of these; consequently, they have a share in the essence of spiritual closeness, in other words, in a common way of thinking.

Authoritarian corporations are further removed from the type of the association than cooperative or egalitarian corporations. Authoritarian corporations may be based solely on the power of one or a few natural persons who look upon and treat all other persons who belong to the association as their slaves, servants, or subjects; and *these* may regard themselves as such and be kept only through fear in a kind of union with their master or masters, held together with one another by means of this common fear and the antagonism arising from it. In this case, an organized group, or corporation, corresponding to the sociological concept which has been employed here does not exist: for the meaning of our concept requires the affimation of the corporation by its members. Such affirmation is given only if the subjects or subordinates regard and acknowledge the authority (1) as natural, that is motivated by actual and necessary circumstances, in particular by natural conditions, as grounds for the social conditions, in other words as justified. For this, there are two normal, or ideal, types: (a) the familial: the image of the ruler is that of a father whom his children love and honor, to whom they owe nourishment and protection—and are also willing to reciprocate—whose anger they fear, finding his chastisements and punishments as well as his rewards and beneficent deeds just; (b) the religious form, that is, an imitation of the patriarchal or matriarchal authority. If all, masters and subjects, approach the throne of the Highest Being like children and servants; if they look up to God—the only one or the highest—as to a father, then there will spring from the imagined superiority of the Invisible a consecration and sanctification of the dominion of the visible overlord; the worldly authority will be supported and elevated through the supernatural authority.

(2) The other condition for an authoritarian corporation to continue in its existence, in spite of distance and difference between rulers and ruled, is that the ruled are not too dissatisfied with their condition and that they regard their state of satisfaction or even happiness, their prosperity and progress, to be due, in correspondence to the favor and grace of their invisible masters—the gods—to the favor and grace of their visible masters, who may even be thought of as appointed and protected by the invisible ones.

A cooperative corporation, too, differs from an association, unless it is different only by name, through its communal (*Gemeinschaft*-like) character, and perhaps also because of a communal origin. Its prototype is the brotherhood which is held together because of common parents, forefathers, ancestors, or which at least believes that it can trace itself and that which is its common heritage to these, and ultimately even to a mythical progenitor, if not a god. As a fellowship of worship (*Kultgenossenschaft*), even an authoritarian corporation may represent a brotherhood. Most likely, however, a brotherhood is based on common action, whether in combat—comradeship—or in peaceful cooperation. Neither its familial nor its religious foundation is of such special significance here as it is for the authoritarian corporation. Yet the authority which a group claims over individuals, the corporation over its members, can develop into domination by single natural persons or by one individual over the rest. Thus, once again, the kind of dominion arises that requires natural or supernatural confirmation —or both.

Both authoritarian as well as cooperative corporations differ from associations above all because of the universality of their character. Associations are intended and meant to be only means to

certain specific ends for their subjects, they are in their whole structure *Gesellschaft*-like, whereas authoritarian and cooperative corporations, unless they have become alienated from their origin or
from their original authenticity, belong to the type of *Gemeinschaft*
and are essentially based on it.

It is one thing if the concept of a spiritual or secular commonwealth (*Gemeinwesen*) is referred to the ideal type of an association (*Verein*) in such a way as we have done, something else
again if the same concept is subordinated to the general or generic
concept of association. To the strictly rational way of thinking
which dominated scientific thought about social relations and associations from Thomas Hobbes to Kant and Fichte and their successors, such a subordination seemed to be absolutely necessary.
This individualistic approach manifests itself in its purest form
in the dualistic construction: on the one hand, of a natural state of
man, a state of perfect freedom and anarchy; on the other hand of a
civil and political state which in logical consequence is conceived by
certain theories as one of ideal perfection: a perfect order is established and maintained therein through a common will, that is, the
will of all concentrated in the will of a single natural or fictitious
person. Between these two lies the agreement of the many, which
as a rule is conceived and designated as the social contract, as was
still clearly the case with Kant; for Hobbes, the agreement—according to the last form of his system—consists at first only in the
formation of an assembly, that is, in the tacit or expressed understanding that this assembly is to create the constitution of the association which is to be established, namely the state, by means of its
permanent competence in arriving at binding decisions until the
task is completed. The quintessence of this competence is that
agreement or disagreement with a suggested statute by the majority of the members of the assembly is considered to be the pronounced collective will of the entire assembly and is made apparent
as such. Whether the members of the assembly ever announce their
own will, in their own name or at the same time in the name of a
multitude that has given them the commission to do so, is not essential for the concept. But it must be presupposed that the totality
of the individuals who, as it were, want to make peace with one an-

other be "represented" by these members of the assembly. The constituent assembly has complete freedom to decide by majority vote as to which form of constitution it decides to adopt, unless all its members have received and accepted the binding mandate to decide in favor only of one particular form of constitution or to dissolve.

In the historic reality of recent centuries a tendency has become apparent which may be called a tendency toward the realization of the conceptual image. Only seemingly, at least only to a small degree, has the image itself contributed to this. That realization has gained momentum only when the image already was about to fade and when other less clear and logically less well-thought-out theorems had competed with it or even replaced it. Far more than under the influence of the theory of natural law, that realization has been gained under the influence of the general social development which is inadequately interpreted as the development of individualism. Individualism is the precondition of the new social structure, of the change in social relations, social collectives, and social corporations, of their constitution as *Gesellschaft*-like rather than as *Gemeinschaft*-like relationships, collectives, and corporations. Especially, individualism is the precondition for the most comprehensive political corporation, namely, the state. The significance of the state rests with the fact that it is the expression of the thought that the associational society (*Gesellschaft*), or the collective of the individuals living together in exchange and trade and a variety of contractually based relationships and corporations, requires a permanent bearer of authority and common will in order to settle controversies which may arise within it, to restrain them, if necessary, by force, to allay self-defense and other ways of taking the law into one's own hands, and to pursue common ends through common means; in particular, in external relations, a common force must be set up to counter any force which one has been subjected to or which is threatening.

Theoretical criticism has asserted with much emphasis and with considerable success: (1) that the actual origin of political commonwealths has been of a different kind; it has been stated that it was untrue that the state had developed through contracts or assemblies of individuals or representatives of these individuals; (2) that the essence of the state was not correctly designated by such a concept; to understand the state as a mere means toward the common ends of individuals would be a mechanical approach and therefore unworthy of it. The state, in the words of Georg Waitz, grows organically, as an organism; not, it is admitted, as a natural but as an ethical organism. This theory derives from Schelling's philosophy, which—more than any other in the German language area and elsewhere—has emphasized the irrational nature of life and of living beings and, following Spinoza's great conception, has focused philosophical thinking on it; this was before Schelling got lost in mysticism and theosophy. Sociologically, an ethical or social organism can be spoken of only insofar as its existence is placed into the minds of human beings who consider themselves to be the members or cells, or in their groups as the web of such an organism, or in certain functions or services which transcend individuals, as the organs of such an organism. I prefer to call the corporation whose general nature is described as that of the state a commonwealth (*Gemeinwesen*). Opposed to this meaning, to be sure, is the concept of the state as a mechanism, in its perfection even as a highly competent machine. Yet this concept is not an error or an incorrect point of view by some theoreticians; rather, it is self-constitutive, partly because it has grown out of one or several commonwealths, partly because it arises from special and new needs as a means to their ends. That is the "modern" state— the only possible conceptualization of a commonwealth which maintains itself on the assumption of isolated rational individuals who exchange goods and make contracts with one another; it maintains itself in concrete manifestations, such as laws, institutions, and the like. In reality, this perfect state, conceived as a societal (*Gesellschaft*-like) machine has not yet reached its completion in any country, and will perhaps never be completed anywhere. But all modern states tend to approach the ideal type, even though in different ways.

The closest approach to this form has occurred in colonial countries, because they enjoy greater freedom from traditionalism. "In colonies the individual must become self-reliant once more," says Roscher, and he adds: "similar to the way it was at the beginning of every human culture." What Roscher does not see is that in these beginnings individuals were strongly tied to each other by tribal and familial spirit, by habits and customs, by superstitious beliefs and delusions, and that even the rationalism which develops in civilized societies remains inhibited by elements of this kind. Their effect, to be sure, decreases at a certain stage of development, and for this decrease, and also for the maturation of a sober, practical, and calculating rationalism and "individualism," a colonial country offers far more favorable conditions than an old country.

10

SOCIAL VALUES:

ECONOMIC VALUES

Social Entity as the Subject of Social Values

BY VALUES, we understand real or ideal objects as far as they are affirmed, that is, approved, appreciated, loved, admired, revered, or regarded and conceived of with other expressions of love, affection, and pleasure. In these appreciations are contained experiences of the psychic life of individuals. But many values are held in common by many people, for example, objects of nature or of art, in the appreciation of which men of every kind and origin, of any country or zone may have a share, without in other respects having any connections or relations with one another, without even knowing each other or of each other. *Social* values presuppose the existence of a social "entity," that is, a relationship between at least two or possibly several persons, a relationship which exists in the imaginations and thoughts of the participants and to which a common value is attached. As subjects—or shall we say: as members —of such a relationship, they are united in the affirmation of this object, be it that they aspire to or want and desire it, therefore, that they wish to have it in common; or that they have and possess and have in mind to keep it and that they are ready to protect and defend it against the power or hostile intention of others, such as external powers of nature, animals, or humans. Social values are partly economic, partly political, partly spiritual-moral in character. All these are internally related and may blend one into the other. In

---

Translated from *Einfuehrung in die Soziologie*, book 3, chap. 1, pp. 135–49 (§§21, 22, 23, 24, 25).

the present context, we will start with economic values, because they are of high generality.

Common desires, aspirations, and intentions to possess a thing may be based either on hostile or on social feelings—on mutual negation as well as on mutual affirmation. The French King Francis I is supposed to have said wittily: "Mon frère Charles et moi, nous sommes tout d'accord; car nous voulons tous les deux la même chose: Milan." ("My brother Charles V and I, we are in complete agreement; for we both want the same thing: Milan.") Indeed, it happens with regard to the most varied phenomena of social life, that the craving for the same or similar values disunites people and becomes the cause for various, sometimes fatal hostilities: whether from jealousy and envy, one-sided or mutual, in the way of competition or rivalry, where one begrudges the other the possession of an object, hoping to cut him out, to precede and defeat him; or where one wishes to take away, steal, or rob an object of value from another person who has it; or it may be that discord arises in a partition, where the point is for several to divide between them an object, or where pieces of an object are to be divided in equal or varying parts; this occurs easily, because one or several or all want more—or want what they consider to be better—than the others, and are dissatisfied with their share, and angry and annoyed, often convinced, rightly or wrongly, that the distribution had been handled unfairly and that they were wronged. This applies obviously to material or economic values, the enjoyment of which is by its nature individual and exclusive, in other words, a *private* pleasure. To be sure, there exists the custom of common eating and drinking, and this constitutes a popular way of living together, so that the Romans called a feast a *convivium* (a living together). But to like food and drink, to relish and to enjoy it, this everybody can do only for himself. Discord in this case is not likely to arise, among human beings, from a selfish wanting of more, except among children; and yet the "feed trough" has become the image of an object of value around which men throng greedily, quarrel among each other, so that one tries to snatch away from the other his bread—the fodder.

Already among children, one easily observes the contrast between peaceful possession and the enjoyment of common values, and the wish to have it all to oneself or to have more of it, which so often becomes the cause of controversy and noisy contention. The superior power and authority of mother or father or of some other adult person that is respected and feared by the children usually resolves and settles the dispute, even if only for a short while.

Varieties of Property

Wherever permanent living together can be observed, we find the concept of "property" developed as something that in fact or by law "belongs" to one or several persons. By law, that is, according to a social will which everybody normally recognizes as valid, and which has sufficient power to prevail and consequently to settle disputes. Always and everywhere there exists individual or private property as well as collective property in objects which are appreciated as individual or social values. Here arises the big question—an important sociological problem: what comes first, private property or collective property? "First," to be understood, on the one hand, in terms of time, on the other hand, in terms of logic. Something may be later in time but logically, that is, in its imagined essence, earlier. For instance, it is an old argument: what comes earlier, the hen or the egg? Every hen, as one knows, grows from an egg, and yet in its essence, or as it is said, in the idea, the hen is undoubtedly earlier than the egg; even "historically," at any rate, earlier than the egg that is laid by her.

Consequently, regarding property, I consider both cases as logically possible: the one that collective property is considered to be earlier, and private property as arising from it. And the opposite case, that private property is thought of as natural and original, and that all collective property arises from it, in such a way that several persons contribute their share to a common good which they then consider and conceive as their common property. The one as well as the other is logically possible; this means, at the same time, that it is legally possible, if we understand by law that which is established by common will and which is strong enough to assert itself and to be enforced: a configuration of the social norm which occupies a wide area in social life, of living together, by means of the general, or at least sufficiently weighty, authority of the judge as arbiter in disputes: an authority which is manifested most clearly as the uninhibited execution of the will contained in the arbitration.

The different relationship between collective property and private property presupposes a different relationship of persons to one another and to their own collectivity or group. Men can conceive and regard their belonging together, and their union, and thus perhaps their commonwealth or state as something real and necessary, as a body whose members they themselves are. This means that they want it as such and affirm it: this again will be most easily absorbed in their thinking if and insofar as they feel and conceive themselves as essentially belonging together, as is the case when they consider themselves as brothers and call themselves by that name. Indeed, it is relationship through common descent which most easily allows for such feelings and thoughts to grow. In that case, we have common property which, as undivided inheritance, naturally appears as collective property, from which the private property of brothers and sisters derives in the case of subdivision. But also in case of a complete division, something of the idea of collective property remains, as long and insofar as the consciousness and willingness of belonging together and of brotherhood is maintained. Such a feeling, however, may also develop from other causes: not only from *being* together (*Zusammenwesen*), by which I mean the sentiment of belonging together because of blood relationship. It can also develop from living together and acting together, each of which, as a rule, is conditioned through, and evolved from, being together but from which it is more or less detached.

Thus, what I call *Gemeinschaft* among human beings develops also from neighborhood as the general expression of living together, and from friendship, comradeship, fellowship (*Genossenschaft*) as the general expression of acting together. In all relationships of this kind the strict exclusiveness of private property is frequently broken and modified, for instance, through gifts, hospitality, interest-free loans, and many kinds of unilateral or mutual aid: through the gratuitous lending of utensils. In this sense the Greeks had a proverb: common, or communal (*gemeinschaftlich*), is what belongs to friends; and similarly, there is a saying: it's all the same among friends. However, over and above such restricted relationships, these feelings of communality (*Gemeinschaft*) are retained with regard to common goods, even those of an economic nature and pertaining to a great nation, as is expressed in the phrase: "We shall be one people, united as brothers," and in the feeling of the necessity and duty to stand together in defending one's country, the very soil which one inhabits together, even if only a small segment of the total population actually has a share in private property.

I have called the feeling that thus evolves as a willing by the name of essential will (*Wesenwille*), in order to express the thought that it is based on the essence (*Wesen*) of the human mind and of its relation both to fellow men and to things to which it considers itself bound and wishes to be bound. In my system the elements of essential will are: *(1) liking:* this is what we usually call love. But it covers a wider area, being not only the lively and frequently passionate affect which is indicated by the word love but also a quiet feeling of comfort and contentment, which may pass the threshold of consciousness only on the occasion of disturbances and inhibitions, that is, when a loss is threatened or has become a reality. In this subconscious feeling lies the transition to the other element, namely, *(2) habit*, which is often called man's second nature; where we consider as natural that common approving relationship to what we have and enjoy as being part of us, such as the organs or limbs of our own body. It is well known that habit, by means of continual practice, makes all activities easy, strengthens and heightens our abilities; on the other hand, habit lessens suffering, makes what is unpleasant and burdensome bearable, sometimes even dear. Habit strengthens the bonds which tie men to other men, and men to things. This psychic fact, therefore, is of as great and universal importance for human living together as the original element of agreement, that is, liking.

To these is added a third element of essential will: *(3) memory:* that is, the remembrance and the knowledge based on it of the value of the person or thing to which a person feels himself bound. Value here means the good quality, the reliability which is also recognized and appreciated as genuineness and which indicates in perseverance and constancy, in trials, in dangers, and in the midst of evils either that a quality of this kind has been experienced or, at any rate, is confidentially expected. It should be understood that even utility can be an important mark of value in this sense.

Social Foundations of Property

It is psychologically necessary that human beings regard as common property or as social value that which they use and enjoy together, defend together, and have acquired or created together. It is equally necessary, however, that the single individual regards as his special and private property that which he uses and enjoys by himself, holds and defends himself, and, above all, what he alone has acquired and created. These basic elements, or foundations (*Gruende*), of property may harmonize, but they can also collide. It is a general phenomenon that men living together, at least insofar as they acknowledge one another as belonging together, for instance, in the sense indicated above, as brothers, blood relations, members of a tribe or a people, that such men consider the land they inhabit as their common property, because they are determined to defend it. Moreover, the knowledge or at least the opinion is widespread that perhaps not they themselves but their forefathers have acquired and conquered it and taken possession of it; that it is, as it were, "purchased" with their sweat or even with their blood. Moreover, they consider it to be a social value, insofar as they love it as their homeland and as they feel bound to it, perhaps through the burial grounds, in particular those of their parents and ancestors, and therefore feel in duty bound to hold it in high regard.

From these motivations a social consciousness has developed which assumes that the land is, or should be, common property and that this is ideally the right thing. This joint dominion over the land is what is meant when the term original or primitive communism is used, and when the doctrine is asserted that this is generally the original institution, and private property is something late and unnatural, an artificial and enforced limitation of a normal equality, which is expressed by the idea of brotherhood. In actual fact, this original communism is chiefly, but not exclusively, connected with land. In this respect it assumes various shapes and forms, depending on the kind of existing communal (*Gemeinschaft*-like) corporations, which change naturally, especially by becoming larger; as a rule, this happens because more children grow up than are needed as substitutes for dying individuals: a natural increase which essentially is unlimited. The increase of population also has the effect that there is a transition from close and near relationships to distant and far ones, and that even in the most favorable case of a general spatial staying together, the living together somehow gains a wider meaning; it no longer implies living under the same roof or even personal acquaintance as between neighbors; acquaintance, however, normally leads to sexual relationships, to friendship, to social intercourse, and to all kinds of habitual cooperation. The wider spatial dispersion, of course, diminishes the common consciousness, or feeling, that the land is common property, whereas for those living in narrower circles it is retained more easily and more firmly. These kinds of "intercourse" which are mentioned go along well with fully developed private property, the exclusiveness of which may be mitigated by mutual gifts as an expression of congratulations, and in the form of hospitality, patronage, interest-free loans, but also through charity in the ordinary and extraordinary course of events—actions which are possible and real, then, even outside of actual *Gemeinschaft*.

Parallel with this development and caused by it, the feeling of interconnectedness through dwelling together, the general character of which I have designated as neighborhood, happens to appear more and more alongside, and to some degree in place of, the feeling of belonging together through blood relationship (kinship) or through being together (*Zusammenwesen*). In the general historical connection of cultural development, the village community becomes the predominant social corporation in place of the kin group or the clan (gens or sib). Through agriculture the village community has a special connection with the *Mark*, that is, the area which is considered the common property of the fellowship (*Genossenschaft*), even if in addition to cultivated fields this area comprises forest, meadows, water, and wilderness. Indeed, the uncultivated pieces of land are retained in the common consciousness as *social* values, as communal property, even more easily than the tilled soil, as long as the need does not arise, internally or by imposition from the outside, for the land to be parceled out.

For, separate or private property, especially that of a single family, whenever it detaches itself from the clan, particularly if the father of a family appears as the head and master of its belongings, is as natural and as original as the separate existence of every kind of *Gemeinschaft* and its common goods. Thus, within the village community, even where its members appear in other respects as equals and entitled to the same rights, the individual family possesses its own homestead: house, yard, and garden; and the family acquires a special property in the plot of land which in the beginning is only assigned to it for a limited period—until a new and definite division is made somewhat later. This has been the actual development of agri-culture as distinct from agri-nature, as it existed for thousands of years, and is still the case in some areas.

But private property in the tilled land is surrounded by the common property of the village community, and its use is conditioned and dependent on the collective will of the community. This is, purely externally, indicated by the existence of mixed holdings that make strict coordination of all work on the village lands, that is, a compulsory common tillage (*Flurzwang*), a necessity. Plowing and harvesting have to be performed simultaneously by every family. Many and significant remainders of this institution can be observed even today with all peoples who gain their livelihood mainly through the cultivation of grain. This state is usually referred to as communal tillage or champion farming (*Feldgemeinschaft*) and has become the object of endless learned interpretations and disputes.

From Communal Tillage to Private Property

In this connection, communal tillage is particularly important for us, because due to the legislation of the modern state it has been subjected for the last two hundred years to the great process of dissolution. From this the pure, complete, and absolute, that is, unconditional, private landed property has eventually evolved. This development is only one, but one of the most important, of the features which characterize the ascendancy of *Gesellschaft* over *Gemeinschaft* as a sociological phenomenon; in economic history, the same process is designated as the rise and progress of a social order, which, by general consent, is now called capitalistic. For the ownership of capital as far as, according to origin and general character, it is owership of money, as a natural and general private property, stands in contrast to the natural and general communal (*Gemeinschaft*-like) property in land. On the other hand, through the combination of shares as a means to a common end arises from private property the associational (*Gesell-schaft*-like) property.

One may say that common property of the land, even after a derived private property in arable fields and in meadows has developed and become established within the actual community, will assert itself and retain its special significance with regard to forest, water, grazing land, and waste. This is the case independent of possible feudal privileges concerning the same land which may have developed from the overall property of the community or some other more comprehensive cooperative corporation, or fellowship (*Genossenschaft*). Such claims could arise from rights due to conquest or to formal transference, for instance, on religious grounds, to the priesthood. In other words, common tillage and the common property of the land as the economic unit of the village community, sociologically speaking, will remain the manifestation of *Gemeinschaft* as long as it dominates and conditions the economy of each individual peasant or farmer by means of the system of mixed holdings and obligatory common tillage; also the economy of secular and ecclesiastical overlords, who have their share in the land which is communally tilled even though it may not be communally owned. Then there is the common pasture ("common"), which is of great value to the poor copyholders (*Hintersassen*) who, with the increase in population and through settlement in the service of the feudal lords, are left more and more without a share in arable and pasture lands or have to make do with what is insufficient for their household and who, as a result, depend on the sale of their labor. The common pasture has been kept in existence in some areas of Germany as well as in other countries as a remainder of the old system of communal tillage (*Feldgemeinschaft*), and has resisted the division of the common until far into the nineteenth century. This division was the result of legislation in the interest of intensive cultivation, the so-called consolidation of holdings (*Feldbereinigung*), which involved compulsory participation and exchange. It not only abolished the common (*Almende*) as far as it consisted in arable fields and pasture but also destroyed the ancient privilege of free cutting of wood in the forests, and in most cases divided the common pasture. However, in some regions, especially in the mountains, as, for instance, in the Alps, it resisted destruction and has remained a strong and enduring element in the Swiss economy.

The enthusiasm for the unconditional private property, under the common influence of the modern liberal legal doctrine and the system of "political economy," has dominated public opinion as an expression of the common consciousness of the educated upper classes in favor of a capitalistic economy. This enthusiasm no longer has its former force and self-assurance; it has been shaken by the combined effect of the retrograde tendencies, never quite extinct, which are supported mainly by the interests of the old gentry (*Herrenstand*) and the much more powerful effect of the labor movement. A socialistic mode of thinking has gained more and more ground, even if it is shaky ground. Even apart from these two movements—the retrograde romantic movement and the labor movement, which is predominantly based on large industry—a general movement has grown powerfully. For one, it is a movement in favor of the reform of the law concerning landed property and against its mobilization, which is the result of the most unimpeded freedom of disposition in several important countries, including Germany. In particular a new appreciation has grown of municipal and other corporative private property, including state (or national) property, as against the more specifically private property of individuals and families: the thought has arisen that the "tax state" and the "tax community" should be superseded by a state and a municipality working for its own good and thus for the good of all; thus, instead of sustaining public bodies, according to the principle of private law, from the income and the property of individual citizens, so that, although these contributions are compulsory, they remain dependent on the solvent rich—rather, the public corporations should be established alongside and above the power of the wealthy private owners as independent powers representing the multitude of more or less impecunious citizens—in other words, as the power of labor against the power of capital.

Private property, on the one hand, has a purely individual meaning, as there exists a property of objects which a person has to have for his own use only, such as his comb and his toothbrush, or his food and drink. Socioeconomic theory is not concerned with this kind of property. However, the other kind of private property is of immeasurable social significance. It is the power inherent in a man or a number of associated persons enabling them to make other people give up what they have and to engage in many kinds of voluntary actions. This *Gesellschaft*-like private property is crystallized as the possession of money. Money is essentially an idea, the idea of the *Gesellschaft*-like commodity, which corresponds to all real commodities because each is soluble into a quantity of it, and which consequently can be divided into equal quantities. Its essence does not change by its being represented by some definite and concrete commodity, whether its substance is valued for its inherent quality or whether this substance, in itself unessential and worthless, has nevertheless obtained by means of a form of social will—convention or law—the quality of validity. This is possible only if the owner feels sure, more or less permanently, of this validity, that is, of a sufficiently definite value for which the money could at any time, or at least during an unlimited time, be exchanged for a variety of other goods. In this sense, money is nothing but purchasing power, therefore essentially the potential for the acquisition of goods. Potentiality signifies a certain degree of probability, and even the above-mentioned ideally complete subjective certainty is in reality—objectively considered—at best a high degree of probability. But the claim or the demand to obtain a commodity, therefore also any kinds of goods, including the generalized commodity, money, has possibly an equally or similarly high degree of probability in a *Gesellschaft*-like system, especially one that is protected by the laws of the state. The most definite kind of such a claim is the one that is stated in terms of a certain sum of money. The more the objective probability of fulfillment of such a claim approaches the objective probability of the validity of a certain sum of money, the more, then, a subjective certainty derives from the objective probability, the more will the value of a claim equal the value of the sum of money required for it. The concept of private property of money, therefore, extends through the property of claims to the concept of wealth.

In a *Gesellschaft*-like sense, there exists common property in goods of any kind, thus also in sums of money and in claims: in other words, common or *Gesellschaft*-like wealth. The special property of the individual does not arise here from common property; rather common property is formed out of the contributions or investments of several individuals. In the same way that his wealth signifies nothing else for a person than a means for obtaining goods or pleasures or the services of others, thus the investment, the share, is a means to a comparable end which the investor expects and hopes to attain more easily through a combination of means.

Among these ends, one is of special significance: it does not aim directly at obtaining goods in order to possess, keep, and enjoy them, but in order to dispose of them again, and this with as much profit as possible. To this end, money is an especially suitable, if not the only, means to obtain, by its use, a larger amount of it, which is profit. Applied in this way, a sum of money is called capital. Insofar as money is the more capable of such achievements the more it is amassed, capital fulfills its end as associated capital, the capital of an association (*Gesellschaft*). For us it is of interest only in that it represents an important form of private property: the property of an association or a corporation in which several private owners have shares, so that the property of the individual is perpetuated in the *Gesellschaft*-like property, even though it amounts to no more than a mere claim. At least there is a claim to a share in profits whenever the association (*Gesellschaft*) acknowledges, through its proper representatives, the existence of such a profit which can be divided and distributed. The difference and contrast between *Gemeinschaft* and *Gesellschaft* are reflected here in the different kind of social value, as a value of economic commodities, and the different kind of relationship toward individual value and property.

It must suffice to draw attention here to the worldwide significance of this *Gesellschaft*-like property as the power of capitalism. Capitalism, whose elementary manifestations are to be seen in trade and in the lending of money, rises to perfection as the capitalistic production of commodities, from which follows the capitalistic domination of the means of communication and also of intellectual life inasfar as the latter is based on both communication and production. The essence of capitalistic production consists in the fact that, just as other commodities, labor, too, as the ability to produce commodities, can be bought. Through the combination of its services and of the material means of production through which it works, new commodities are produced by means of individual or societal (associational) capital, the sale of which, as a rule, results in a profit of greater or smaller extent; the aim always being profit as large and at the same time as safe as possible.[1]

[1]   Toennies means to say that profit from invested capital is the basic principle of capitalism.—Eds.

11

SOCIAL VALUES:

ETHICAL SOCIAL VALUES

Institutions, Persons, and Things

I DISTINGUISH as such, (1) institutions, (2) persons, (3) things, (4) memories, (5) signs.

Institutions.—The political values (for example, fatherland, state, constitution) are at the same time ethical values insofar as they are acknowledged and approved by a moral consciousness; this means, not only from habit, or conventionally, or merely from moods, or for their usefulness and comfort, but from an attitude of respect and reverence. A sentiment of this kind, as a rule, preferably is bestowed upon old age, including that of institutions. It may also be based on a feeling for, or in recognition of, its expediency, on trust and hope, and it is, like ethical sentiments in general, related to aesthetic feelings, notwithstanding many differences between the two. Toward no other institutions is this sentiment so strong as it is toward religious institutions, if we refer to those who relate to these institutions as believers. Reverence in this case expresses itself through the predicate of holiness, meaning venerability and inviolability—predicates attributed to religion itself, and above all to the Church as a union which is even declared to be supernatural; a social entity, then, of the highest sublimity. However, the actual sanctified objects are not so much invisible entities but invisible persons imagined as visible, supermen or gods, objects of all kinds of cults, according to their nature exaggerated creations of a veneration otherwise offered to human beings that are

---

Translated from *Einfuehrung in die Soziologie*, book 3, chap. 3, pp. 169–86 (§§30, 31, 32, 33).

admired and feared: thus to the aged, to ancestors, to the dead in general, to kings and princes. At this point the veneration of humans changes into the veneration of gods or at least demigods. All institutions, thus also the state, the community, are human institutions, but acquire easily, especially when sanctified by age, the quality of divinity.

Living persons.—Living persons can also be appreciated as economic values, can even be objects of property, as slaves or serfs, who because of their usefulness, but possibly also for their own sakes, are appreciated, loved, and even pampered. This is most likely the case if sexual relationships are involved. Living persons are also regarded as political values in popular consciousness and in the considerations of statesmen, especially because of their significance for military purposes, for the defense of the country, and even for the conquest of foreign countries. It is in close connection with this that persons because of their high rank, hereditary or acquired, are regarded as social values, particulary when they are called upon to exercise the functions of a master and ruler, whether directly by virtue of the glamour in which they appear or because they have attracted admiration, gratitude, and awe through their achievements, apparent or real. This has happened at all times, in the first place to victorious military heroes, especially when they appear as saviors from great dangers and as liberators from serious troubles, such as oppressive foreign rule or other tyrannies. A particularly high esteem is bestowed upon the military profession and generally on men bearing arms, not only by women; in this respect, women are representatives of the common people. Admiration of heroism may be extended to persons who have nothing heroic about them: colorful uniforms and shining armor excite the senses and engage the imagination, especially of women and children.

Other persons may appear equally venerable, namely, those who have made themselves known as benefactors or saviors in wider or smaller circles; to these belong, the more superstition attaches to them, sorcerers and priests and eremites who are considered holy and men and women who are thought of as sages, radiating beneficial effects or feared because of harmful ones, such as witches and sorcerers. But political leaders, statesmen, or leaders of parties, too, can arouse praise, enthusiasm, and love, and are paid homage to and esteemed as if they were gifts sent from heaven. Gradually, moreover, in periods of advanced urban civilization, while the circle of those who appreciate and honor in the old manner becomes smaller, such admiration is bestowed, although to a lesser degree, on other achievements which are considered to be in some way useful or enjoyable or both, and on persons to whom they are attributed: achievements in science and art, in particular those that appeal to the masses and are accessible to popular understanding, like dramatic art when it moves people to tears or produces hilarious laughter. All in all, the more life becomes public, the more the attention of those who read or attend at spectator arts is drawn to strange and extraordinary objects and persons, partly quite naturally, partly by various kinds of artifices, the sooner will objects of admiration become objects of a cult of some sort, even if often only for a short while, as we contemporaries have experienced constantly in the rush and fickleness of present-day metropolitan life. Even as early as in the *turbida Roma* of the emperors, one man was raised to the throne of admiration today, and another tomorrow, and to many a man hosanna was shouted who was, the week after, considered a candidate for crucifixion. Thus we observe today that some champion, like a skilled swimmer, especially a lady swimmer, or a victorious boxer or wrestler, would be praised and feted more than, say, a meritorious poet, musician, or artist, who may be waiting in vain for applause. Even today, as happened more easily in times past under simpler conditions, men may be held in esteem for their virtues by small circles, perhaps as teachers or masters in their art or as plain citizens, even if nothing but the beneficial effect of their life and conduct is observed, and they are contrasted with the many others who have the opposite effect. Sentiments and thoughts of this kind have sometimes bestowed upon such men and women a halo which in churches has given them the quality of saints, by means of which they could attain a sublimity superior even to that of high secular rank and its glamour.

Deceased persons.—All effects of this kind by which living persons are transformed into social values are concentrated to a higher degree upon distinguished persons who are no longer alive. In a way, *worship of the dead* has always been practiced, at least by a small group of relatives and friends, if only as the last respect paid to the deceased, through care for and decoration of his grave, even if otherwise he was a most obscure person. The intensity and duration of a cult of this kind are largely dependent on the prosperity of the bereft; the rich may set a magnificent memorial to a stillborn child, and in other ways, too, burial places are often used as conspicuous demonstrations of an elevated status as much as for their aesthetic effect. Among such admirers—apparent or real —of their dead, most naturally princes and kings and the like have always been noticeable: the tomb of an otherwise insignificant prince of Caria has given his name to what was after him called a mausoleum. Herbert Spencer has suggested that temples evolved from burial places; this is quite probable, transitions being manifold, even if almost imperceptible, from the gifts accompanying the corpses to the contributions and sacrifices dedicated to them. Of these, wreaths and flowers are the remainders in our time: from sacrifices offered to the dead to sacrifices offered to the gods. Ancestor worship has been retained as a noble custom probably by the largest part of the human race. It makes its appearance in all regions where the Church cultivates the traditional superstition of the cult of souls and tolerates it as part of its ideology. It is most probable that these cults represent the original form of a religious mode of thinking which has receded in the high religions of the Orient and Occident increasingly behind the more glamorous cults of deities of a more universal validity and their prophets, or even of an only or trinitarian God, or his Son, or the Holy Ghost.

Things.—Thus objects of many kinds may be spiritual (*ideell*) and ethical values for small or large social entities. For holy pictures and reliques are valued and honored not because of their exchange or money value, which, to be sure, may play its part, but like other, even possibly insignificant, objects, for their own sake or for the sake of the associations with which they are connected in the minds of those who honor them. Their use value is not essential or may be nonexistent; their value is of an affective nature, perhaps for a few, perhaps for many. The same holds true for all objects of secular or religious adoration, such as temples, church buildings, chapels, and memorials of every kind; it holds for holy objects of religions, equally for unholy ones, if they once belonged to men of worldly fame: they may be valued as private property or, if they are represented in museums—as saints are in churches— as social values. In the imagination of the faithful, pictures always symbolize relics of the person, the god or the hero whom they represent. "The identity of the god and his idol remains a wide-spread assumption far beyond the stage of primitive religion." Even "apart from similarity, participation or physical contact are sufficient for creating such a causal relationship." (Spencer) Thus rises "the practice of regarding nails, hair curls, clothes, arms, or implements of a person as if it were a complete substitute for this person"; one believes one can gain power over him by means of such objects, one loves and admires them for this reason, and they become ideal social values.

In matters like these, memory is the initial factor, even for someone who has not known the long deceased or mythical person, that inclines the soul to devotion. In the same way, memories become social values of a spiritual (*ideell*) or ethical nature, even if a factual substance is lacking.

Memories

Common memories.—As memories unite a pair of friends or a married couple, a family small or large, and many are cultivated lovingly, so there are no *Gemeinschaft*-like collectives or corporations that do not revere or even keep sacred some common memories; these are memories of common actions and suffering and of persons who had been prominent in their circle. Here, too, fighters and saviors are in the front row, but others may also be praised as popular benefactors; to them a memorial is set in some form, they are remembered in speech and song, and celebrations are held in their memory. A feast is especially destined to keep alive or reawaken memories: in the family, birthdays, weddings, and other anniversaries are celebrated; rarer occasions are silver and golden weddings or a birthday if it signifies a considerable number of years. Such days have the effect that even more distant relatives, friends, and acquaintances, not to mention strangers, take part in the festive day of remembrance and feel impelled to demonstrate this on account of their sentiments but occasionally also because they suppose that this may be useful to them. In this way, a whole country may express its sentiments toward eminent men and women who enjoy its admiration and upon whom it feels obliged to bestow its gratitude. In particular a people who, as a nation, has a common memory can give expression to sentiments of admiration and gratitude by means of monuments or works of art or through festivals; an example is the unveiling of a monument on the occasion of a centenary or the day of remembrance of a birth or death that occurred several centuries ago. Mnemosyne was revered in Greece as the mother of the muses and, as one of the muses, Klio, the muse of history. In fact, it is the principal function of history and that of the muses in general to cultivate and promote the common memories of a people. This is most noticeable for wider circles where a people really live together, in the sense of a knowledge of its past, a knowledge dependent, like all knowledge, on the wish to know, on a lively interest which therefore presupposes a certain degree of education and can thus be promoted through instruction. Instruction is ususally carried on under religious or political sponsorship; as a result, it may be directed either to cultivate mainly the memory of religious values and their carriers—founders of religions, church dignitaries, priests—or toward the memory of princes or, in a long-established republic, of persons who are of historical importance in the history of that republic. In this sense, the arts, especially poetry, which in themselves are social values of great significance, are likewise of value for the purpose of enhancing and glorifying common memories. Poetry belongs to a festive celebration, together with music in which its charms are heightened, like a beautiful garment belongs to a beautiful figure.

Gesellschaft-like entities, too, gladly take advantage of the opportunity to celebrate jubilees and to imitate the outward manifestations of *Gemeinschaft*-like life: partly for reasons of sentimentality regarding the persons involved, partly because it is good for business and serves as publicity. In this way, all *Gemeinschaft*-like life, living together, celebrating together, is constantly in danger of conventionalization; more often than not, it rigidifies and ends up a mere shadow of itself.

Fame

A social value, which as a quality, an ornament, as it were, is ascribed to things or persons, natural things as well as works of art, is fame. One must understand fame as an expression of social will, because its foundation is acknowledgment, gratitude, the admiration of many, in a higher sense of an entire people, in the rarest and highest instance of all humanity. Fame exists often to a far lesser degree and extent than is imagined, particularly by those who believe they possess it. Even where it is genuine and real, it attaches only to the name, whereas the real merits which it is meant to designate may be known to only a few and appreciated by even fewer. Also, fame is often of a fleeting nature, swiftly blown away, like the rumor which carries it. Fame is meant to signify ethical value, in contrast to notoriety. Yet, both have to do with being much talked about, and with the imagination of something interesting and memorable that attaches to the names and their bearers. Thus, the value of fame is easily overestimated; not only because its genuineness, as that of other highly esteemed objects, is more frequently assumed than might correspond to the truth; even more so because it usually is of shorter duration than one may think. That is why the fame of the dead has always been considered to be greater than that of the living, and it is not infrequently bestowed on people who were little known and little talked about during their lifetime. Thus, posthumous fame is considered to be the true fame: the memory and gratitude of later generations for achievements which have proved their value, increased their significance, and are diffused far and wide.

If Schiller, a poet-historian, makes a Homeric hero say, "Of all life's goods, fame is the greatest," he was thinking, in the first place, of martial fame, of the heroism which has always been the prime object of popular admiration. But much heroism of this

kind, thus also the fame which is attached to it, fades in the course
of centuries, like the splendor and glitter of precious things which
once had made the deepest impression on their contemporaries.
More lasting is the fame which is a reward for lasting achievements, especially if their memory is celebrated in song, or if still in
our day and in the days to come the works of great poets and
thinkers continue to delight and warm their readers' hearts, as
they have made happy their long-lost contemporaries thousands
of years ago.

Shortlived celebrity sounds off, but, apart from varying duration, shows varying extent and magnitude, sometimes conceived
of as heights—as pointed out in Homer's "Tu gar kleos uranon
hikei" ("His renown rises to the heights of heaven"). In truth,
many men consider it a privilege merely to have their name mentioned, better still, to have it mentioned often, most of all, to have it
passed on to posterity. Herostratos the Ephesian, obsessed by this
ambition, set fire to the temple of Artemis, and although at the
time the cities of Ionia took it upon themselves never to mention
his name, yet he was "successful." Many an ambition is no more
noble than that.

Signs and Symbols

Signs.—As a fifth and a very significant type of social value
I regard social signs. Social signs are distinguished from individual ones: sense perceptions and memories are effective as signs
with reference to objects or movements, thus also with reference
to human actions, if they induce the preceiving or remembering
individual—animal or human—to a certain kind of willing or feeling, thinking or acting. The most important effect of this kind is
the inference, for which in many cases signs become the cause without their perception attaining the level of consciousness. A sign
is what is effective as a sign. One concludes from signs that something exists, or used to exist, or is going to exist. On the one hand,
signs are natural, that is, those that were not, and probably could
not be, willed to be signs, such as a meteoric appearance that
rouses pleasant or somber expectations; on the other hand, signs

are willed, that is, they are made, given, set, with the intention that
they have the effect of signs, meaning that they are interpreted and
understood as such; often they also mean that something ought
to be done. Such signs may be natural signs made for some useful
purpose, like the affectation of a gesture, or they are invented for
their purpose and are actually artificial signs. The former, like the
latter, are individual signs as long as by their very nature they have
the effect of signs and are understood as such. They do not become
social signs because several individuals apply them, not even when
these individuals use them simultaneously for a definite purpose,
for example, in order to make some impression upon animals or
humans. A natural or willed, especially an artificial, sign becomes a
social sign only by serving several individuals, on the basis of a
quality which is commonly known and serviceable to these several
individuals, in such a way that it has the same effect on all participants, that it is understood and consequently correctly interpreted
by all.

Only a social will creates social signs. Consequently, the most
rational and therefore the most clear and distinct kind of social
willing is the decision made by several persons conjointly that a
thing or action ought to be a sign for them, the decision makers;
this is the simplest origin of a social sign. Not essentially different
from this is the agreement, except that, like the decision by a small
number, it may be between only two persons. Agreed-upon signs
have always played an important and manifold part in social life.
They are most significant if the agreed-upon signs are secret
signs, that is, if it is of their essence to be known exclusively to
those who have agreed upon them. In this way love signs, for instance, if a flower or color of a certain kind was agreed upon, may
serve as a sign to meet at a certain time or place. But intimate
signs, even if they are not agreed or decided upon, may be accepted as valid in some circle of persons if their meaning is shared
by giver and receiver.

Language.—This is the most significant system of such signs
imparted through audible sounds, possibly designed only for one-
sided understanding like commands which are also understood by
some animals; as a rule, however, they serve for mutual under-

standing. The fact that humans, even tribes that otherwise are very crude, possess a more or less comprehensive system of such signs, valid within smaller or larger circles, for a long time has been regarded as worthy of admiration and as evidence for the supernatural source of language and thus of the human beings themselves who possess such a precious gift: it was believed that it could be explained only as stemming from a supernatural source. The shallow opinion of those was mocked who ascribed even to language a natural origin by supposing a fictitious assembly which might have decided to call one thing a house, another a table, a third an animal, and so forth. In an argument of this kind, language was shown to be a prerequisite for language, which is an impossibility. Nobody wanted to and nobody was able to acknowledge the simple truth that artificial signs would develop from natural signs, and social signs from individual ones, through imperceptible changes and through gradual growth—and that social will was to come about similarly. One might remember here the sign language of deaf-mutes: partly, gestures are understood by these, as by human beings in general and even by higher animals, for instance, as signs of anger and of benevolence; partly, gestures and what is added to them as the somewhat arbitrary expression of emotions, desires, and expectations through movements of one's movable limbs, especially one's fingers, are interpreted on the basis of their being together and hanging together with other, especially more natural, signs that had been understood previously. The correctness or incorrectness of such interpretations enters into consciousness by way of experience: the correct interpretations will be more easily repeated and become automatic through habit; thus they can be learned.

If in this way a quasi-language of gestures can develop, it is even more likely that the language of words has been developed from elementary beginnings not different from animal cries and from whimpering or faltering sounds. We experience every day how infants announce their feelings, moods, and desires, even though they may be comprehensible only to the mother, and that they learn gradually to understand language and to speak it; only gradually do they enter into the long-existing community of those for whom these sounds have validity and who have, as it were, invented and agreed upon such a system that in its further development becomes more varied and complex. Even an adult, and whoever progresses to improve his education, continues to learn more words and their meaning, and the older child learns foreign languages, at least their elements. Only a certain blindness and man's natural inclination to prefer explanations of natural facts by means of imagined beings to those resulting from real persons or things or processes, which was nurtured assiduously by priests and theologians, could have found the origin and growth of such a system of signs more miraculous than the origin and growth of any organic being, including that of a human being out of something that is not yet a human being. Interpreters of this kind are always ready to assume miracles, that is, divine intervention.

Social signs which mean that something is to be or to happen, to be done or left undone, according to the will of a natural or collective person authorized or believed to be empowered to issue such commandments or prohibitions, lead us into the sphere of social norms: for comparable to individual orders or commandments, social regulations may be made known not only through the general system of language but also by means of special signs, the meaning of which is mutually familiar.

Signs as signals.—Here simple artificial signs for the ear (acoustic) or for the eye (optic) prove to be particularly useful, and therefore may achieve great importance as signals in war on land and sea, but also within a peacetime army or in some other system of communication; the reason being that they are particularly suited to be perceived quickly and distinctly and, after having become known through habit, to be understood clearly and regularly. They are of great value also because of their international intelligibility, as soon as they have become generally accepted. An example is the book of international signals in which signals are compiled that serve to promote communication between ships of various flags on the high seas and between ships and land signal stations. Whereas here, then, a general understanding from man to man, whatever language they may otherwise speak or know, is favored, on the other hand, it is evident that the common language is not discrete enough to be kept concealed from the enemy or from persons whose understanding of it is undesirable or even harmful: especially written words are dangerous because an otherwise strange language, which may be hard to understand if spoken, can be more easily comprehended if transmitted in writing. In such a case, writing in ciphers proves to be the suitable means for keeping secret information secret; a coded dispatch, therefore, is an important instrument in diplomatic relations. Similarly, the use of a foreign language, written or oral, may often be sufficient in safeguarding a secret as long as one is sure that unauthorized persons who may see the document do not understand this language and are not particularly interested in having it interpreted to them.

Signs as documents.—The use of signs has always been considered necessary where authority asserts itself, therefore always where a dispute is decided by the judgment of a court, and where a sentence is passed that inflicts a punishment. Certain forms are always prescribed, and these forms in spoken or written words which have become formulae are the signs for the validity of such decisions. Thus, still today the defendant or accused is called before the court by means of a certain *formula,* and judgment is pronounced to him in certain *formulae;* using certain fixed forms, he may appeal the judgment until it becomes valid through a higher court's decision. All this, at one time prescribed by customary law, is now provided by enacted law. Even a law attains validity only through the observance of fixed forms; certain signs are required which confer legal power. In the course of cultural evolution, all these forms have acquired their regular structure, first in writing, then, after printing became customary, as a printed document. Documents are testimonials, and testimonials, written or oral, serve as proof of facts, especially of such facts that are chiefly facts of validity and therefore not provable by means of visible or other sensual evidence. Every proof requires signs which are meant to bear witness that the more or less firm opinion, at best the conviction, is the result of the truth of an assertion, therefore also of a fact; and vice versa. Thus, testimony before a court of law serves as a means of proof, particularly if its power is augmented by means of forms which are required and accepted as signs of the truthfulness of the witness: the most common expression of the significance of the oath in social life. In all these cases, we deal with the development of communication among men for the purpose of peaceful living and acting (working) together. They become all the more important, the more acting together in closed ranks is required for the sake of unity; therefore especially cooperation in battle. This is the reason why we observe in an army particularly pronounced regulations of commanding and obeying; obeying both general rules and individually issued but socially sanctioned single commands. Therefore, here, too, we see the effectiveness of signs: signs of domination and signs of servitude, expressed partly in words, spoken or written, partly by other, mostly visible, signs. A promise and, in consequence, the solemn vow refer in particular to obedience. Here is the place also of the promising oath and its counterpart: the negative promise of a threat of punishment. This, too, is to be discussed in connection with social norms.

Signs as symbols.—The third and particularly remarkable kind of social signs is symbols. These are visible signs represented by certain objects whose significance is to be understood in such a way that they indicate something that cannot be designated or expressed directly, especially if it must not be mentioned in words. This is the reason why the symbol claims enhanced value and gains its special validity regarding everything that is supposed to be mysterious, for instance, as far as the communication with invisible and unreal beings, such as gods, is concerned, whether they are feared or revered. This is why religious symbols cause a pious shudder in the heart, for the believer a necessary and dutiful effect of the supposed presence of intimate and familiar as well as of ghostlike and uncanny powers. But worldly and visible representatives of power, too, obtain their share, although only more or less so, in such supernatural magnificence. To them, too, symbols are of service, especially on festive occasions when they are called upon to represent gods and to display the splendor of their own power in brilliant guise. This task is the immediate concern of priests, especially high priests, who are believed to be in direct contact with their deity, to know their secrets, and to mediate their power.

The word symbol derives from the Greek, and can be traced to a verb meaning "to throw together," therefore also to put together, to contribute, to communicate, from which is further derived the meaning of "concluding a treaty," and many other related meanings. The important sense of the word derives from the fact that it means two fitting halves of the small plate or ring by which hosts and guests would recognize each other. Thus even in the origin of the word there is an element of something that secretly binds persons; hence it gained the significance that made it develop its particularly religious connotation.

Religious symbols, in the first place, are connected with the worship of images: in the same way that the statue of a god is thought of as being the deity itself or at least as being consecrated by it and as being in magic contact with it, and thus as capable of performing miracles as the deity itself. They are the outcomes of fetishism, which endows some objects with sacred power and which survives among civilized peoples in the shape of charms or amulets. In other words, religious symbols are to a lesser or larger degree inspired by that way of thinking of primitive peoples which is at the bottom of all mysticism, namely, the conviction that nature everywhere is filled with efficacious ghosts, or spirits, and that these spirits haunt, that is, do good or evil to, people according to their whim and mood, that they are always and ubiquitously present, preferably in the dark and at particular places, not only at holy ones but also at some that, on account of their age or because they are the residence of important personages, have gained an uncanny kind of quasi-holiness. There is always a basic desire and endeavor either to banish, to exorcise, or to propitiate and befriend them, and often one kind of spirit has to deter and overcome the other, as the symbol of the Cross overcomes the devil. Of a cruder kind are animalistic symbols, in which may be included phallic ones, the use of which, in the form of mimic acts, images, and symbolic ceremonies, even the real act of coition, is so widely spread that one might be tempted to trace it back to an idea fundamental in ancient religious belief that even the maintenance and increase of nature's and man's fertility were not explainable through natural causes but through supernatural ones, namely the spirits. The idea is that fertility, if desired and longed for, could and should be promoted through spirits.

Although the incantation of spirits by magic words: more or less articulate sounds, incomprehensible and mysterious enunciations and holy names, seems to have the same effect as have symbols, nevertheless these always have a special meaning: they condense into chants, and thus stimulate inspired powers, as the images of the gods inspire the plastic arts. Pictures evolve into script, and letters like spoken words, can become sacred and have a magic effect. They, too, become symbols, especially when, as creedal writings, they are destined to become the expression of the common and obligatory doctrines of a religious union or a church, and when they are believed in as such. From this has developed the meaning which symbols have gained by means of such creedal writings: the body of symbols which Roman Catholicism places under the authority of the Holy Ghost and the Apostolic Office, and which have become an essential and infallible part of ecclesiastical and divine truth: therefrom develops the concept of symbolism as a special theological doctrine, claiming validity as a science.

While symbols easily acquire the character of holiness because ceremonial acts attain through them a particular solemn significance, other signs are related to them which claim an important significance because of their content. Without religious solemnity attached to them, as for instance, acts of state, they achieve special dignity in public and private opinion. Of this kind are distinctions which, as the bestowing of titles and orders, are given as rewards for merits, as compensation for damages suffered, and as a means of creating a serene or at least confident mood in perilous situations or during difficult enterprises. Thus they belong into the larger area of signs by means of which a person in authority may show his approval to those under him and employed by him, so as to encourage them to continued diligence and zeal, whether in his own interest or in a common and worthy cause. Here may be included good grades and school reports, meant to give pleasure to children, just as bad ones make them feel bad, so that they try to improve them.

In all these instances, we have to do with social signs, that is, signs that are meant to be generally understood, partly by means of the words by which they are expressed, partly without words, that is, as decoration: for, like all words, they are easily and frequently misunderstood: not only unintentionally, as in the most numerous misunderstandings, but also intentionally, especially when they are considered to be undeserved and deplored as such— misunderstood insofar as their general validity cannot be contested, for which reason the criticism is often ascribed to envy and grudge. These social signs always retain their significance in a centralized order, therefore chiefly in the army and similarly regulated large administrative bodies where order is definitely based on superordination and subordination, hierarchically descending from the chief to the private. Therefore, the abolition of titles and other decorations, as befits a democratic constitution, is a great risk for the government of a state which rests on such a constitution! It loses a strong instrument of social control, that is, a means of ensuring the cooperation of such persons who have to obey orders continually and more often than giving them, down to the multitude of the lowest category, who have nothing to do but obey. Of course, there are other ways of expressing satisfaction and giving praise, and of showing approval as well as disapproval; but the visible, and, in the case of titles, audible, form, as a rule, is for the consciousness of him who receives such praise of a very special value. In the same way, the privilege of wearing a special garment, even if it is connected with a special duty and especially if the garment is supplied free of charge—the livery—may have the effect of a distinction because the uniform impresses the public as a sign of worth and dignity.

The symbols of power—crown and scepter—designate the monarchic form of government; its decline is symbolized by the fact that, even if this form is still in existence, the crown and scepter are rarely visible any longer. However, like all symbols, they remain alive in the imagination and in art.

12

SOCIAL NORMS:

GENERAL CHARACTERIZATION

Commandments and Prohibitions

BY NORM we mean a general rule of action and of other kinds of behavior: it prescribes, either generally or for certain cases that are definable in advance, what shall happen or not happen, inasfar as this happening is based on the willing of reasonable beings, namely, men for whom the norm is intended to have validity. The essence of the norm may be generally conceived of as negation or inhibition, that is, as a restriction of human freedom; for the positive commandment, too, negates the otherwise existing freedom to act as one pleases, therefore to act differently from what has been commanded, above all, to act contrary to commandments. *Omnis determinatio est negatio.* A prohibition blocks one particular way, permits all others or leaves them open. A commandment blocks all other ways except the one indicated and prescribed which, being the only permitted one, at the same time is the way that one is forbidden not to go. The relation, then, between prohibition and commandment not only is that of contrast, but the commandment, at the same time, is an extended prohibition.

A single prohibition or commandment is not a norm, not even when directed toward many. If "silence!" is commanded at a gathering, or if soldiers are ordered to "stand at attention," this means only that silence or attention is required for a while, not forever, or that it is always to be observed in certain situations. However,

Translated from *Einfuehrung in die Soziologie*, book 4, chap. 1, pp. 189–203 (§§34, 35, 36) ; slightly abridged.

if the order says, "Whistling at a gathering of this kind is prohibited," or "If a soldier is addressed by a superior, he has to stand at attention," those would be norms. The hallmark of norms is generality.

Why are some norms called social norms? How are they to be distinguished from individual but also from asocial or alien norms? Not because social norms are decreed out of their united will by several persons who are socially connected with one another—such norms could be alien as well as social norms. Social norms are distinguished from others because the persons for whom the norm is meant to have validity are among those who themselves will and establish them; they are based on autonomy. They may be based on the autonomy of the participants directly or indirectly. Directly, if the many are really and fundamentally united in wanting these rules or norms. Indirectly, if the norms that are brought to them from the outside are acknowledged, affirmed, and agreed upon by them.

To command and to prohibit are actions arising from volition, actions evident in the most varied manifestations of social life: they may be expressed as an individual command or as a norm, as an alien or as a social norm. We may consider them, first of all, as applied by one person toward another, an everyday event. Everybody can attempt to restrict everybody else's freedom in this manner and, if the attempt is successful, restrict it actually. Whether a commandment or a prohibition is successful, that is, whether they are complied with, does not concern us here for the time being. The attempt to restrict the freedom of another person in this manner is one of many forms of the endeavor to influence the will of another person positively or negatively. Other ways are: request, advice, admonition, warning, demand, summons, invitation, correction, instruction, persuasion, recommendation, provocation, encouragement, seduction, bribery—all are attempts to move or to induce someone to do or not to do something by means of words, spoken, written, or expressed in some other way. Words may be supported by actions, their influence strengthened, under certain circumstances even substituted: by means of gestures, by touching the other person, for instance, the request by means of folded hands, clasping the other's knees, kneeling down oneself, prostrating one-self. Other examples are: advice by means of a cheerful or thought-ful or sad countenance; admonition through cuffs, ear pullings, knocks, and hits; recommendation and provocation through ef-fects upon the senses, such as figures, pictures, sounds. All these could be reinforced by means of words of different content; through praise and blame, flattering and scolding, but especially by means of promises and threats. Promises, provided the request, advice, command, or prohibition, or any other form of influence has been yielded to, open up the prospect of such activities on the part of the person who made the promise as are expected to be desirable to the other; conversely, threats, in case of noncompli-ance, open up undesirable prospects. The same effect as emphati-cally promising or threatening words may have hope and fear that are aroused without such words, be it the expectation of good or bad results from the requested, advised, ordered, commanded, or forbidden actions, or perhaps the hope or fear of actions of peti-tioners, advisers, commanders, and so forth. Especially, such senti-ments may lead or contribute to obedience, through fear rather than hope, if it is assumed that the restriction of freedom is unwel-come and that obedience, therefore, is offered unwillingly. Hope presupposes a more voluntary decision, joyful obedience, or a grateful following of advice, stimulation, admonition; fear, on the other hand, presupposes a somewhat less voluntary action or omission, a willing under pressure.

What distinguishes command and prohibition from other kinds of attempts at influencing another person's or several other per-sons' will? Both command and prohibition are attempts at com-pulsion, applied with the intention of effecting, by means of words, an action or an omission as a certain consequence; and this inten-tion is connected with the expectation of rousing in the other, or others, the feeling of compulsion or of having no choice. The other person expresses this sentiment not only through "I must" but even more aptly through the words "I ought," which, apart from the feeling of necessity, contain the implication that this necessity has been induced by another will, even though in a derivative way the actor's own will could be regarded as such another will.

If all negation is considered to be hostile, to command and to prohibit are likewise hostile. All other kinds of attempts at moving the other's will toward something are friendly insofar as they do not disturb the other's freedom to act either according to the influence that is being exerted or otherwise; they are friendly insofar as they merely give expression to selfish or unselfish desires —which the other may or may not fulfill, as he pleases. Even he who tries to bribe or seduce does not claim more than to make his desires more effective by the means and artifices which he applies. To be sure, the one who prohibits, too, expresses a desire, but he combines with it the intention of excluding the liberty to act contrary to his desire.

From whatever cause, or for whatever reason, an order or a prohibition may actually be followed, it is not part of it that the person who obeys concedes to the person who commands a "right," in other words that he grants the permission to give orders— whether in general or in particular; nor is it part of it that he admits a duty, that is, an obligation he agrees with, least of all that he feels it to be his duty to obey.

What is meant by saying that I concede someone a right, that I ascribe a duty to myself? To concede a right is more than to give permission or to leave something to someone's choice. It means the admission that the action I permit is right. . . . An action is correct if it is logically incontestable. It is logically incontestable that man, as far as he possesses reason, is the master of his own actions. To be master of himself also means that he can prohibit himself from doing something: and thus is expressed a fact of our own self-consciousness, which used to be designated as the mastery of the reasonable part of the human soul over its unreasonable parts, namely, its drives and passions. Modern psychology, which covers, or intends to cover, with the concepts of sensory perception and emotion all psychic complexities and which calls compound perceptions ideas or images (*Vorstellungen*), expresses the same fact by asserting the existence of inhibitory ideas, or simply inhibitions, as a criterion of a normal human being, namely, a human being in possession of reason. These inhibitions are of different strengths in different persons, and at different times in the same person. But to the extent of their weakness or failing, a man is a pathological or unreasonable being, regarded from the point of view of the theoretician who takes his measure from a normal human being, that is, one capable of being master over himself. Therefore it is right for me to be master of myself, give myself orders; and if I call this reasonable willing, it is implied that the freedom of will is a right to will, that is, to regulate my actions and thus my body and my limbs; in other words, normal and expected inhibitions are present and effective. If I give someone the right to give me orders—and this is to mean more than that I give him the right to speak ineffective words—then this means that I also will what has been ordered, and if the feeling of "I must" and "I ought" has been roused through the order, then this feeling implies an "I will," that is, over and above the willing of the doing, a willing of what ought to be done (*Sollen*). This means that I am conscious of my duty. If I obey my own command, then the feeling of "I ought" or of being obliged (*das Gefuehl des Sollens*) is directly a sense of duty, for it is not different from the "I will." To the extent that the other person has the right to give me orders and I feel duty-bound to obey, the other's command is the same as if I were to give myself orders. It presupposes a relation between us that approaches more or less that of identification insofar as we are in agreement in relation to what we are willing to do and what we ought to do (*Wollen* and *Sollen*). Inversely, from such positive relations which are, for this reason, called social relations evolves the unilateral or mutual right of prohibition and command and the unilateral or mutual duty of obedience.

Other Varieties and Manifestations of Norms

It is an essential feature of a social relation for two or more persons to move or to endeavor to move each other mutually and constantly toward actions or abstentions from actions. But it is not an essential feature for this to occur in the form of ordering and prohibiting. Other forms, as a rule, may be sufficient to prevent certain actions and to encourage others. Even without any attempts at being effective in this sense, by means of words or actions, the existence of a relationship, especially the presence and closeness of a person to another, or the exchange of letters, may have the same or a similar effect, especially where experience allows one to know or to imagine which actions or omissions are welcome, which ones are unwelcome to one's companion or partner. Further, different forms of expressing wishes sometimes merge or overlap: "Your wish is my command," even if the wish was only guessed by the other's looks. Requests can become so earnest, so urgent, so tormenting, that they are at least as sure of success as an order intends to be, and they may be made with the intention of compelling the person to whom the request is directed. This is all the more so, if the latter is an invisible being, existing only in the imagination, like a god, especially where words are supported by actions such as sacrifices and witchcraft . . .

That requests are powerful is indeed an obvious notion to the pious, childlike mind: if children feel sure that through constant repetition they can soften a benevolent father, and even more the good mother, or, as they call it, make them change their mind, then they ought to be surely successful in changing the mind of a saint or even the all-bountiful god himself, and move him to interfere; because these invisible beings do not scare away or reprimand bothersome supplicants, or attempt to instruct them about the uselessness of their desires. It is well enough known that a power is attributed to prayer which, indeed, it may have in the mind of the supplicant.

The request, as petition, is the natural mode of action of those that are smaller and weaker toward the stronger and bigger. Conversely, on the part of the stronger, the request is often only a polite form of command. If a monarch makes a request, this is, as a rule, understood to mean an order. Even an advice may be equal to an order. If the advisor has the power or is supported by those in power, like the British cabinet, or the prime minister in its name, the counsel given to the sovereign implies such urgent advice to take the advice that approval and agreement are taken for granted. Refusal (a *veto*) does not occur and would be almost ridiculous. But even if the advice has not become a mere form for a binding order, it can be obtrusive and experienced as compulsion. The same applies to the use of other methods of influencing the human will. They are often preferred to the form of an order, (1) because the prospect of seeing the order executed is not good, and the probability of effecting its execution small, (2) because an even more favorable effect in this regard is expected from a milder form such as admonition, warning, request, and because, in contrast, for him who is supposed to obey, there is a special thrill in defying an order; pressure arouses counterpressure; attack, resistance—an order may be taken as a sign of hostility; whether this is the case and to what extent, depends in part on the nature of the social relationship, whether it is communal (*Gemeinschaft*-like) or associational (*Gesellschaft*-like).

Out of every social relationship, therefore also out of every circle (if by that is meant a totality of persons who are connected in social relationships such as the family or a circle of friends), out of every collective and every corporation grow and directly develop rights and duties of their "members," who are given this name insofar as they acknowledge their belongingness to the relationship. Every social relation implies for its members the request to behave and to act according to the norms which prevail in it; consequently, these may be understood to be the will of the relation, collective, or corporation itself, which, even without the form of an order, has the effect of being understood and acted upon accordingly. The meaning of every social relation, at the very least, is to refrain from force as the crudest form of hostility unless this force has been recognized as being rightfully exercised and therefore justified. But the demand for some positive contribution is almost indissolubly connected with it; essentially, the contribution is mutual aid. Thus, the social relation itself imposes prohibitions and commands; it restricts the freedom of the individual. In the final result, it means the same thing when we say that within a relation the companions and partners, one regarding the other, undergo identical restrictions of their freedom. But indeed it makes a difference, whether they do it merely as an expression of their personal desires or in the spirit and for the benefit and, as it were, in the name of the relationship. However, what the relationship demands can be proclaimed by the companions and partners in other ways as wish or desire.

The social norms of every relation, that is, of every social entity, are founded in part on its individual, in part on its general nature. They are conditions of life of the one as of the other, and as such more or less known to the members. The individual nature itself can be determined by general criteria which are not general criteria of the social entity; the purely individual remainder consists in the nature, character, and the way of thinking of the individuals themselves and of individuals in reference to one another. Further, what the social relation between only two persons requires in accordance with its individual nature may take the form of a social norm, but only insofar as it is approved, that is, recognized and willed in this quality by both partners. For instance, every marriage has its very individual existential conditions, so that it may maintain itself and remain healthy; further, it has existential conditions of a relatively general nature; finally, there are general existential conditions, arising from the essence of marriage as a supremely significant communal (*Gemeinschaft*-like) relationship. Individual existential conditions may be based on the state of health of the wife or the husband and on peculiarities of their personalities deriving from it: they require mutual consideration in living together. Relatively general existential conditions are provided, for instance, by a considerable difference in the age of the partners, by a difference in character and mode of thinking, therefore also of religious faith or the lack of it, tribal origin or even "race," descent by estate or class: all these differences require certain concessions, forbearances, and resignations. Finally, the general nature of marriage, which is founded on mutual dependence, bestows upon the spouses rights and privileges relating to one another, and imposes duties upon them which extend to all true marriages, even if they may be in part rendered invalid or modified because of special conditions of life.

Equally, a social circle imposes duties and bestows rights; likewise, a collective: even if membership, for instance, of a party— for example a [Catholic or other] religious party—(*Religions-*

partei)—is usually determined by birth, therefore quite involuntary, nevertheless the influence of such a collective and of its members has the effect that, as a rule, it is felt to be of one's own choice and based on one's convictions, which, however, have only been developed by those influences. For, like a social relation, even if less immediately so, a collective produces a sentiment and consciousness of duties toward it, especially the duty to be directed by it, to recognize and defend its honor, to observe its interests, and in certain circumstances to do battle for it. Corresponding to these duties are the privileges which are the consequence of the fact that the same duties are imposed on the other members of the collective. The collective, then, is based on the extended idea of mutual aid which is the hallmark of every social relation, thus of every circle, especially the family. The collective is extended to a number of personally unknown people, comprising also the deceased, whole former generations who are venerated especially because they are ancestors and possibly founders and who therefore are celebrated as originators of certain rules, norms, and regulations that are acknowledged as having binding validity.

Expressed more formally, although frequently far less significant, at times trifling, are the duties and privileges which a corporation may impose and bestow upon its members, by whatever name it may be established, and there are many that may be given to it as a fictitious, or moral, or legal person. In the first place, the corporation rests directly on the common and joint will of its members, whether they have created it or whether they are acknowledged by their entry and admittance or in certain circumstances by the privilege of birth and sheer existence, as members by the other members, therefore also by the fictitious person itself. As a "person," the corporation has the right, as a rule limited but possibly unlimited, that is, the capacity bestowed upon it, to impose rights and duties upon its members, thus, to command and prohibit. The further the corporation is removed or different from other more simply constructed social entities, the more is its function restricted to ordering and prohibiting, in other words, to the creation of norms; these tend to assume the character of coercion, which is justified insofar as it corresponds to the mind and will of those who submit to it. However, this is often based on a mere assumption, and the application of the general assumption to a concrete case may be a disastrous mistake. Good examples of the ideal, or fictitious, person and thus of the corporation itself, existing, as it does, in the first place, and perhaps exclusively, in the consciousness of its members, are the secret societies and conspiracies. In spite of this sole basis of their existence, in spite of their rejection of the more general corporation (for example, the state) on which they rest, by which they are conditioned, and whose authority they acknowledge in their volition and consciousness, these societies exercise great power over their members and impose heavy obligations upon them. They even become masters over the life and death of the conspirators, and, as their lawgivers, they demand continual and unconditional obedience.

Consent as the Prerequisite of a Normative System

We started off with the simplest case of one person giving orders to another, who has acquired the right to do so from the latter, so that consequently the obeying person feels duty-bound to obey. This idea is enlarged with regard to social entities and finds its fulfillment in them. The assumption was made that the command, if it implies a general rule, is to be called a norm, and that it becomes a social norm through the consent of him who conforms to it. A system of social norms presupposes general consent, unanimity of wills among all those for whom it is supposed to have validity, for instance, for a people, even for all mankind, insofar as it is conceived of as civilized mankind and its members as capable of comprehension and communication.

However, consent is something very complex, as is volition in general. The consent which is meant here in particular can extend over a whole scale, from passive tolerance, possibly to a considerable degree unwilling and conceded only reluctantly, to active, emphatic, and even joyful affirmation. Another scale, but connected with the first one, is one from nonrational expression of affirmation to a completely rational one denoting conscious overcoming of repugnance and agreeing to something which for the willing person is the means to a possibly distant though ardently desired end and which thus, in spite of repugnance, may be of decisive value. However, even nonrational willing may occur wholeheartedly, namely, without any thought of contradiction, rather as something taken for granted because it is felt and thought to be altogether wholesome and good, in the sense that it is believed to be morally necessary. Of this kind is consent on the grounds of liking, love, and related sentiments, such as reverence, a sense of one's own weakness and of the need for protection and help. The basis for such sentiments are the aforementioned inequalities: differences in age, sex, and, often connected with them, differences of physical and mental power, especially superiority of knowledge and experience in applying it, but also of all other means of power that one person has while the other person has not, and of which one person has more than another.

An ancient case in this regard is the superior position of the mature man as the *pater familias* and master of the house over a woman or the women, over sons and daughters, servants and maids; consequently also the power of the chieftain over an entire clan, tribe, or people: the picture of patriarchal dominance, often compared to a small kingdom. Conversely, princes may feel like fathers of their subjects and they may claim the dignity of patriarchs, even if they themselves are youths. Patriarchalism is not, as has often been said, something original from which the rule of emperors, kings, and princes has grown organically: this is the doctrine and concept of a people with an old and highly developed civilization, the Chinese, which, however, has had but little influence in Europe. Europe has never allowed this doctrine to prevail completely, although it had the support of the high and religious authority of Jewish tradition—as well as the attestation through the Jewish God of Christianity. This concept passed into Islam and is the basis of ideas about oriental despotism which have become prevalent in Europe since the seventeenth century. The revolution and the Enlightenment, which was the basis of revolution, have identified the absolute monarchy, which by then had glamorously risen in the modern countries, with those despotic systems and rebelled against it. It was a widely accepted but erroneous idea, possibly nourished by reminiscences of the Old Testament, that this free and arbitrary rule was something original and derived from patriarchalism. In actual fact, the European monarchy had always been restricted, and was so even where it appeared to have reached its most completed stage, as in France of the Bourbons.

From early times the cooperative fellowship (*Genossenschaft*) had been in competition with authoritarian rule (*Herrschaft*), and had continued to be alive in the consciousness of the people and therefore in reality. Its historical manifestations were: (1) the fellowship of a clan or sib, the significance of which has declined long since; it survived only among the nobility, part of which used to be the sib called a dynasty; (2) the village community and the larger community of a *Landschaft*, within which the Mark fellowship (*Markgenossenschaft*) maintained itself, even if the village community had been absorbed by the manor and had become subject to the nobility who succeeded in asserting their domination over the egalitarian principle of the fellowship; (3) the city, or urban community, by far the most important and increasingly more powerful configuration of the principle of equality and fellowship, in which some roots of the budding modern state are to be found, whereas other roots took their nourishment from tyranny, as it was developed early in the municipalities of Italy. The idea of a republic has never been alien to the idea of the state. It is an egalitarian idea based on fellowship (*genossenschaftlicher Gedanke*), achieving importance in the participation of the estates in government, most of all in England, where it destroyed, through a conservative rebellion, the already highly developed beginnings of monarchic absolutism. The "State" was a new name for the unity and solidarity of a nation, insofar as the nation had become conscious of constituting and representing a unity and defending and protecting its ancient and common law against the administrative uniformity fostered by the ruler and his statesmen, therefore against a standing army and a police force. Communal (*Gemeinschaft*-like) egalitarian structures survived in the great aristocratic families who, in Scotland more than in England, maintained their ancient constitutions; they survived in village communities and cities—although often in a distorted way. In the state, one great unified egalitarian configuration (*Genossenschaft*), overroofing and overshadowing all other configurations, had come into existence or was about to come into existence. As a corporate body, the state is the antithetic complement of civil society. Therefore it tends to throw off its monarchic shell, which has served its purpose.

13

SOCIAL NORMS: LAW

Law as an Effect of Custom

CUSTOM is social will itself, distilled from habit, usage, and practice. This effect of custom is customary law, which has its equivalent in codified or statute law. In the course of normal development, statute law tends to prevail, although custom, representing a more basic form of social will, actually has a much more far-reaching and penetrating significance. This is because custom is the "law" sanctioned by age, often allegedly by a boundless past which over a long period of time has become firm as a rock and, as long as it lasts, apparently indestructible. It is assumed to be the eternal creation of the sense of justice, the consciousness of right, and of the soul and mind of a people (*Volkseele und Volksgeist*). Statute law (*Gesetz*) is different insofar as it is sanctioned outside of or even against, tradition, only by reasonable design, by its *purpose:* it appears to be something new, looking toward the future rather than the past. If law is given or even forced upon people by a single person or by a few individuals, it may offend the remainder of the people, hurt their sense of justice, and do violence to their conscience. If law is the expression of the will of the majority, then, at least, it is only the minority who suffers because of it; but this minority may comprise elements who have the power to express their disapproval, even their disobedience, effectively. It could happen that for this or other reasons, perhaps because of the weight of their arguments or because of the pressure of chang-

Translated from *Einfuehrung in die Soziologie*, book 4, chap. 3, pp. 209–24 (§§40, 41, 42); some brief passages are omitted, others have been contracted.

ing condtions, the established law and order are imperilled by this resistance. Added to this are the mobility and instability of the majority, especially if its composition changes and if this change is caused by the addition of new elements who had not been committed previously. Any innovation, because of its very nature, is always opposed by habit, tradition, ancient custom, and thus also by customary law. This is why the new likes to dress up as a restoration of the old; conversely, restoration turns against innovation, even if innovation claims, with or without reason, to be, and to stand for restoration of, the yet older.

Innovation in law has a better chance of success, if it can claim, and if it succeeds in convincing people, that it is of supernatural origin: this has had enormous historical importance for all relationships of authoritarian rule (*Herrschaft*), especially if these have prevailed over relationships based on fellowship (*Genossenschaft*). At first it appears to be the natural prerogative of the ruler to issue orders and to establish norms and, in the role of a judge, to make decisions as he sees fit and deems right. Soon, however, habit asserts itself in a large circle of the community. and habit endows law, if it is conditioned by fellowship, with the power of creating a common will, possibly with reference to a precedent: the way in which the predecessor, for instance, the father, has ruled, is said to have been good, and the new ruler is unpopular merely by not being and acting like him: all the more so where there used to be greater respect for tradition. The ruler who is endowed with higher authority needs special accreditation, because he is more remote and less well known. Always the dead prevail over the living, and the visible powers are replaced by invisible ones who are shunned and feared.

The less the ruler is capable of achieving his goals on his own, and the greater the number of innovations he wishes to introduce, the more indispensable is the resort to the gods. If a people in its totality is the subject of custom and customary law, it prevails over, and restricts thereby, the arbitrary power of the ruler; whereupon the ruler soon asserts himself and reinforces his power through religion. Of the judge's authority, the part which is supported by religion enables him most effectively to reform and overcome customary law: the simplest way of achieving this is for the judge's person itself to be endowed with holiness and the splendor of priesthood. This very point can be observed in important manifestations in the life of ancient and highly developed civilizations, as in India and Ireland and many other places where the king was the highest judge, where he was at the same time, either by himself or by the grace of his god, invested with the dignity of a priest or where he could act with the favor and support of the priests. The Indians and the Irish have also in common that priestly wisdom, which included knowledge of law, was taught and transmitted in schools. The importance of these schools was due to the fact that they were run in a familylike, that is, in a communal (*Gemeinschaft*-like), manner; priestly wisdom thus partook of the natural and genuine holiness which distinguishes any piety relationship. It has always been known and confirmed again and again that religion and law are closely related and that they have even merged to the extent of identity. This has perhaps become nowhere as obvious as in ancient India. "A king and a Brahmin who are thoroughly versed in the Veda, these two uphold the moral order," says one of the oldest books of ancient Indian law. Nowhere has the authority of priesthood manifested itself so bluntly, even to the point of elevating itself openly and emphatically above its gods. In the book of law of Vishnu, we read: "The gods are invisible ones. The Brahmins visible ones. The Brahmins support the world. It is by the grace of the Brahmins that the gods live in heaven."

The antique city-states (polis) and, although more reluctantly, Rome, which in the end became the most powerful of them, at an early time separated law from religious creed and cult. This was achieved by granting all superstitious ideas, ceremonies, and rituals, especially sacrifices their impact upon the people, together with a remnant of royal dignity, which had traditional validity. However, the judge, as a civil servant of the republic, was bound even more strictly to the will of the citizenry, as established by customary and statutory law. Totally different was the effect of the system developed in Palestine, which brought the theocratic ideas of the Orient to its greatest perfection. Law and the courts remained undeveloped. People sought justice from the elders, from the king or, preferably, from the priest. This was called, as we see also in the law book of Hammurabi, "To take the matter before God." Sacred law, of course, was entirely in the hands of the priests. As all culture in the newer countries of Europe has been nourished from these two sources, the Roman Empire and late Judaism, from which Christian faith and the Church had sprung, thus it also came about that law and the courts to a great extent fell under ecclesiastical influence. There were, then, these two kinds of law: the native customary law, in its colorful variety, mainly originating from Germanic tradition; and canon law, which is completely based upon alleged revelations and alleged decisions of the head of the Church. Because of the prestige of the ecclesiastical courts and owing to their demands, canon law was extended gradually upon large areas of civil law, especially concerning matrimony, succession, loans, and the taking of interest, which latter was regarded as a mortal sin. These were the very areas in which the Church insisted upon its moral authority, without, however, being able to impede social development; the secularization of these institutions continued irrevocably, just as the secularization of all life, including the Church itself.

Natural Law

A most remarkable and important phenomenon in this area is natural law. As a rule, deliberations about law are left to the special profession of juridical scholars, but natural law is a philosophical discipline which looks for the universal and necessary elements in law. The theory of natural law, as it is nowadays thought of outside Catholic theology, has developed both from and against theological and scholastic natural law. Troeltsch calls this modern natural law profane natural law, which is correct inasfar as it has shaken off ecclesiastical fetters. More adequately, it is called rational natural law, thereby indicating that it has resumed the direction which it had pursued in Greek philosophy and Roman jurisprudence. The decisive innovation in this sense did not emanate from Grotius, as is often asserted, but from Hobbes, although Grotius' treatise on law has indeed been an epoch-making work. It was Hobbes who gave the classical form to this doctrine of natural law around which associational (*Gesellschaft*-like) thinking, which has since grown, has crystallized.

The Hobbesian doctrine starts from the assumption that every man by nature tends to be the enemy of everybody else, because of mutual fear and mutual distrust. Consequently, the natural condition of man must be thought of as a general state of war, a war of everyone against everyone (*bellum omnium contra omnes*). Frequently, this doctrine is misinterpreted and misunderstood, partly because Hobbes himself only gradually became clearly aware of the strictly abstract and schematic character of his own doctrine, and partly because he never quite ceased to connect his abstraction with the development of human civilization out of savagery and barbarism, an idea which was much discussed at that time, when the first circumnavigation of the earth had occurred. He interprets his theory more correctly when he compares a stateless and lawless condition between individual persons with the actually observed condition between individual independent states. He asserts ideal validity (*ideelle Geltung*) for the law of nature, that is, for the sum total of rules of behavior which can be derived from men's own interest by drawing correct conclusions. These rules, however, have only limited and insufficient force, as long as there is no authority which changes this law of nature into positive law, thus enforcing conditions of peace.

Natural law culminates in the statement that reason demands the affirmation of the state or, if it is nonexistent, its creation. Hobbes mentioned only what he might have elaborated upon, namely, that the true meaning of international law lay in its being recognized as an incomplete institutional arrangement among states, similar to the incomplete natural law which was prevalent prior to the existence of states; there is no superstate in existence which would have the recognized authority to decide conflicts between states and the power to prevent violent hostilities, much as a federation might claim legal superiority over member states. . . .

The analogy of international law and rational natural law is part of the thinking of natural law, as is indicated in the customary ex-

pression *jus naturae et gentium*. Kant, who in this as in other respects
develops his legal theories in close relation to those of Hobbes, in-
troduces international law as follows. A state perceived as a moral
person in the condition of natural freedom, and thus also in a condition of constant war, has the right to make war as well as the right
to compel others to abolish this condition of war, and thus should
make it his task to create a constitution as the foundation for a
lasting peace. The distinction from the state of nature of individuals or families was merely that in international law the concern
was not only with the relation of one state to another state but also
with the relation of individuals of one state toward individuals of
another state, and of individuals toward the other state itself. To
consider this, only such rules were required as could easily be derived from the concept of the state of nature. Kant therefore presents as the elements of international law: that states exist by nature
in a nonlegal condition, thus in a state of war, even though this may
not always be war in the sense of actual hostility; that for this reason a league of nations, according to the idea of an original social
contract, was needed, "indeed not to interfere with domestic troubles
but in order to protect each other against attacks from the outside."
Yet, he adds as another element of international law that the league
would not have to have sovereign power, as in the constitution of
a state, but should form a fellowship, a federation; a union that
could be terminated, and thus would have to be renewed from time
to time—a right *in subsidium* of another original right, namely,
to prevent the degeneration into the condition of actual warfare
between the member states. Kant calls this in parentheses a *Foedus
Amphictyonum*, thus referring to the coalitions of Greek city-states,
which were based partly on international, partly on constitutional
law; if he had experienced the *Deutschen Bund* (German Federation), 1815–1866, this might have occurred to him as an example.

Hobbes would have rejected the very thought as completely
insufficient [because alliances were exposed to the threat of internal conflict and because one alliance was to call forth a counter-
alliance, so that the danger of war would continue to exist and
might even increase. This danger could be eliminated only by
means of a complete unification, which requirement, in turn, was

to make the establishment of an independent, unrestricted, and sovereign organization an absolute necessity. Further, no valid claim against sovereignty could be permitted to exist; as soon as such a right was conceded, the state of nature would be continued —nobody would then be entitled to make the ultimate decision, let alone to enforce it, and the right of self-help, which leaves the ultimate decision to sheer force, would remain in effect or would be reestablished.][1]

Today, Hobbes might refer to the end of the German Federation, as likewise to the terrible Civil War which somewhat earlier tore the "United" States of America into two federations. He would hold the same opinion about the reconstituted federalism in America, as about the present [1930] German *Reich*, although the combination of federalism and centralism in both countries has been changed somewhat toward the latter, that is, from a league of states toward a federal form of government.

Natural Law in Gemeinschaft and Gesellschaft

One may attempt to develop, in contrast to associational or rational (*Gesellschaft*-like) natural law the idea of a communal (*Gemeinschaft*-like) natural law: the task would be to examine whether another basis for the concept of the origin of law could be considered besides the one which opposes individuals to other individuals as isolated persons, that is, as persons who share no common rights, except those which derive from specifically concluded contracts and agreements. Indeed, one is free to assume that men, whether one regards them as equal or unequal, are by nature friendly toward one another; that not war of everyone against everyone but peace of everyone with everyone was the state of nature. To be sure, such an assumption was immanent to the thinking

[1]   In the German text, Toennies refers to Hobbes' position concerning international law prior to referring to Kant's point of view in this regard; the editors have reversed the sequence and abridged the passage dealing with Hobbes. We have also omitted Toennies' reference to the ideas of "Paneuropa" and the "League of Nations" as an exemplification of the Hobbesian argument.—Eds.

of the Middle Ages which Hobbes and his followers attempted to overcome. Regularly, it was associated with the Aristotelian thesis that man is by nature a political being (*zoon politikon*), that is, one destined for life in the *polis*, later expressed by the Latin version indicating that man was a social being (*animal sociale*). Hobbes opposes this view expressly; in the book which has had the greatest effect on world literature, *De Cive*, he attempts to repudiate the Aristotelian idea in detail by maintaining that man in contact with others is not looking for anything but advantage or honor (*Ehre*). Indeed, each needed the help of the other, but whoever was able to would rather strive to rule over others than to ally himself with them; the origin of great and lasting societies was mutual fear, and the origin of mutual fear lay partly in natural equality, partly in the natural inclination to harm one another. However, it is remarkable that in the later great presentation of his theory (*Leviathan*) Hobbes did not return to this kind of reasoning. Besides the three main causes of strife, namely, (1) competition, (2) distrust, (3) vanity, Hobbes maintains, in logical pursuit of his psychological theories, that there are also three "affects that incline men to peace," namely, (1) fear of death, (2) desire of such things as are necessary for commodious living, and (3) the hope of obtaining them by their industry. Here, too, he is looking for a likely transition from the state of nature to the political state without presupposing a natural benevolence of man towards man: man is supposed to be clearly egotistic.

However, it is possible to start from the opposite hypothesis of natural altruism, and from this to arrive at a system of social norms as natural law. It would mean that in every social relationship which is founded on mutual affection and an ensuing feeling of obligation, a germ of objective law is contained and that this germ could grow under favorable circumstances of life and develop into law. One could take one's departure from the actually observable source of communal relationships—whether these are based more on domination (authoritarian) or on fellowship (cooperative). One assumes, even in an attenuated form, a natural inclination of man toward man which makes nonhostile behavior, that is, mutual toleration and peacefulness, possible, as long as there are no particular causes inciting to animosity and violence. Under these assumptions there would be here a germ of law, but with a much diminished chance of growth and development, because it could be suffocated and killed so much easier by counteracting motivations. Within these limits—intimacy among a few, and weak sympathy of every man toward every man—various more or less vital germs of *Gemeinschaft* may be thought to exist. An objective law (*Recht*) derived from such a germ might be designated as communal (*Gemeinschaft*-like) natural law.

But what would be the characteristics of such natural law? It would not distinguish and separate subjective rights from obligations in such a way as is required in associational relationships, where the law of contract contrasts the subjective right or claim of one party with the duty or obligation of the other. On the contrary, the right would directly imply the obligation: the right of dominion (*Herrschaft*) would involve the legal obligation to use it for the benefit of the subjects; the duty of obedience would contain the legal claim to protection and assistance. In cooperative relationships, this reciprocity and unity of right and obligation would be even more obvious as a communal force; rights and obligations would equally and in unison derive from mutual goodwill and the necessity of cooperation. Objective law as a system of social norms in this case would mean that such rules are recognized as natural and necessary, so that the form of control which claims validity as judicial authority would know such rules and apply them when making decisions.

This communal natural law would establish as supreme principle that men, as rational beings, are united in narrower or wider circles, collectives and corporations for protection and defense, that thus all would stand up for one, and one for all. Everybody would be placed in his proper station, with rights and duties connected with it; every man would have a natural right not only of existence but of participation, with corresponding obligations.

Such rules of living together are likely to develop most purely and most completely, because most easily, within the narrowest circles, thus mainly within the family; therefore the first place in civil law would be accorded to marriage and family law, and consequently also to the law of succession insofar as it would be accepted as natural and just. The law of property would be next: here naturally common property and, as far as feasible, common usage and usufruct would have to be assumed as communal natural law; such common property can also be extended for essential and important objects to wider circles and corporations. Common property would always remain necessary and natural insofar as people who live and work together are attached to each other emotionally and perceptively and are determined to let law prevail. They would demand for themselves no more than what is regarded as appropriate for each, assuming that what is to be appropriate had been determined according to mutually acceptable rules. Thus, a nation that would want to be justified in perceiving itself as one large family, as *ein einzig Volk von Bruedern*, ought to submit itself to a natural law which treats land and other essential necessities of peaceful living together as common property, in such a way that it may be disposed of and used according to recognized rules which are regarded as lawful and just.

Besides land, other objects can be administered communally as common means, serving the purpose of common living and working, thus as a means of production, so that these also could be obtained by smaller groups: communities, families, or even individuals as a mediated, conditioned, and revocable possession. This would presuppose that the total labor of such a group, as, for instance, a nation, would be subjected to a suitable regulation which would serve the general welfare but nobody's profit and which would have the purpose of distributing the result of the total thus regulated labor as might be considered proper according to communal (*Gemeinschaft*-like) natural law. The simplest principle of just distribution is absolute equality, which naturally would be modified by given circumstances to relative equality, thus being adjusted to actual inequalities due to ability and achievement.

Thus communal natural law, in this respect not essentially different from associational natural law, would be subsumed under the valid and accepted concepts of reason and wisdom. These are demanding concepts, asking for a—no matter how motivated—measure of self-control and self-restraint in favor of an idea, which even in *Gemeinschaft* would be recognized as ultimately serving the individual's true welfare and benefit. This idea as applied to action, especially the peaceful regulation of man's relation to man, and to things appears as the idea of justice which is inseparable from the idea of natural law. According to the Aristotelian distinction, for associational (*Gesellschaft*-like) natural law, the idea is the justice of exchange: commutative justice, as Greek usage puts it. In communal (*Gemeinschaft*-like) natural law, on the other hand, distributive justice prevails, the justice of fair distribution within the unity of common ownership and common use. The maxim *suum cuique* in the case of *Gesellschaft* means that each member of society shall keep what he has gained, unless it is conclusively proved that it has been earned dishonestly. In the case of *Gemeinschaft*—respecting distributive justice—it means that each member of a community (*Gemeinschaft*) may and shall earn what has been assigned to him by law and equity.

Characteristic for the difference between the two ideas of natural law is thus their relation to moral concepts. This is demonstrated by the different meaning which the concept of justice has in different contexts. The justice of exchange enters into associational relation, as it were, from the outside: it requires merely the conditions of concurring wills and of the proper understanding of the advantages of contracts, in other words, the abstention from force and deceit. On the contrary, the justice of distribution is concerned with the objects themselves; it is, if one may say so, the precondition of life in a *Gemeinschaft*. Corresponding to this difference is the relationship of morality and law within the two systems of natural law. The idea of associational natural law has nothing to do with morality except that it leaves to the latter the problem of evaluating by its norms the actions of its subjects. This includes the actions of judges, insofar as it is assumed that judges ought to be just. Law itself does not claim to be moral in an associational (*Gesellschaft*-like) context. It merely wants to be useful, that is, fitted to a purpose. The purpose is a peaceful living together, without force, but not a living the good life together, replete with goodwill and the desire to provide mutual aid. This is precisely what the idea of communal (*Gemeinschaft*-like) natural law requires. It merges morality and law, but necessarily submits law to morality. Law becomes here an instrument of the spirit of self-control and the limitation of the individual, thus of education for and practice in applying the virtues which are required for a good living together.

The development of the theory of rational natural law has actually meant the separation of law and morality; consequently, the development of law modeled after this kind of natural law means the elimination of the moral elements which had previously been contained in it. It is in this respect exclusively that we shall consider theory. Hobbes had treated natural law as almost identical with morality, so that according to him the individual as a citizen, within the sphere of freedom granted to him by the state, had the obligation to apply rules of honesty as a means of his own self-preservation, just as he who wields political power must shape positive law according to these rules. Christian Thomasius, following Pufendorf, has undertaken a clear and sharp separation of law and morality. Pufendorf tried to mediate in this respect between Hobbes' theory and that of Grotius, which still adhered to the premise of the inherently social nature of man. But Thomasius divided the whole complex of what ought to be into that of *justum, honestum*, and *decorum*. This point of view remained prevalent in the German theory of natural law. The philosophers Kant and Fichte, especially, have insisted upon the strict separation of law and morality. Indeed, Fichte, otherwise Kant's successor and disciple—although his discipleship is of questionable quality—has gone farther than Kant in this respect. The separation is more radical with him. He denies expressly that any legal relationship should be based on morality, that is, on the moral duty to keep one's word. He demands that jurisprudence establish means by which legality can be preserved even if trust and good faith should have disappeared entirely. That is why law ignores morality, and morality even transcends law because the truly moral man does not recognize any law that could compel him.

This theory has become more effective in Kant's rendition. In the most generalized way, Kant distinguishes the idea of legislation as (1) ethical: which makes an action a duty, and this duty the motivating power; and (2) juridical: which does not include the motivation in the law and thus **permits** another motivation than duty. In the same way he differentiates between the morality and legality of actions. Kant, like others, uses as his foremost example that of contract. He maintains that ethics did not comprise a legislation of all duties, although the duties themselves were part of ethics. Thus, ethics demands that an obligation promised in a contract should be complied with, even though the other party might not be able to enforce it. But ethics derives the legal principle that *pacta sunt servanda* and the corresponding duty from jurisprudence and takes it for granted. "It is not a duty of virtue to keep one's promise, but a legal duty, compliance with which may be enforced." This latter attribute has been presented as the distinctive feature of law prior to Kant, as after him, and more recently, by Stammler. On the other hand, on the authority of older concepts of law it is contested that this is an essential feature, although nobody denies that it describes the reality of modern positive law, which is completely determined by the power of the state, and that it postulates in this respect the separation of law from morality: rules of law are enforceable, rules of morality are not. One can say that this separation is part of the modern development of law, although it is not generally sustained. One should, moreover, not overlook the fact that positive morality—that is, public opinion in its communal or associational manifestations—does not lack the means that are necessary to enforce its demands and its judgments, thus to punish transgressions. However, it is certain that the state increasingly has become what it ought to be according to the concept of the younger school of natural law: *the possessor of all enforcement rights.*

14

SOCIAL STRUCTURES OR
INSTITUTIONS:
GENERAL CHARACTERIZATION

Pairs of Concepts

BY SOCIAL STRUCTURES (*Bezugsgebilde*) we mean all institutions and other systems of social action to which social entities refer and in which their more communal or more associational character may be discerned, including the possible transition from one type to the other.

For economic life and, further, for social life in general, places and localities are of the greatest importance because work is performed there, business is engaged in, and all kinds of social activities occur. Village or town—sparse or dense population—small town, medium-sized town, metropolis—these differences shape economic life in various ways; most of the other institutional configurations develop in accordance with these. Recognizing this, Marx writes: "The basis of all highly developed division of labor, which is mediated through the exchange of commodities, is the separation of city and country. One can say that the entire economic history of society is summarized in the movement of this contradiction," to which statement, unfortunately, he adds, "but we are not concerned with that here." (*Das Kapital* I, 4, p. 317, German ed.)

To the separation of city and country correspond the most important differences in political life as well as in spiritual and moral life; to a considerable part these differences arise from the separa-

---

Translated from *Einfuehrung in die Soziologie*, book 5, chap. 1, pp. 261–64 (§51, 52); the first part of §52, apart from the opening sentence, is omitted; the second part follows in the next chapter ("Effectiveness of Factors").

tion of city and country; they are their effect. Separation, antagonism, conflict are always most noteworthy, notwithstanding the fact
that all phenomena are interdependent and belong together; this
is especially obvious with regard to seemingly purely intellectual
differentiations. There, interdependence is noted because fundamentally different movements of thought and action, on the one
hand, complement each other, while, on the other hand, they retain
liveliness and mobility by means of critique and polemics.

A series of conceptual pairs could be enumerated which would
serve to illustrate this kind of differentiation. The facts which correspond to the concepts belong partly to the economic sphere,
partly to the political as well as to the spiritual and moral sphere.
Only a few of these conceptual pairs are mentioned here. The most
important examples are:

1. in economic, that is, in general social life,
   village—town
   small town—metropolis
   mother country—colony
   primary—secondary production
   production—trade
   household—market
   small enterprise—large enterprise
   precapitalistic—capitalistic modes of production and
                       trade

2. in political life,
   folk society—state society (*Volksleben—Staatsleben*)
   aristocracy—democracy
   federalism—unitarism
   conservative parties—mutative parties
   customary law—revolutionary legislation

3. in spiritual-moral life,
   feminine mind—masculine mind
   belief in miracles—knowledge of laws of nature
   religion—scientific way of thinking
   Church—sect
   orthodoxy—heresy
   art—science
   distributive justice—commutative justice

How These Concepts Are Related

It should be understood that all these conceptual pairs are somehow interconnected; most directly those which are vertically aligned, because they belong to the same basic category. But even more important are the interconnections among the basic categories themselves and their reciprocal interaction: partly the general interconnections and interactions, partly the specific ones between corresponding conceptual pairs; finally and especially those within each conceptual pair.

(1) A single conceptual pair should be interpreted in such a way that primarily the necessary and essential *relationship* of its members is open to consideration; this means especially that the second member in the conceptual pair is the younger one, which has developed from the first one and continues to do so. One must therefore be particularly attentive to transitions and connecting links, and generally to the manifold appearance of reality contrasted to the concepts that are not intended to do anything but to represent outstanding phenomena in relatively fixed types. They must never be interpreted otherwise but as means to provide hitching posts to the thinking about things; they offer something like a yardstick, the application of which is supposed to do two things: to clarify the confusion that reigns in the world of experience, and to make the data of experience comparable.

(2) It is important to be cognizant of the differences between the members; they are frequently more striking than the natural unity and the similarity by which they are linked. What is meant here are the relations of the generations of man to one another as well as the relations between whole historical periods that join a series of generations. One might think here, in the first place, of the relation between our European so-called modern era to the so-called Middle Ages, but also of the relation between new countries, especially colonies, to old ones; or of the in many ways analogous relation of late antiquity, in particular that dominated by Rome, to an earlier epoch which culminated in Athenian culture. In some regards, even if the dimensions are totally different, one may think of the relation between the cultural configuration of northern Europe that had grown out of the decline of the Roman Empire and the older cultural configuration of southern Europe, with its roots in the East, especially in Egypt and Asia Minor.

(3) Another leading consideration is separation and *contradiction,* the latter developing the more easily and strongly the greater the differences are or turn out to be; these contradictions appear in many a shape and form. They are most alive and fraught with fate if they burst into open *conflicts;* these, again, are very varied and can lead to a variety of consequences. They are not always reflected in the subjective consciousness of men as dislike, repulsion, or hatred, but frequently they are, if to a lesser or larger degree. The most significant phenomena of contradiction are closely connected with the reciprocal interactions between the three basic categories.

(4) A reunion or, one even may say, a *reconciliation* of the two diverging and possibly antagonistic wings of a conceptual pair is possible and may at times be desired and attempted. Reconciliation may be understood as a synthesis in the Hegelian sense, succeeding the antithesis and evolving from it. Such a synthesis may have a purely ideological basis and effect, that is, it may arise solely from the desire and will of some persons that participate or do not participate in it. Its strength and effect, however, are much more likely to come to the fore if the inclination toward union arises from the contrast itself, that is, out of contradiction and conflict that are inherent in a situation, like the desire to reestablish a peaceful condition after a long war. This is true even if during wars the desire for the end of hostilities appears to be, or at least is discernible, more strongly on one side, namely, with those who are defeated or about to be defeated; so that what formally seems to be a treaty, in actual fact signifies the victory of one state or principle and the submission of another. As a rule, and most likely, this victory will be that of the more recent reality or idea which, however, at the same time indicates its internal transformation. It is in the nature of things that sooner or later a new split will occur, and therefore possibly a new contradiction.

These developments can be completely described only historically; but this falls outside the frame of a theoretical introduction.

One can merely attempt to clarify typologically the relation of the conceptual pairs and especially the relation of the basic categories to one another. We know of no cultural condition wherein the three basic categories of economic, political, and spiritual life and institutions are not simultaneously present and intermingled.

15

SOCIAL STRUCTURES OR

INSTITUTIONS:

EFFECTIVENESS OF FACTORS

Economic, Political, and Spiritual Aspects of Social Structures

IT MAY reasonably be said: *the economy* is everything, it governs and determines all spheres of human activity. For none can be imagined that is not to a considerable degree economic activity. All kinds of political activities have obvious economic aspects; the same is true of religion and other varieties of spiritual culture, as embedded in ecclesiastical and educational institutions and associations; it likewise applies to all institutions that are devoted to the arts and sciences. They must be served by physical labor, and even more by mental labor, and these constitute elements in the totality of economic life.

In another sense, *politics*, too, may be conceived as a general activity of human reason and volition, as something involved in the regulation of many human activities: in the management of every household, every industrial enterprise, every business becomes discipline, thus leading and following, ordering and obeying, the more necessary, the more the extension of such activites grows: political insight, foresight, cleverness find a place in every kind of administration; it is of the greatest importance in municipal, and even more so in state government. Often, politics has been compared to the art of steering a ship, and certainly the helmsman of a ship, the driver of a car, the railway engineer, to all of whom persons and goods are entrusted, need a certain measure of political reasoning. And finally, in large institutions and organizations that belong to

---

Translated from *Einfuehrung in die Soziologie*, book 5, chap. 1 (cont'd.) and chap. 2, pp. 267–83 (§§52, 53, 54, 55) ; slightly abridged.

the sphere of the spirit, there is the more scope for politics, the more such an institution represents an organization and system of human activities which resembles the administration of a commonwealth, and the more it requires cleverness, even craftiness and cunning, in order to preserve itself, because its foundation is questionable. The most celebrated case of this kind is the Roman Catholic Church, whose leading minds have long been renowned for being masters in the art of diplomacy and political wisdom. Its system of super- and sub-ordination constituted as a hierarchy has become a model for all governmental organizations, therefore also for the bureaucracy which is characteristic of the modern state.

Finally one may say truthfully: the *spirit* (Geist) is everything. Human living together is spiritual in the most general sense, that is, through language, thought, reason, and by means of deliberation and decision. This is true regarding the simplest and most general economic activity, and even more so the more human labor becomes employed in large and at times gigantic industrial plants; finally, regarding the totality of political activity. Spirit has its own special sphere; the most general in witchcraft and religion, on a different level in educational and instructional processes and in formal schooling, finally, in its most liberal form in the arts and sciences. To be sure, artistic, scientific, and scholarly activities are individualistic to a high degree, and many a person involved in them desires nothing so much as to be left alone. But he is not capable of placing himself outside human interaction; he needs understanding, sympathy, support, often, as a rule even, also of the recipient, of the customer ("the art goes a-begging"). The artist or scientist wishes to preserve his skills and his knowledge, hence to pass it on through disciples and pupils. Often enough he is dependent on the municipality or the state in order to attain the income and honor which his self-consciousness desires. The actual positions of the artist and the man of science in the social life of today are frequently unsatisfactory and are felt to be so. The positions which artists and scientists need in order to have a stimulating effect and to serve as leaders are all too often occupied by those who do not possess the qualifications that are required.

Effectiveness of Factors: Historical Materialism

If, then, economics, politics, and the life of the spirit are always connected and have a unified effect, the question suggests itself: which of the three basic categories is the relatively independent variable, that is, the one most easily, most probably variable, without or even against the influences of the other two? What, on the other hand, are the effects of this variable on the other spheres that orient themselves on the changes of the first, even though they may endeavor to hinder or to reduce it and perhaps follow the road but slowly and reluctantly; in other words, adapt themselves to what is the unalterable new?

This is the field of controversy which, during the past few decades, has stirred up a great deal of discussion and occasioned an immense literature in books, brochures, journals, and newspapers, comparable perhaps only to the discussion around the question of the origin of man some time earlier. Then, as now, a new idea which in both cases was not actually new has collided with a rock of traditional views and obstinate prejudice, without, however, being shattered thereby.

The belief that an idea, or ideas, was something that changed independently, that approached truth more or less closely, that would be transformed into doctrines of faith or into opinions which then would dominate political as well as social and economic life, this was the effect of speculative philosophy in Germany; in other countries, it was rather the remainder of a theological way of thinking. It seemed like a degradation of man when an interpretation of history arose and claimed validity which called itself materialistic and expressly denied the autonomy of ideas by maintaining that the manner how every day's work was conducted was the primary factor and that the changes in the organization of work were a direct expression of the necessary relations of production which corresponded to a certain developmental stage of the material forces of production. The totality of these relations of production, as Marx says in a sketchlike presentation of his theory, makes up the economic structure of society, the real basis upon which the legal and political superstructure develops; certain societal forms of consciousness corresponded to that structure—and with a change in the economic basis, the whole colossal superstructure was bound to be turned over more or less rapidly. The doctrine has often been interpreted as though it meant that only the base, the economic substructure, and the movement of economic phenomena was truly real, and that spiritual phenomena were nothing more than reflex effects of that actual reality. We cannot blame only the sometimes too ardent disciples of the doctrine for these interpretations; its learned originator himself is responsible for the misunderstanding because of his use of the expression "the real basis." Nevertheless, the interpretation is undoubtedly erroneous. In the preface of the short treatise *A Critique of Political Economy (Zur Kritik der politischen Oekonomie)*, Marx says that, in detaching himself from jurisprudence and Hegelian philosophy, he had endeavored to do justice to French socialism and communism, and that he had come to the conclusion that legal institutions and forms of government could not be conceived either as developing of their own accord or as emanating from the general evolution of the human mind, "but rather that they had their *roots* in the material conditions of life, the totality of which Hegel . . . summarized under the name of civil society." Here he uses another simile than the architectonic ones of foundation and superstructure. It would be odd to present only the foundation as real and the building itself as but a reflex and mere appearance—possibly a case of castles in the air—but it would be clearly nonsensical to declare a tree to be unreal and only its roots to be real. On the other hand, one might say with good reason that law as an order of living together—settling disputes, ensuring discipline, meting out punishment—was of essential significance in every kind of living together insofar as it is a working together, whether these rules among men have their origin in a tacit or emphatic unanimity of the companions or perhaps in the personal will of a chief or of a council of elders in a clan.

Wherever we meet social life, we do in fact find such rules in force: they grow in force through practice, similar to other less severe social norms which we combine with customary law into the general concept of custom. They are the expression of the necessary requirements for living and working together. The requirements have a tendency to expand when men are working together, warlike or peacefully, so that law will more and more take the place of force, especially when peaceful settlement of conflict takes the place of hostilities; thus punishment through organs of the commonwealth replaces the revenge of one clan against the other. Marx clearly expresses this necessity for law when he says that property relations are only a legal expression for the relations of production, and that these, in turn, correspond to a certain stage in the development of the material forces of production. Property relations, therefore, are said to be essentially evolutionary forms of the forces of production. One may argue that this is not a clear way of expressing oneself. But the idea is obviously that *private property*, whether of land, of homes and gardens, tools, implements and instruments, finally, of money, can be useful to society—even after it has become effective as capital in trade and credit operations—in the development of production or in the enlarged and increased production of goods, if the number of socially interacting persons remained equal, and even more so if their number were increasing. Even free and absolute private property might be useful and serviceable as a normal organ of society in a definite if limited epoch of history, if and when it represented a stage in the evolution of the forces of production, that is, as we might say in modern parlance, if it makes sense sociologically.

The Influence of the Economy on Law

Economic life most easily influences politics, therefore public law, which is more order than law; and mostly by this mediation only, economic life influences the real, that is, private law, after it has become differentiated from public law. Like the application of law, and like all life, economic life is in constant movement, therefore changing. Economic life, and this must be emphasized, is more diverse and more comprehensive than the life of law, but it is also more flexible, more fluid, and sometimes even like air: for it is always determined in part by desires and will; by the interests and feelings, then, of innumerable persons, among whom the important ones are of course the strongest; these may be individuals of decisive influence, and they could therefore most easily and effectively change existing institutions. Law, as it is pronounced by the courts, is, like custom, rigid and firm in its original substance, not easily changeable. Even gods and their priests, who are most likely to have the power of changing existing rules, would rather confirm and sanctify what is customary and in effective usage. It is a different matter if the secular rulers, such as kings and their ministers, who can, by means of their power, which is usually enhanced by wealth, disregard law and tradition; if by virtue of their influence upon judges or by means of special orders and decrees, behind which stands not only the power but also the alleged favor of the gods, they can abolish the old and create new law. This may be so on the strength of their irresistible whim and fancy or in the name of the state with which they identify or whose servants they claim to be; the state, they mean, is a master who cannot easily harm them.

In several regards, serious conflicts may develop between customary law, sense of justice, and traditional legal doctrine, on the one hand, and the reason of state (*Staatsraison*), on the other hand, even if reason of state is only the whim of a monarch in disguise, and if, besides the formally established law, mere acts of government and administrative practice take the place of the law. A permanent change in the valid law will be successful only if it corresponds to existing power relations, and the power relations will be at least in part economic power relations, either old and established by tradition or new: struggling, advancing, and endeavoring to manifest themselves in political power. Thus, those at first politically weaker will indirectly become politically stronger if they succeed in winning as an ally or even force into dependence one or several of those political forces which are based on traditional economic conditions; if, for instance, a more recent economic force is capable of splitting the alliance between the aristocracy and its head, the monarchy, which was based on more ancient economic relations of power; if, then, financial power—that of either commercial or industrial capital—strengthens and supports the monarchy, in order to receive favors from it and to be reinforced or, in reverse, if financial power pays for services already rendered.

The one great example of a transformation of law as a result and effect of changes in economic relations and conditions of life is offered by the history of the last few centuries. The underlying cause is the growth of industry, trade, and capitalism, and the urbanization which goes hand in hand with it. When drawing the conclusion that the effects of this development are most obvious in the sphere of public law and, above all, the constitution and the administration of the state, and that subsequently and by means of legislation they gradually extend to and transform all branches of law, we must not conceive of either one or the other effect as having been anything but a long-drawn-out and slow process to which various more or less powerful elements have made their contribution. One of the earliest and at the same time most distinctive phenomena in this regard, in Germany and England as well as in other countries, is the decline of the peasantry in contrast to its previous ascending development, which had been in happy agreement with the growth and prosperity of the cities. The deterioration occurred because of the increasing refinement and urbanization of the nobility, especially where it gathered at the courts and thus developed a greater need of money. "Their" peasants became the obvious object of oppression and exploitation. Heinrich Brunner (*Grundzuege der deutschen Rechtsgeschichte*, p. 216) explains that since the end of the Middle Ages in large parts of the Holy Roman Empire the legal security of the various strata composing the peasantry had been undermined.

Whereas formerly there had been a tendency to convert peasant farms into hereditary possessions, or their de facto heredity was on the way to becoming legal, a regressive tendency asserted itself after the fifteenth century, when the landlords endeavored to abolish the hereditary quality of peasant farms or at least to impede the development of that hereditary quality. This drive was promoted by Romanistic jurisprudence, which, even if not actually hostile to the peasantry, had no use for the complexity of the forms of peasant property in Germanic law. Since for evaluation this Roman law offered only the concepts of hereditary tenure and temporary lease (leasehold), its application had a leveling effect; it forcibly subsumed numerous intermediate forms under the heading of temporary lease.

The adoption (*Rezeption*) of Roman law was another and a new symptom for the preponderance which the Roman cultural inheritance maintained in church, in speech, and in the fictitious continuance of the Roman Empire (which had lost its universal significance in favor of the developing national states long ago).

This spirit was reinforced by the progressive development of the cities, that is, of trade and commerce. This development required, even at that time, a unified civil law; the same necessity became apparent in the nineteenth century. The influence of princely power worked in the same direction, and of all factors of legal life, it was this power that would protect and favor lawyers trained in Roman law and promote their legal interpretation and jurisdiction. This interpretation served imperial privileges, and did not recognize the constitution of the estates (*Staende*) which had developed throughout the Empire. The jurists established the maxim, *Quod principi placuit, legis habet vigorem*, which would please every prince and support him in his struggle against the nobility that limited his power. Paul Laband, the most eminent scholar of political law at the turn of the century, maintained that "the development of the absolute state and the adoption of Roman law in Germany are one and the same historical process." Laband also has drawn attention to the fact that the adoption was accomplished mainly by the princely courts of justice, where the *doctores* soon gained the upper hand. They assumed, as may be read in Janssen's *Geschichte des Deutschen Volkes* (I, p. 560), an attitude of actual hostility toward Germanic law. Brunner, too, admits that Germanic law was pushed aside and neglected by the learned and semilearned jurists who were sitting in the courts. But it was by no means the case that princes and their statesmen always and outright supported the efforts of the nobility to suppress the peasantry, to rule over it at will, to reduce it as they pleased by eviction and by not resettling deserted farms.

However, Roman law has not had the same effect everywhere. Max Weber pointed out (in his posthumous *Wirtschaftsgeschichte*, p. 291) that in France royalty made the eviction of peasants extremely difficult for the landlords, by means of her legists who were trained in Roman law. And in a later phase, German territorial princes, too, occasionally interfered successfully. They had a strong interest in preserving the peasantry; first, because the transformation of peasants' land into seignorial lands rendered it tax-free, since the nobility had retained the privilege of serving on horse for the land which they possessed by feudal law; second, because the peasantry provided the best infantry. From this privilege of the nobility, officership as a chosen profession had emerged, especially service in the cavalry. But that it was possible for the nobility to increase its power over the peasants, and thereby its income to such an extent, was indirectly the result of the long-standing battle which the princes had to fight against the nobility and against the estates (*Staende*) in general until they established, in the words of the soldier king (Frederic I of Prussia), their sovereignty as a *rocher de bronze*. In Brandenburg particularly, as early as the sixteenth century, but more so in the seventeenth, the relationship had developed in such a way that the nobility was forced and often willing to relinquish its previous political privileges and its right to participation in government for private manorial rights and castelike privileges. In the local community the estates retained their magistracy, but in government their power was annulled (Schulze, *Preussisches Staatsrecht*, p. 43). It was a compromise: private privileges were increased in order to decrease public ones. Only after princely power had become sufficiently strong, could it attempt to curtail those private powers again, as happened toward the end of the sixteenth century through forcing resettlement of abandoned peasant farms and through prohibiting the transformation of peasant land into manorial land. And in the territories of the west, where the power of the landed gentry had been defeated earlier by the sovereign, that is, by the central governmental power, this sovereign power had started at an earlier date to assume the role of protector of the peasants versus the manorial lords. However, only after the successes of the French Revolution, did this progress lead to the abolition of the restrictions on transfers of land. (The Prussian edict of 9 October 1807 permitted the free sale of rural property.) This also meant the breakdown of the institution of *Leihezwang*, that is, the protection of peasants. And it is remarkable how by means of this newly established freedom, the power of the estate owners (*Gutsherren*) which they had formerly possessed and claimed as lords of the manor (*Grundherren*), was reestablished.

During the time of general reaction that followed the peace [of Paris, 1815] and the founding of the German Federation (*Deutscher Bund*), the estate owners managed to prevent the so-called regulation of the smaller peasant holdings, with the result that a great number of these were bought by the estate owners in the course of the next generation. Only because of the popular unrest of 1848, unrestricted ownership was legally extended to the smaller holdings that had survived until that time. Just as the regulation of the larger peasant holdings, because peasants had to buy their emancipation by yielding from one-third to one-half of their land, resulted in a considerably enlarged ownership of land by the great landlords and in much reduced holdings by the peasants, so the process which in its beginning the lords had fought against so violently turned out to be definitely in their favor in the end. Knapp indicates through the title of his book *Die Bauernbefreiung und der Ursprung der Land-arbeiter in den aelteren Teilen Preussens* (*The Emancipation of the Peasants and the Origin of Agricultural Laborers in the Older Parts of Prussia*) that the greater part of the owners of the smaller peasant farms and their children became day laborers, and that the great majority of them was left with no land whatsoever. It is well known that in the whole area of Prussia, recently much reduced, east of the River Elbe, the peasantry is of little significance and that this remained or became the area of large estates and of large agricultural enterprises.

In England, the course of development was very different, but a similar goal was reached; the political result was similar to that emerging in Prussia in spite of Prussia's conquest of large, predominantly peasant provinces: the overwhelming influence of the landed gentry upon legislation. As early as in the sixteenth century, the solution of the agrarian problem was effectuated in favor of the economic power of the landlords which then grew—especially after the confiscation of the estates of the monasteries—to greater and greater dimensions. The legal position of the peasants, although practically always personally free, since ancient times had been similar to that of the so-called lassitic farmsteads in Prussia: they were copyholders, in contrast to freeholders, who were in the minority. The right of ownership was doubtful, and different in almost every manor because it was dependent on its particular customary law and on additional statutes. The main question was whether the right of inheritance was protected and the giving of notice admissible.

It was natural that the landlords were in favor of the restriction of peasant prerogatives, but the peasants themselves in every district in favor of the extension or at least preservation of their prerogatives. This class struggle, like others, assumed the form of a struggle between right and right, with the new law (*Recht*) definitely considered to be a wrong (*Unrecht*) in the popular consciousness. Although Roman law was not adopted in England because the London bar rejected it successfully, principles similar to those of the later Roman law were established under the name of Equity, especially at the younger High Court of the King's Bench which has been preserved as an absolutistic element, notwithstanding the victory of the estates over the crown. The inheritance of the peasantry had become the rule, even where it remained rather doubtful legally, as long as it was in the interest of the landlords themselves, and this was the case as long as the lords themselves administered their land, the so-called domain, and therefore depended on the services of the peasants. But as early as in the fifteenth century, because of the increasing significance of the export of wool to Flanders, grazing became more economic than tillage, and the landlords succeeded in asserting their will more and more, although the Courts of Plea in particular often decided in favor of the peasant's right of inheritance, on the ground of the custom of the district. Generally, however, larger acreages of property were established or leased by formal contract, in part long term but mainly in such a way that the lessor reserved the right to annual cancellation or renewal of the contract, the so-called tenancy at will.

Stammler's objection to historical materialism, that some sort of law is inherent, more or less, in all social relations, that the economy is to law as matter to form, is indicated in Marx's own sketch, when he calls property relations nothing but a legal expression of the existing relations of production, and adds that the relations of production change within the property relations, and are, to begin with, developmental forms of the forces of production, even if they may become their fetters.

The true facts, and this is what matters, are not contested, namely, that material relations change sooner than the forms in which they occur or, in other words, that material changes will eventually, even after heavy resistance, be followed by changes of form. Rights will always be fought over, not only in the councils of governments or in parliaments. Courts of law, too, even if the judge is considered to be a person of ideal impartiality, will interprete the law either in favor of the economically strong or in favor of the economically weak. Not infrequently, the judge may be inclined—for reasons of fairness, sympathy, good nature, humanity—to decide rather in favor of the weak and the poor. But by social position he belongs to the ruling class, and will sympathize, although perhaps not consciously so, more with the way of thinking and with the interests of his class. A popular or labor movement will not be likely to rouse his sympathy, not only because of its rough ways but also because of its indifference, if not hostility, toward ideas which are dear to him. Moreover, it is psychologically unavoidable that a judge is influenced in his judgment by the skill and eloquence of an attorney; and it is obvious that the strong are better clients for lawyers than the weak, and therefore in a position to choose the most skillful counsel.

The reality of the relations between the economy and the law, which is not completely identical with, but touches closely on, the dependence of political power on economic power, has been recognized and acknowledged a hundred times, although a fundamental and systematic theory has been shunned and rejected. The idea can be found expressed again in the brilliant inauguration speech by Georg Jellinek, *Der Kampf des alten mit dem neuen Recht* (*The Struggle between the Old and the New Law*) (Heidelberg, 1907); he expects that the future, too, is destined to experience new struggles between the old law and the new. "New historical and social conditions will, in the days to come, as always, produce new systems of law."

The Material Basis of Spiritual Life

Not only the law but also the mind, the spiritual life which is expressed in thought and creation, as well as morality and public opinion—all of this changes along with the economic foundation of social life. The sketchiness of the simile used by Marx becomes more obvious when he speaks of religious, artistic, or philosophical, in short, of ideological, forms, within which men become, as he thinks, aware of the conflict between a state of higher development of the forces of production and the relations of property, and fight out the conflict. For one could call it "fighting"—unless it is done with swords, guns, and cannons—only insofar as it is a *disputare*, a thinking differently, therefore talking and advising differently, and willing differently. Consequently, literature which is more and more written for the day, is the main battlefield where the different tendencies, and thus the social forces, those of conservation and those of change, those of the traditional and those of the new, those ways of thinking based on faith and those based on reason meet, as long as the one has not been silenced or killed off altogether by the other. But total killing hardly ever occurs. Whole generations may be silent and die. But new generations emerge who in part have already received and learned from those preceding them, in part will gain from new facts the same sentiments, impressions, and emotions. Attitudes and convictions are to a high degree hereditary, and so are, therefore, opinions, insofar as they spring from the same social facts, thus also from the same relations of production.

The relationship between the material bases and the higher manifestations of the mind, or spirit, might be conceived perhaps best of all according to the analogy of the relations that can be recognized between, on the one hand, the vegetative system of the human body, and the human needs and passions based on it and, on the other hand, the animal and mental system. This may be expressed in the words of Schiller, the much praised idealist, which he addressed to the Duke of Augustenburg, words that in abridged form are included in his collected works (*Briefe ueber die aesthetische Erziehung des Menschen*), namely: "Man is very little when he lives in a warm abode, and has eaten his fill, but he *must* have a warm abode and enough to eat, if his better self is to stir in him"— a sentence that reappeared later in the epigram "Man's Dignity": "No more of this, I ask you. Feed him, house him! Once you have covered his bareness, dignity comes of its own." Even more impressively he says the same in verse:

> Until philosophy succeeds,
> Nature is ruling with its creeds.
> The motive power she supplies
> By hunger's pangs and lovers' sighs.[1]

In a forceful way, the great poet, whose study of medicine early familiarized him with crime, expresses a similar thought in the violent words, "Something man must call his own, or he will murder and burn."[2]

In political life, the poor and suffering have acquired a voice only since the middle of the nineteenth century, after having been represented possibly in religious disguise or through priestly and, perhaps even more often, secular humanists; or else, they have let off steam directly through revolt and riots. It is part of the obvious advantages of the democratic state that the poor can, and are permitted to, present, in an orderly and regulated manner, their charges and complaints; that they can oppose laws which might make their situation worse, and promote better ones. Thus, only in more recent times, after the right to vote has become universal, do the political parties represent a relatively clear reflection of the economic situation. With all that, the picture is often disarranged and distorted. But whereas at a time when care was taken that the poor should not have any representation, the party of the status quo and the party of reform faced and opposed one another, these former opponents

---

[1]   Friedrich Schiller, *Poetical Works*, translated by E. P. Arnold-Foster, p. 290; wording of translation slightly changed by editors.
[2]   "Etwas muss er sein eigen nennen, Oder der Mensch wird morden und brennen."

now move closer together under the pressure of common troubles and dangers. A powerful voice rises on behalf of the masses from the so far silent campsite, the voice of poverty, the voice of labor, not seldom the voice of despair. In this instance, the truth of historical materialism is most clearly evident, and it is only worthy of contempt if the property-owning classes or their advocates stigmatize the materialism of the have-nots, so as to be able to indulge in their alleged or hypocritical "idealism." The reverse relation is often and to a certain degree more real: the love of pleasurable consumption (*Geniessen*) makes common, and a sumptuous way of living insensitizes one's ears to higher and nobler sounds than those of luxurious enjoyment and greedy desire; poverty and deprivation may create more favorable conditions, for some kind of people at least, to devote effort, labor, and sacrifice to the love of the arts or of knowledge, and to strive for them, as long as hope lights the way. Indeed, often it is this hope in the guise of pure idealism that gives the proletariat its self-confidence and the trust in its advancement.

IV. Empirical Sociology

16

STATISTICS AND SOCIOGRAPHY

EDITORS' NOTE. *The following selection is taken from a paper by the same title in the* Allgemeines Statistisches Archiv. *The first half of the article has been omitted because it deals with a problem that was much discussed in Germany at that time but has little interest for American readers today. The issue was whether statistics was merely a method or a special social science. Toennies as well as the dean of German statisticians, Georg von Mayr, took the latter position. There was, however, disagreement about the substance of this science. Von Mayr claimed that the collection and systematic arrangement of official statistics—of all enumerable and measurable social phenomena—could constitute a scientific discipline. Toennies, on the contrary, wanted to revive an older meaning of statistics; in the eighteenth and early nineteenth century* Statistik *in German meant the description of a country, or part of a country, of its natural features as well as of the population, the economy, political organization, military power, and other social institutions, in short, of anything that might be of service to the "statesman." Sometimes figures were given, but that was not essential. This was the real issue in Toennies' controversy with von Mayr.*

Statistik *in the modern sense was for Toennies a method. Realizing that the older meaning of the term could not be resurrected, Toennies adopted the term* Soziographie *from the Dutch sociologist Rudolf Steinmetz. Unfortunately, Toennies remained rather vague and perhaps undecided about the actual content of* Soziographie. *Sometimes he gives the impression that* Soziographie *would comprise empirical, comparative inquiries into social problems, that is, pathological phenomena like crime, suicide, prostitution ("Moralstatistik," in* Studien und Kritiken *III. p. 125 f.). At other times he defines the task of*

Soziographie, *which he identifies with* Moralstatistik, *as giving a "statistical" picture, in the* old *sense of* Statistik, *of the moral conditions of a people. "The highest task is to give* a view of the life of a people *but also to comprehend it by* comparative *methods" (*"Die Statistik als Wissenschaft," *in* Studien und Kritiken *III. p. 95 ff.; emphasis added). These overlapping definitions should be kept in mind by the reader.*

Statistics and Sociography

THOSE SCHOLARS who are mainly interested in understanding social life through observation and investigation of facts—that is, by the inductive method, which finds its expression in the statistical method—might rightfully call themselves empirical sociologists. This would be in accordance with Georg von Mayr, who, in one of the last of his varied statements about this subject, had decided to define statistics in his sense (which I, however, contest) as exact sociology. Certainly, the inductive method must strive to proceed as exactly as possible, and quantitative analysis is more exact than any other method. However, empirical sociology harms itself if it regards as its task, as von Mayr does, studying the *general* social phenomena directly instead of limiting itself *first* to a description and analysis of a certain area; this should, just because of the statistical method, be an area for which uniform statistical data are available through official statistics or would be obtainable privately. This would lead back to the old statistics in which scholars in Germany used to be engaged, describing countries and states under the name *Laender- und Staatenkunde.*

Upon such a solid foundation one could imagine building a general theory of certain social phenomena such as population changes, epidemic diseases, suicide, and crime. But this should not be the first object of empirical sociology; it is, rather, a distant and nebulous aim, like the idea of a general grammar. To know the specific grammar of a given language with which we are familiar, thus especially our mother tongue, is in its finer details already a great

---

Translated from "Statistik und Soziographie," *Allgemeines Statistisches Archiv* 18 (1929) : 546–58; abridged.

and difficult task. In the same way, for empirical sociological studies, our own country in which we were born and reared will always present itself intellectually as the nearest and most easily penetrable subject, not considering emotional attachment.

Within any larger area there would be ample opportunity for comparisons; indeed, one can arrive at a number of relative generalizations: as a rule, these will soon become weaker and more fluctuating if an attempt is made at comparisons with neighboring countries. It is understood that knowledge of the results of such studies (which one may continue to call statistics) will not only be of great interest and value for empirical sociologists but to a certain extent be indispensable.

What is essential is the starting point, the basic question at issue. Necessarily, one must start from the objective facts, not from the subjective wishes of the scholar. The truth is that the basis of insight into this subject matter must be the sort of knowledge of the country and its people which the scholar possesses either as a native of a particular country, as a citizen of a state, or which he has acquired through a sufficiently long stay in a country, through adequate knowledge of its language, and through diligent study. Only on the basis of such intimate knowledge will he be able to properly understand and apply what he may find as reliable material in official and other sufficiently dependable sources. He will not utilize this in the first place in order to derive general conclusions, that is, for the finding of universal laws in seemingly arbitrary human actions. His first aim must be to describe the inhabitants of a particular country, their characteristics, their living conditions, and their changes—as we actually do when we, for instance, describe the status and movement of a country's population. Even though it seems not only permissible but indicated to combine descriptions of this kind with those of other countries, to examine their similarities and differences, yet the more intimate study of the characteristics of a country or a state, a province, or even a community will always require limitation; the scientific character of such investigations will only benefit from such limitation.

We are unable to assign to "statistics" a particular subject matter. The discipline called statistics could, if it existed, not be limited to statistical method, even though this method should be preferred wherever applicable. But a science cannot emerge from mere application of a particular method. If the description of social reality is the object of such a science, then every available means of analysis ought to be utilized.

If we substitute the word sociography for the word statistics, unquestionably it would become equal in rank with theoretical sociology. However, if one prefers a broader concept of sociology, one would have to subsume under it both theoretical (conceptual) and empirical sociology, which latter I regard as identical with sociography. However, this concept appears less commendable for teaching purposes, and generally for academic planning, than the other one, which at least for these purposes limits the term sociology to its conceptually constructive aspects.

Personally, I frankly confess that I think empirical sociology is just as important as theoretical sociology, although I have become known far more through my work in theoretical sociology than through sociography and statistics in the old sense. Indeed, I recognize sociography as basic concerning the study of facts and their interrelations, thus of cause and effect, which, after all, remains the ultimate goal of knowledge. It is true that this study has to be preceded by groundwork (though not necessarily in the mind of each individual scholar) which must consist essentially in purifying conceptual thinking from the residues caused by using language not specifically made for conceptual thought. Every science simply has to speak its own language in some way—as some of the sciences are already doing in a most pronounced way. The development of the humanistic and social sciences is greatly handicapped because with their subject matter this is exceedingly difficult. Here we cannot avoid using a language overloaded with metaphors and associations and beautified and enobled as the language of literature, on which to some extent scientific thought likewise has to rely.

When in 1909 Max Weber was asked to become a special member of the newly founded Heidelberg Academy of Sciences, he declined this offer, giving as his reason that this academy had been established according to a traditional scheme which necessarily would have to be disadvantageous to the systematic study of the poitical and social sciences. These, he emphasized, were especially in need of support by such foundations, because both the utilization of materials hidden in statistical offices and the collective investigation of new facts were so expensive that the individual scholar could not possibly finance them out of his own pocket. "How much more productive" he wrote, "would it be if a modern academy were to support such pressing investigations which might throw light on the present, instead of exhausting its resources for specialized historical and philological studies, which a single person can so much easier do by himself." This result of an overwhelming historicism appeared to him by its very nature (since the academy owed its existence to the living forces of the present) as a contradiction in itself, and he felt it to be his duty to label it as such.

In his basic thought, Weber had a predecessor in another prominent scholar: Fr. J. Neumann of Tuebingen. He gave a lecture at Basel thirty-eight years earlier, entitled "Our Knowledge of the Social Conditions Surrounding Us." In this lecture he points out, on the basis of his complete mastery of the at that time already abundant statistical material, the lack of solid knowledge, especially concerning the conditions of the laboring classes. He places the responsibility for this lack of knowledge not only on insufficient material but also on the deficiency in studying and utilizing the available material: there would be plenty of urgent tasks before us, if we wanted to achieve a knowledge of social conditions around us, adequate for present needs.

The intention of my present paper points in the same direction, nineteen years after my esteemed friend Max Weber expressed himself; I would like to give to the totality of these studies a more unified character by uniting all of these endeavors around the concept and the word sociography. Its special character would be emphasized if it were recognized and promoted by state and society. Apart from chairs for sociography (although chairs for sociology might be established earlier), special research institutes, which I would like to name sociographic observatories, might be serviceable; I would propose to establish them for areas corresponding to a Prussian administrative district (*Regierungsbezirk*).

The time available for my paper prohibits my discussing why I am not in favor of combining such observatories with the existing statistical bureaus, although I am glad to say that except for this proposition I agree with my colleague Wuerzburger. Neither do I have sufficient time to develop my thoughts on what profound benefits, even blessings, such research and the money dedicated to it could create if the research were done strictly according to scholarly principles, completely independent of any administrative purposes; benefits not only would accrue in material welfare but would also be of a spiritual and moral nature; the observatories would serve the people. I only want to mention the general maxim, valid everywhere, that, in order to improve and heal, one must know the causes of the evil first, and that diagnosis is the most difficult task, as for the physician, so also for the action-oriented social scientist.

For a long time, statistics has provided valuable services in this respect, but has also caused trouble and confusion where it has been applied uncritically. Its transformation into sociography would be more effective in preventing abuse than has heretofore been possible. If statisticians were to adopt the concept and name sociography, their professional status would by no means be degraded but would, rather, be upgraded. To achieve this is the intention of my attempts and of the defense of my position.

17

THE PLACE OF BIRTH OF

CRIMINALS IN

SCHLESWIG-HOLSTEIN

EDITORS' NOTE. *The following selection from* Deutsches Statistisches Zentralblatt, *is presented as an example of Toennies' empirical studies. To be sure, it is a highly condensed report on one of his major investigations. The research on criminals in Schleswig-Holstein occupied Toennies for many years. The data were collected by Toennies himself in the penitentiaries at Altona and Rendsburg, which served the Prussian province of Schleswig-Holstein. The careful reader who is familiar with Toennies' theory will notice that the classification of criminals by type of place of origin (urban, rural, and by size) reflects the distinction between persons from communal* (Gemeinschaft-*like) and associational* (Gesellschaft-*like) backgrounds although it is not exactly identical with it; the differentiation between natives and nonnatives is also related to this distinction. The typology of* Frevler *(offender) and* Gauner *(swindler, crook), on the other hand, is based on the assumption that the kind of crimes committed by the former tend to be motivationally related to essential will, the crimes committed by the latter to arbitrary will. All this is not stated in so many words but rather implied. The terms* Gauner *and* Frevler *are Toennies' personal choice. They do not conform to German legal terminology; nor do the English equivalents render Toennies' meaning. The underlying meaning is the distinction between (a) crimes committed with deliberation and (b) crimes committed in emotion or out of passion. As the classification of sex delinquents (sub b) shows, the distinction is not the conventional one between "habitual" and "occasional" offenders, although it comes close to it.*

The Place of Birth of Criminals in Schleswig-Holstein

THE FOLLOWING report summarizes the results of two enquiries; the first concerns 3,500 male criminals who were convicted to death or to the penitentiary by courts in Schleswig-Holstein during the period of 1874–98; the second concerns 2,483 equally defined cases from the period of 1899–1914.

In both series the individuals have been classified in the same way, according to place of birth. The basic assumption is that the place of origin, which with few exceptions indicates also the place of upbringing, is of significant importance for those who become criminals, as it is for everybody. The importance of this factor cannot be tested for each individual, but only by the analysis of larger numbers who in this respect have common characteristics.

(1) We distinguish first between criminals who are natives of Schleswig-Holstein (*Heimbuertige*) and those born outside this region (*Fremdbuertige*); we call them natives and nonnatives. The distinction is not significant for a small proportion of the nonnatives, who stem from neighboring regions, even from enclaves (of the states of Hamburg, Luebeck, and Oldenburg); these may be different from the natives only insofar as they went through different public schools systems. The great majority, however, of the nonnatives are men who have left their place of origin (*Heimat*), in most cases as young men, and very often have not found a new home. These are uprooted individuals, especially if they have not founded a family.

(2) In both cases, natives as well as nonnatives, we distinguish between urban-born and rural-born.

(3) We classify the urban-born by size of city.

Translated from "Ortsherkunft von Verbrechern in Schleswig-Holstein," *Deutsches Statistisches Zentralblatt* 21 (1929) : 146–50. The tables, except table 3, have been rearranged by the editors in conformity with present-day usage.

(4) We classify the rural-born by size of village.[1]

The total number of all criminals is 5,983; of these, 2,271 are natives (37.6 per cent), 3,712 nonnatives (62.4 per cent).[2]

(5) We further differentiate by type of crime: (a) those who were convicted for theft, fraud, or robbery, we call *Gauner* (crooks); (b) those convicted for murder or other violence against persons, for perjury, arson, or sexual offenses, we call *Frevler* (offenders). Of the total of 5,983 criminals, 1,570 or 26.2 per cent are offenders and 4,413 or 73.8 per cent are crooks.

We find significant relations between the type of crime and the origin of the criminal; tables 1 and 2 demonstrate these relations.

TABLE 1

	NATIVES		NONNATIVES		TOTAL	
	N	%	N	%	N	%
Offenders	767	48.9	803	51.1	1,570	100.0
Crooks	1,504	34.1	2,909	65.9	4,413	100.0

TABLE 2

	OFFENDERS		CROOKS		TOTAL	
	N	%	N	%	N	%
Natives	767	33.8	1,504	66.2	2,271	100.0
Nonnatives	803	21.6	2,909	78.4	3,712	100.0

Offenses are more likely to be committed by individuals whose psychic structure is that of native and settled; crook-type delicts, far more likely by nonnative and homeless persons. This is not contradicted by the fact that the number of nonnative offenders surpasses the number of native offenders; the difference is much smaller. Not only the nature of the delicts but also the age and

[1]   For details see for the first series "Verbrechertum in Schleswig-Holstein" in *Archiv f. Sozialwissenschaft und Sozialpolitik*, vol. 61, 2 (1929), p. 322 ff. and "Uneheliche und verwaiste Verbrecher" in *Kriminalstatistische Abhandlungen*, book 14 (1930); for the second, "Die schwere Kriminalitaet von Maennern in Schleswig-Holstein in den Jahren 1899 bis 1914" (with E. Jurkat) in *Zeitschrift f. Voelkerpsychologie und Soziologie*, vol. 5, 1 (1929), pp. 27–39.
[2]   Toennies gives all proportions in pro mille.—EDS.

everything else that is of importance for the psychic structure of the criminal tend to be different for crooks than for offenders.

In order to explain the higher proportion of nonnatives in various crategories of criminals, especially the crooks, the following factors are to be considered.

(1) The frequency distribution of nonnatives in Schleswig-Holstein by age groups; according to the census of 1900, which distinguishes five age groups, this distribution is different from that of the natives. Among the nonnatives we find a high proportion in the second and third age groups. If we relate the criminals to the three middle age groups, we still find a strong prevalence of nonnative criminals.

(2) The greater mobility of the nonnative and the recidivity which is characteristic, especially for the crooks, produce constantly a fresh supply of criminal individuals, whereas recidivity among the natives tends to bring identical individuals before the criminal judge.

(3) The higher rate of endogenous criminality in the regions of origin of the nonnatives is hardly a decisive factor, and its effect cannot be measured.

(4) More important is the place of residence of the nonnatives who tend to concentrate in the larger cities of Schleswig-Holstein.

(5) The correspondence between the distance of the place of birth of the nonnative inhabitants of Schleswig-Holstein and the proportion of the nonnatives among the criminals within this province; this holds for the crooks without exception, for the offenders to a lesser extent.

Table 3 shows the percentage of criminals among the aver-

TABLE 3

Zone	Crooks	Offenders
1. Hamburg, Luebeck, Oldenburg, both Mecklenburgs	1.74	0.48
2. Hannover, Bremen, Braunschweig, Westfalen, Lippe, Rheinprovinz	2.42	0.63
3. Provinz Sachsen, Brandenburg, Berlin, Pommern, Anhalt	2.75	0.83
4. Ost-Preussen, West-Preussen, Posen, Schlesien	3.51	0.98
5. Koenigreich Sachsen, Sachsen-Weimar, Thueringen	3.67	0.65
6. Hessen-Nassau, Hessen, Baden, Wuerttemberg, Bayern, Elsass	3.55	0.66

age (1874–1914) number of male natives of the respective region residing in Schleswig-Holstein 1874–1914. [The zones are arranged roughly according to the distance from Schleswig-Holstein.—Eds.] These findings are not affected by the fact that the age distribution of the nonnative population varies with the zone of their origin. The increase of criminality with distance of zone of origin is maintained if we relate the criminals to the nonnative residents (in Schleswig-Holstein) of the three middle age groups.

The same correspondence which exists between the numerical relation of natives to nonnatives and those of offenders to crooks can be found in the relations of rural-born to urban-born individuals among native as well as among nonnative criminals and among "offenders" as well as among "crooks."

Among the total number of criminals, the rural-born prevail: 3,425, as against 2,558 urban-born, or 57.3 per cent, as compared with 42.7 per cent. In evaluating this finding, it must be considered that the latest year of birth of these criminals is 1894, that most were born much earlier, since the majority are more than thirty years old. The median year of birth for the group of 1899–1914 may be assumed to be 1880, and 1860 for the earlier and larger group; we may thus assume 1871 as median year of birth for the total group. At that time about 64 per cent of the population of the German Reich were living in rural communities, statistically defined as places of 2,000 inhabitants or less. Around 1890 the rural-born who survived the twentieth year of life must still have been two-thirds of the population, the urban-born less than one-third (or 67 per cent and 33 per cent respectively). This means that the proportions which we find in our universe of criminals actually indicate a heavier load for the *urban* communities; this holds for the relation of native urban-born to native rural-born (40.4 per cent versus 59.6 per cent) as well as in the case of nonnative urban-born as compared with nonnative rural-born (53.5 per cent versus 46.5 per cent). But the nonnatives are in significantly higher degree urban than the natives; one should, however, remember that in Schleswig-Holstein the proportion of urban-born among the living, especially for the earlier period, must be estimated as far below the average [for the German Reich.—Eds.].

Similar relationships are found for the rural-born crooks as compared with the urban-born crooks and for the urban-born offenders in comparison with rural-born offenders. The proportions for crooks are: rural-born 48.4 per cent, urban-born 51.6 per cent; for offenders, urban-born 39.9 per cent, rural-born 60.1 per cent. Interesting relations analogous to those found by the analysis in terms of rural and urban origin are revealed by the further enquiry into the *size* of places of origin, both cities and rural communities. We define as larger cities all those that (about 1871) had a population of 10,000 or more, and as larger villages all rural communities of 500 inhabitants or more.

The table 5 demonstrates the differences in the proportions of criminals corresponding to the size of communities, urban as well as rural.

The fact that large proportions of native offenders and also of crooks stem from large villages demonstrates the predominant contribution of villagers in general to the criminality of natives (endogenous criminality). The important fact is that among natives as well as nonnatives relatively more crooks than offenders originate in the larger villages and especially in larger cities than in smaller communities [while smaller communities tend to produce larger percentages of offenders.—EDS.]

TABLE 4

	NATIVES				NONNATIVES				TOTAL			
	Offenders N	%	Crooks N	%	Offenders N	%	Crooks N	%	Offenders N	%	Crooks N	%
Urban born	239	31.2	681	45.3	387	48.2	1,597	54.9	626	39.9	2,278	51.6
Rural born	528	68.8	823	54.7	416	51.8	1,312	45.1	944	60.1	2,135	48.4
TOTAL	767	100.0	1,504	100.0	803	100.0	2,909	100.0	1,570	100.0	4,413	100.0

TABLE 5

	NATIVES				NONNATIVES				TOTAL	
	Offenders N	%	Crooks N	%	Offenders N	%	Crooks N	%	Offenders N	Crooks N
URBAN-BORN										
Large	27	11.3	127	18.7	117	30.2	585	36.6	144	712
Small	212	88.7	554	81.3	270	69.8	1,012	63.4	482	1,566
SUBTOTAL	239	100.0	681	100.0	387	100.0	1,597	100.0	626	2,278
RURAL-BORN										
Large	117	22.2	227	27.6	136	32.7	476	36.3	253	703
Small	411	77.8	596	72.4	280	67.3	836	63.7	691	1,432
SUBTOTAL	528	100.0	823	100.0	416	100.0	1,312	100.0	944	2,135
TOTAL	767		1,504		803		2,909		1,570	4,413

V. Applied Sociology

EDITORS' NOTE. *Applied sociology was conceived of by Toennies as a dynamic theory in contrast to, but not always clearly distinguishable from, the static theory which is elaborated in pure sociology. Public opinion, being both a manifestation and a changing aspect of Gesellschaft, surely is of a historical character and therefore belongs to applied sociology. The paper on "Power and Value of Public Opinion" is representative of Toennies' varied attempts to come to grips with the concept of public opinion, not to conduct public opinion research. The paper on "Historicism, Rationalism, and the Industrial System" develops in a wide sweep of argument the principles which in Toennies' view govern the emergence of the new industrial society of our time. In its concluding sentences, it reveals Toennies' confidence— so contrary to the general assumption that he is a pessimist—that mechanization and automatization may ultimately be conducive to the liberation of the intimate forces in human nature, which are presently neglected.*

By way of contrast, the paper on "The Individual and the World in the Modern Age," the clearest of Toennies' sociological interpretations of the course of modern history, ends on a note of resignation. What is progress in one regard is decline in another, and the response of the scholar necessarily will be in line with Spinoza's principle: Non lugere, non ridere, neque detestari, sed intelligere.

18

THE POWER AND VALUE

OF PUBLIC OPINION

PUBLIC OPINION is difficult to define; it is more convenient to determine what it appears to be, to find what it is believed to be rather than what it *is*.

Public opinion appears as a power in societal life, a very important power. Ever since the period immediately preceding the year 1789, which was a turning point, this has often been emphasized—most vividly and intensively by the then minister of the treasury, Necker, who played such a great role immediately prior to the French Revolution and during its first phase. Equally emphatic was Jean Joseph Meunier, who publihsed his *Appel au Tribunal de l'Opinion publique* in Geneva in 1790. Also, Abbé Morellet and the famous Abbé Sieyès participated in what one may call the discovery of public opinion; in Germany, one might name Forster, Wieland, Garve, and others. Many writers in the last quarter of the eighteenth century and throughout the nineteenth century followed suit, until in our days the belief that public opinion is strong and forceful has been widely accepted. One can say that this belief has become part of public opinion itself.

Translated from "Macht und Wert der Oeffentlichen Meinung," *Die Dioskuren, Jahrbuch fuer Geisteswissenschaften* 2 (1923) : 72–99; abridged.

Toennies says in a note that the principal ideas of this treatise are likewise contained in his comprehensive work, *Kritik der Oeffentlichen Meinung* (Berlin: Julius Springer, 1929), but that the *Dioskuren* paper represents an independent investigation which may be considered complementary to the larger work.

The power of public opinion is placed side by side with the power of governments or, where governments are dependent on legislative bodies, side by side with these; one frequently even hears it said that public opinion is the supreme and decisive power, at least in democratic countries, and that it is the court of last appeal in important political matters. Public opinion is thought of as a thinking being, and it is frequently either adored or maligned as if it were a supernatural, quasi-mystical being. As the skeptic and cynic Talleyrand put it, "I know someone who is wiser than Voltaire, more intelligent than Napoleon and all the ministers of state that we have had and will have, and that is public opinion." Napoleon himself, after his downfall, bent his knee before public opinion, when he said on Saint Helena, "Public opinion is an invisible and mysterious force that is irresistible; nothing is more mobile, unsteady and powerful; and capricious as it may be, it nevertheless is far more frequently true, reasonable and just than one is inclined to assume." (Las Cases' *Memorial*, I, 452). Herewith, not only the power but also the value of public opinion is affirmed.

Now, does this view imply a clear idea as to what public opinion *is?* To be sure, there are theories of public opinion, and these theories, like others, have their history, which is worthy of a specific treatment. But the general judgment about the power of public opinion knows nothing about these theories. It is satisfied with indistinct and fluctuating ideas. One believes that there are certain signs by which public opinion can be recognized.

Public opinion is recognized by what one *hears* everywhere, if one "talks to people" and is attentive to what they say; especially important is their judgment about a particular event, and especially so if this judgment implies a definitive approval or disapproval and if it appears as an unopposed and unanimous judgment.

Many judgments seem to go without saying, such as, for instance, those pertaining to morality and propriety. Patriotic-political judgments, to be sure, claim universal validity much more rarely. Their intention is to be subjective; they are supposed to express the emotions and the manner of thinking of a people, especially of a politically organized nation, regarding matters that do not concern other nations, do not interest them, and presumably are not understood by them; or that are necessarily negatively evaluated by those whose interests and modes of thinking—which usually are derived from interests—are likely to be opposed to one's own. Consequently, one considers in every country one's own judgment to be the right judgment, and one considers it the duty of one's compatriots, as "good patriots," to share in this judgment, not to contest and not to doubt it; on the other hand, one understands that one's judgment cannot be shared by other nations, or at least that it cannot be shared and affirmed by enemies; one can even understand that the judgment of enemies is of an opposite character. However, hatred of the enemy easily leads to the assumption that he harbors a mean and corrupt manner of thinking and that his adverse judgment is derived therefrom; especially from his ill will "against us," which is manifested in the very maliciousness of his state of mind. Indeed, the common judgments of a collectivity, like the judgments of individuals, are largely based on their common wills, desires, strivings, loves, and hatreds, on the sentiment and consciousness of common needs and interests, insofar as these are shared by an entire people; it would seem that one must expect similarity in judgment as certain or at least as very likely. However, even if this is the case, and if one further assumes the existence of common needs and interests, views will diverge because these are felt in varying strength and gravity, and because the thoughts of men, in the majority of instances, do not widely differ from their emotions. To sum up, a converging and general judgment, even in patriotic-political matters, can be expected with some assurance only where very strong needs and clear interests are felt with elementary force, so that they impose themselves, as it were, on the common consciousness.

Thus far, we have based our consideration on the observation that one believes to be able to recognize public opinion according to what one hears. However, one also believes one can recognize public opinion according to what one *sees*, such as large gatherings of men in the streets, demonstrations, marches, and so forth.[1] One must understand, however, that popular sentiment and public opinion are related, but by no means identical, phenomena. Public

[1]   In this context, Toennies gives a colorful description of collective behavior in time of war.—Eds.

opinion manifests its societal and political power by means of its approval or disapproval of political events, by demanding that the government take a certain position and abolish certain abuses, by insisting on reforms and legislative measures, in brief, by "taking a stand" on certain questions of public policy, after the manner of a spectator or a judge. Public opinion as power is thought of as a court of appeal, placed over and above popular sentiment and separated from it; public opinion may be dependent on popular sentiment, but is essentially an intellectual force.

Public joy and public mourning must not be equated with *the* public opinion. The visible signs of these affects must not be thought of as signs of public opinion, except in the very general sense that every affect contains an opinion and that every opinion, that is, every thought, assumes affective coloring. Accordingly, precisely what one sees is frequently misleading and leads to incorrect judgments. One sees a mass of people in a large city, seemingly, even obviously, caught by one single sentiment, and filled with it. One calls this mass "the people," their assembly within a space holding, say, a thousand persons, a popular assembly. But even if this multitude really represented the "people" of the city, it would not constitute a representative assembly of the population of the city or country. We have a true representative assembly (*Volksvertretung*) only in an assembly based on legally sanctioned elections. Such an assembly is considered with some justification as an organ of public opinion. But by all means not always. Parliament in eighteenth-century England—even the House of Commons—was exclusively an organ of the gentry, while a broadly based (*gemeinbuergerliche*) public opinion was already in evidence, as an indefatigable and strong critic of Parliament. Behind that public opinion stood an invisible assembly of the educated and thinking members of the people.

Third, one believes one can recognize public opinion by what one *reads*. The power of public opinion is frequently equated with the power of the press. Both were called "the sixth great power" as early as in the period (1815–67) when the European concert was performed by five great powers. The power of the press is more obvious than the power of public opinion. The power of the press is especially significant because behind a newspaper, especially a big newspaper, stands the power of a political party, which frequently is also a party of economic and intellectual life or at least is closely connected with these; and a political party exerts a great and often decisive influence upon the workings of government. Behind the party stand strong and influential personalities, overt as well as covert leaders of the party, even whole groups of them; they are strong and influential, partly because of intelligence, knowledge, and experience, partly and more frequently because of wealth; and influential wealth, in turn, is based either on landed property or on mobile capital; and capital has different validity and effectiveness depending on whether it is lending capital, crystallized in banking, commercial and communication capital, especially shipping, finally mining and industrial capital, the latter concentrated in what one calls "heavy industry."

Capital in all its forms has gained predominance within modern states; but industrial capital has become the most characteristic manifestation of the power of capital over men to such a degree that industrial capital frequently has been equated with capital generally; in the same vein, capital has been identified and confused with wealth. Indeed, wealth based on landed estate and wealth based on capital frequently merge and are combined in a few large hands. Especially, great wealth based on land holdings (*latifundia*) participates in a variety of capitalistic enterprises; very great capital wealth, on the other hand, is intent on acquiring landed estate because it is prestigious and, especially in earlier stages, politically influential. With all that, capital enjoys a natural advantage over landed estate with regard to the power of the press for the following reasons: (1) commerce, communication, banking, industry are more intimately connected than is landed estate with the spirit of modernity and thereby with the press; (2) commerce, and capital generally, is closely related to the world of information and communication, which is served by the press and thereby to the doings in national and international politics; (3) the newspaper itself is, and becomes more and more, a capitalistic enterprise; the main business of a newspaper is advertising, which is a tool of commercial and industrial capital; (4) the press is in line with the great body of literature inasmuch as it is carried along by the progress of scientific thinking and stands in the service of a predominantly liberal and religiously as well as politically progressive consciousness; consequently the press *ab initio* has been an effective weapon of the cities, especially the large commercially oriented cities, against the feudal forces that are rooted in dominion over the soil; the press addresses itself primarily and preferentially to an urban, especially a metropolitan, public because this is the public that is most eager to read, most accustomed to and capable of reading, and therefore most inclined to do battle by means of script and speech.

It emerges that the power of the press primarily appears to be a means by which liberal thought and parties exert power over conservative thought and parties; conservative and ecclesiastical thinking are closely related, while liberalism goes hand in hand, partly with a freer and less church-oriented religiosity, partly with an agnostic world view connected with the natural sciences. Now, if and inasfar as public opinion is subject to the same influences and developmental causations as the press, public opinion will be reflected in the press, so that the power of the press expresses the power of public opinion to the extent that the identification of the press (and, indeed, of all means of communication.—EDS.) and public opinion becomes understandable and within certain limits justified. The facts meet this prerequisite to a considerable degree. For public consciousness as we may call the common manner of thinking of those who are supposed to be the representatives of contemporary civilization in the advanced countries of the world, is replete with elements that are the fruits of the Enlightenment: thoughts and judgments which two hundred years ago appeared paradoxical, indeed, were detested and proscribed as atheistic and detrimental to the commonwealth but have finally, after a long-drawn-out struggle, emerged victorious. Opposed to these thoughts and judgments were traditional views, sanctioned by religious faith and scientific doctrines which were in concordance with the requirements of faith: views about what is real and possible, right and good, permitted and commanded that today are rejected, despised, and ridiculed by public opinion. Numerous examples of these transformations in every field of opinion can be given. It must suffice here to remind

ourselves of tortures, cruel death penalties, witch hunts, and personal servitude, and to ask the question how any attempt to revive
these institutions, which formerly were uncontested and considered indispensable, would be received by contemporary public
opinion.

To be sure, conservative thought necessarily advocates the restoration of what once has been, but no conservative spokesman will
wish to go so far as to appear "reactionary" and become suspect before the forum of public opinion, as if he intended to bring back the
Dark Ages; for outdated privileges and the oppression that goes
along with them are laid at the door of the Middle Ages by public
opinion, even if most things of this kind have flourished in the
garish light of modernity. To these things belongs, among others,
the absolute monarchy, an institution which in actual fact is characteristic of the modern age and not of the Middle Ages; in contrast, popular representation on the basis of more or less universal
suffrage and a written constitution are considered a lasting and
indispensable liberal accomplishment. In all these respects, liberalism has become a constitutive part of public opinion everywhere, except in areas of cultural transition, where it is still in
the process of spreading from Europe and America to the much
older civilization of the Orient. The power of public opinion can be
seen in the fact that such modern thoughts are considered to be like
a strong fortress that needs to be guarded and defended. In this regard, the press is believed to be the inseparable organ of public
opinion; the power of a unanimous press reflects the power of a
unanimous public opinion, and if both follow the same direction
they are irresistible. The press, then, is *the* organ of *the* public
opinion. It is the power of the "spirit of the age." What we have
in mind here is a latent, if rarely realized, unanimity of the press.
However, the daily spectacle offered by the press is one of contending opinions, even of bitter conflict. And yet, the press is regarded
as the expression and organ of public opinion, almost as identical
with it, even if it is the very picture of discordance.

This latter view contains a concept of public opinion which is
different from the concept that has served us as a point of departure.
Surely, if one conceives of public opinion as the sum total of a

variety of expressed opinions which appear in the light of publicity, one can say that the press, especially the daily press, is its true image: the more factions there are, whose particular mentalities are expressed in particular signs, the more varied will be the picture. This sum total of public opinion is a power, too, in the same sense in which a polyphonic scream, against which the voice of the individual attempts in vain to assert itself and become audible, is powerful as such, even if the voices of which it is composed are but a confused and contradictory disharmony. But it is a power of a different kind than the power of a unified harmony of many thoughts and opinions, the power which we have in mind, if we conceive of *the* public opinion as the generalized opinion of a people or a public as a whole; in other words, if we conceive of public opinion as a form of *social volition*, which is manifested as a unified will in all its forms, as if it were the will of a *person*. In this sense, it is customary to speak of public opinion as a personal power which asserts itself in affirmation and negation, acceptance and refusal.

Only differentiating, that is, critical thinking is capable of forging a scientifically usable concept of public opinion as a unified potentiality: a concept of this kind must be related to common linguistic usage, but must simultaneously dissolve and limit such usage and describe the conceived object so clearly and sharply as only a thing of thought can be described. Obviously, it is not by chance that public opinion, in one as well as in the other sense, is named by the same name; it is indeed the same thing in two different manifestations. An assembly or a court of justice is one thing in the condition of deliberation and another when it decides or has decided. In the latter instance, the assembly stands behind the decision as a unified whole or a moral person; in the former instance, the assembly, more often than not, is divided and torn apart by contradictory opinions and perorations. One can compare public opinion with an assembly of this kind, but the comparison must not make us overlook the dissimilarities.

Assemblies are one thing if they assemble by chance or are called together by some people, and an entirely different thing if they are the embodiment of an ideal assembly (*ideelle Versammlung*). The ideal assembly is the organ of a unified will, instituted

by statute, legislation, or custom. The actual assembly, whether or
not it is the embodiment of an ideal assembly, occupies a particular
space and has some duration; the individuals that belong to it are
recognizable as members of the assembly, either as active participants or as listeners. An assembly, even if it is merely a consultative
assembly, will, and should, appear as some kind of a unified psychological body. As a rule, it is formally opened and closed and a
temporarily limited existence is ascribed to it, as if it were a living
being. Public opinion, on the other hand, is without limitation in
space and time. It cannot be perceived by the senses, and one cannot observe who precisely participates in it. Whoever feels motivated can raise his voice; there is no clearly defined membership.
Public opinion, in this sense, can much sooner be compared to a
consultative assembly, if in such an assembly a discordance of noisy
screams is heard, than to an orderly assembly where a firm chair-
manship facilitates the quiet exchange of thoughts and opinion and
limits quarrel and violent controversy. But a *unified public opinion*,
which must be thought of as an expression of social volition, is to be
compared to an assembly that decides or has decided, inasmuch as
these decisions have binding power, either exclusively for those
assembled or for a larger whole whose "organ" the assembly is supposed to be. In the same way, public opinion claims binding power
for itself.

Public opinion in this sense strives for validity, that is, for acceptance, and tolerates contradiction and deviance as little as a religious doctrine which is pronounced a saving truth. In the one as
in the other case, the disapproval of error soon becomes a moral reproach, which means to say that to believe in something, to think in
a particular manner, is established as an obligation. Initially those
who think differently are presumed to be blind: the deviant does
not see the truth, he does not comprehend that what I see in the
brightest light, what I "show" him, what I demonstrate, is right. Or
does he comprehend but does not "want it to be true"? Does he not
want to admit that it is true because it is inconvenient, indeed,
shameful for him to confess that he has been in error, or because
the untruth agrees with what he wishes to be true while the truth is
contrary to it? In the latter case, his ill will is obvious and his own

conscience must condemn him. However, it is possible, and in many instances probable, that he is simply incapable of comprehending the correctness of my opinion, which is the generally accepted opinion, and that he lives in delusion. Does this, then, mean that he is innocent? Religion, as is known, does not assume this. The doctrine of the obduracy and hard-heartedness of those who close themselves off from revealed truth plays a great role in the history of the Christian churches: heresy is a sin, atheism a mortal sin. In this regard, public opinion resembles religion.

Public opinion may be compared to a dominant faith and, like faith, it is all the more intolerant the more sovereign its rule. This is especially obvious if the dogma is "patriotic" in nature.

Everywhere, patriotism, the belief that one's own country is right and good, is considered obligatory in public opinion, frequently also faith in the constitution, whether traditionally or rationally affirmed, monarchic or republican; finally, hope and confidence in the future of one's country. These sentiments and thoughts are enhanced during a war. . . . There are honest doubters, but as a rule they will be careful not to make their doubts public. "One cannot say that"—at least not say it publicly—but what is meant is: "You must not even think that, your thinking and doubting testify to a deficiency in your conviction." Love, more than faith or hope, is independent of critical thought; it is there or not there, a gift of nature, an organic product that cannot be made or enforced; at best, one can further its growth. And yet, patriotism, the love of one's country, is made obligatory by the public opinion of one's fatherland, as the love of God and his holy Church is made obligatory by religion.

In both instances, the request does not remain without effect. The fear of disapproval and punishment brings it about that at least the expression of the prohibited conviction is repressed; even more so does the desire to find favor with leaders in religious life and public opinion. But the repression of explicit thoughts and sentiments retroacts on the thoughts and sentiments themselves, weakens them and makes them wither; and, as an organ that is not exercised receives insufficient nourishment from the total organism, so atrophies the silenced thought.

The power of public opinion to impose itself stands in direct proportion to the applied energy. The greatest energy is exercised by fanaticism—there is a fanaticism of public opinion, as there is a fanaticism of religion. The power with which these fanaticisms assert themselves internally enhances the power which they exercise externally. But the power of inner cohesion and of outward effect must be kept apart. They may further or hamper each other. To the extent to which cohesion is operative, that is, to the extent to which it is possible to assert the social volition which manifests itself internally as religion or public opinion, to the same extent will this power operate also externally, and vice versa: the more external effect, the more internal repercussion, that is, the more successfully will the social volition impose itself on individual subjects, be they members of a church or religious community or the dispersed individuals of which a public is composed.

Both religion and public opinion are part of the spiritual-moral sphere in social life; they compete within this sphere to the point of conflict. Both exercise the strongest influence on political life, so that *the* religion of a country may become either the only or the most favored, recognized, protected, and supported religion. The public opinion of a country, likewise, is an effective power in political life, and will be recognized as such by other factors especially by the government. Religion as well as public opinion strive to be morally supreme, so that all varieties of religious faith have a powerful tendency to become *the* religion, and all particular expressions of public opinion have the tendency to become *the* public opinion. Both are engaged in propaganda. Public opinion propaganda, especially political propaganda, is modelled on religious propaganda. As religious propaganda propagates faith, so political propaganda propagates opinion.

The means to achieve this end are partly the same, partly different; different also with regard to the historical period wherein one or the other kind of propaganda is predominantly effective. The propaganda of public opinion is highly characteristic for the contemporary period. Its most general and most powerful means is the press, which is engaged in a continuous wrestling match in the arena of public opinion. We observe the continuous effort of the political parties to generalize their opinion into the public opinion of the country; but apart from organized parties, occasionally with their assistance, a variety of domestic and foreign influences are at work in order to bring public opinion to their side, by means of the press. Public opinion is belabored, with the frequent result that *the* public opinion is *made* thereby. It has been said more than once that a particular public opinion has been manufactured, as one manufactures any manner of merchandise. One produces merchandise in order to sell, and one sells in order to make a profit. One produces opinion because one expects an advantage from it if it should come to be shared by many, and this advantage differs little from the profit which the merchant and entrepreneur are seeking. The powers of capital are intent not only to bring about a favorable opinion concerning their products, an unfavorable one concerning those of their competitors, but also to promote a generalized public opinion which is designed to serve their business interests, for instance, regarding a policy of protective tariffs or of free trade, favoring a political movement or party, supporting or opposing an existing government. The government must adapt itself to the interests of capital, submit to them or defend itself against them, always dependent on public opinion, always intent on transforming a possible disfavor into a favorable attitude. In such fashion, every political power, including every political party, whose endeavors usually are intimately tied to economic interests although they are also independently motivated, is conditioned by the enjoyment of power or the desire for it. Consequently, governments as well as parties attempt to influence public opinion in the sense that they seek to transform their particular opinion into *the* public opinion, certainly in matters of considerable impact.

The spiritual-moral powers, likewise, participate in wooing for the favor of public opinion. Organized religion, science, arts, and letters do not merely wish to create a public opinion which is favorably inclined toward their interests and achievements; they want also to influence public opinion with regard to political matters. Public opinion is easily accessible to these influences because it is itself a spiritual force. All powers that attempt to gain the favor of public opinion, avail themselves of the printed [or otherwise communicated—Eds.] word as an effective instrument. It is not the only instrument that can be used, but one that is extraordinarily suitable, extremely flexible, always available for purposes of uninterrupted persuasion, and—according to Napoleon—most effective by means of the most powerful rhetorical configuration, namely, repetition. It happens, however, that public opinion is in evidence *prior* to newspaper propaganda, that it is fixed immediately after an event becomes known, that it becomes virulent *pari passu* with the dissemination of the news. This is most likely where the judgment seems to go without saying, particularly if it is a moral, and even more so if it is a patriotic-moral, judgment; and this is especially so if pre-sentiment and prejudice are ready to believe in the truth of the matter without further ado and to arrive at a particular judgment at a moment's notice. This is most obvious in the case of a negative judgment, a condemnation. That happened in 1894 when French public opinion, along with the verdict of the military court, condemned Captain Dreyfus. It was considered proven that he was a traitor; prejudice against Jews confirmed the conviction; hatred against the victors of 1870 lent to the alleged crime the worst possible coloration, made the very doubt that it had been committed suspicious, rendered contradiction impossible, and unconditional consent a moral duty. Hence, the newspapers had their position staked out for them—it was a command of necessity.[2]

All this illuminates the concept of *the* public opinion. The varieties of motivation and their accompanying sentiments are irrelevant if only the judgment is identical; what is essential, therefore, is the judgment. We further learn from the Dreyfus case, as from others where public opinion appears as a political factor, that unanimity is the unity of those who have a political judgment, that is, those who habitually participate in political life. More precisely, one may say that participation in the formation of public opinion is more effective, the more vivid the political interest, especially if the interest is focused on a particular problem area. Hence, it is stronger with men than with women, stronger with adults than with adolescents; stronger with those whose life chances are touched by

[2]   Toennies treats as another example, the reaction of German public opinion to the Emperor's political *faux pas* of 1908.—Eds.

the matter in question than with mere spectators; consequently, in economic matters more with businessmen than with scholars, but in spiritual matters the other way round; in purely political matters stronger with urban than with rural people, and strongest with the inhabitants of metropolitan areas. Very generally, one can say that public opinion is the opinion of the educated classes as against the great mass of the people. However, the more the masses move upward and the more they participate in the advance of education and political consciousness, the more will they make their voices count in the formation of public opinion. Always public opinion remains the judgment of an elite, that is, a minority, frequently, to be sure, a representative minority, at times, however, a minority that is entirely out of contact with the mass of the people. The great mass of the people, especially of the rural folk, failed to participate in the Dreyfus affair. In the first place then, if we want to determine what public opinion is, we must be attentive to what is accepted and effective (*was gilt*) as public opinion. For instance, it is obvious that in 1878 the issuance of a particular law directed against the Social-Democratic party was considered to be a demand of public opinion in Germany, although, of course, the Social-Democratic party, and consequently a large part of the industrial working class, rejected and detested the very idea of it.

Even with this limitation, it is not difficult to observe that unanimity in public opinion is a rare phenomenon; and what is effective in it most of the time, in the best circumstances, is only the majority of an elite: the predominant, the most conspicuous, the most vociferous opinion. Rarely can one achieve more in the wrestling for the favor of public opinion than this predominance. Every party in the game strives to increase its weight in the scales of public opinion. This has some affinity with the attempt to influence as many voters as possible and, for this purpose, to have as many "organized" members as possible; but there is a difference. Again, the attempt of a party to gain the favor of public opinion differs from the attempt to establish party opinion as the generally accepted public opinion. The party, convinced of the truth and correctness of its opinion, wants nothing but the recognition of this truth and correctness. But is indeed true and correct what is effectively established as true and correct?

One final comment: the intellectuals are called upon to be the leaders in social life; they cannot fulfill their role better than by trying to care for and improve public opinion. We have mentioned, above, those component parts of public opinion whose maintenance is the task of a humanistic ethics. One can easily establish a catalog of those firmly rooted judgments which not even the most resolute enemy of modernity can wish to do away with. These judgments and yardsticks are the fruits of doctrines which the philosophers of the seventeenth and eighteenth centuries have sown and which were propagated by their numerous disciples, by writers, and by secular as well as ecclesiastical popularizers. The philosophers that came later have modified some of these judgments but have annihilated none of them; even the transvaluation of all values, which we experience, cannot touch them.

19

HISTORICISM, RATIONALISM, AND
THE INDUSTRIAL SYSTEM

IN THE FIELD OF LAW the historical approach has replaced
the rationalistic approach since the beginning of the nineteenth
century. This change took place mainly in Germany and was accompanied by the protest against a civil code [*Allgemeines Buerger-
liches Gesetzbuch*]; the latter had been demanded by the new and
liberated national consciousness. When Savigny denied to his age the
authority to codify the law, his line of thought was oddly inconsist-
ent. He contended—in the vein of Schelling's philosophy of nature
—that law is "organically connected" with the essence and character
of a people. In this organic unity with the character of the people,
law, he maintained, is comparable to language; and it is tied together
with the language, customs, and institutions of a people by the
common bond of shared convictions and a shared sense of inner
necessity. This idea should have led Savigny to fight for an unadulterated German law, for its renewal and further development
in the indigenous spirit. Yet, knowledge of Roman law being his
very domain, and intensification of its study by the practitioner of
law being his foremost postulate, he refuted "the bitter complaints
about this foreign ingredient of our law." He contended that a
common civil law of foreign origin was not considered "unnatural"
by modern nations, in the same way in which their religion was not

---

Translated from *Soziologische Studien und Kritiken* 1 (1925): 105–26;
first published in *Archiv fuer Systematische Philosophie*, vol. 1 (1894).
Toennies gave the paper the shorter title "*Historismus und Rationalismus.*"
Some quotations and footnotes as well as some paragraphs and sentences
in the text are shortened or omitted. Subtitles are supplied by the editors.

indigenous and their literature was not free from the impact of the most powerful external influences. Thus Savigny endorsed the adoption and adaptation of Roman law and did not realize that it followed the same trend as natural law (which he despised), namely, a rationalistic rather than a historical trend. Nor did he realize that a foreign law can hardly be related organically to the essence and character of a people, just as a foreign language cannot be so related. Savigny's successors are accomplishing the task which he wanted to prohibit. They write a civil code for the present-day German Reich,[1] the first draft of which is provoking anew the familiar bitter complaints that it is conceived in a thoroughly "Roman" spirit and is, naturally, approved by the "old and uneradicable frame of mind characteristic for natural law which will always prevail among the bulk of the "educated classes" and will also, again and again, shatter the forced historical airs *(Allueren)* of the jurists."[2]

The impact of natural law, as *naturalis ratio*, upon the development of Roman law was comparable to the impact of Roman law, turned universal, upon the formation of German law. Regarding the latter process, not much remained to be done for the new natural law except for a fundamental change in the concepts of public law. Natural law claims to be a private law applicable to the mutual relations and transactions, not merely of men who happen to live within the same political borders but of civilized mankind altogether. In the latest draft of the German civil code, there will, indeed, be found hardly a provision or tenet which could be proven to suit "Germans" while running contrary to the common spirit *(Volksgeist)* of Austrians, Italians, Frenchmen, or Englishmen. In these countries, as well as in Germany, customs are contrary to the code. But few such customs bear a national imprint—national in the sense of modern nations—except, perhaps, the customs of the Anglo-Saxon peoples who have been able to preserve some of the principles of ancient Germanic law. But even so, most of these Anglo-Saxon customs are of a regional or local character. No wonder, then, that nowadays we often *call* "national" that which is in

[1]   Observe that this article was written in 1894.—Eds.
[2]   Gierke, in *Schmoller's Jahrbuch fuer Gesetzgebung* etc., XIII, 929.

actual fact cosmopolitan, all present-day national tendencies being nothing but preliminary restricted versions of international ideas generated by worldwide trade and communication. Moreover, the demands of everyday practice urgently require the formation and continuous adjustment of an international private law.

To the present day Roman law serves as common law in German territories. Whenever a special state law or local law proves inadequate, Roman law is applied as a subsidiary. Thus the latter is assumed to be the basic law which has been transformed in various ways according to specific needs. In that case, specialized law is considered of a higher order than general law. If, however, legislation generates a new general law, that law is supreme, and the principle is upheld that federal law breaks local law, general law breaks particular law. Only by an explicit decree can, in this case, provisions of particular law remain in force.

In actual fact, common law has always broken local law, because the jurists—lawyers and judges alike—maintained it was the true and proper law, the *ratio scripta*, as I believe Roman law has been called. According to Savigny, the jurists, in developing the law, represent the people at a stage of cultural advance. He did not even realize that, by virtue of applying Roman law, the jurists had the same revolutionary and leveling effect which he feared would result from a codification of civil law. The trend about which Savigny had no misgivings—in contrast to his predecessor Hugo— and which he did not intend to check, led then and still leads to the lifting of all restrictions on civil law, on arbitrary property, on private contracts. It is a question of minor importance whether prescriptive law undergoes change in this direction as a result of scholarly efforts, of interpretation and reinterpretation, or because of legislative action. And as the mind of the jurist could conceivably follow a different trend, under a different set of circumstances, so can the mind of the legislator tend toward repealing this entire development.

In political economy, too, a "historical" school has long since risen against the rationalist one—initially claiming it would match the achievements of the historical school of law. But the analogy is very inadequate. A precise definition of the shared features has never been reached. And the historical school of economics [*Nationaloekonomie*] lost its self-confidence even earlier than historical jurisprudence. Indeed, its foremost representative characterizes the descriptive works of economic history merely as "building blocks for a theory of economics," and states the "philosophical-sociological character" of today's economics (G. Schmoller, article "Volkswirtschaft" in *Handwoerterbuch der Staatswissenschaften*). Representatives of both historical economics and historical jurisprudence have occasionally tried to replace by an "organic view" of social life the "mechanical" approach of the theories which they oppose. But "to the present day the philosophical mastery of this idea (the idea of historical-organic law) has remained insufficient" (Gierke, *Althusius*, 317), and "so far, the argument in favor of this conception—considering the state as well as the economy as an organism—has been unable to win a broader recognition."[3]

Now, if the historical doctrines had no other intention than to present law and economy in a historical perspective, nobody would deny this to be a significant contribution. However, their cutting edge apparently consists in contending—while forgoing, more or less explicitly, conceptualization and theory—that no other approach is at all possible or fruitful. And yet the champions of historical law and historical economics attempt to draw practical conclusions from their historical views—oddly enough, contradictory conclusions. The historic importance of the historical school of law—which it nowadays renounces—consisted in its opposition to arbitrary action by the state and its insistence on leaving the formation of civil law, in all its essentials, to the people and to its natural organ, the profession of law. The historical school of economics, on the other hand, essentially is a school of social *policy*. It grew out of the opposition against the doctrine that the wealth of a nation would increase most if the state did *not* interfere with the natural fluctuations of trade and commerce but pursued a policy of laissez-faire toward the people and particularly its organ, the entrepreneurs. Everybody knowing his own economic advantage and natural confrontation of supply and demand resulting in

3   Cf. v. Scheel in Schönberg, *Handbuch der politischen Oekonomie* I, 104.

an ever renewed balance, the unrestricted competition among sellers would necessarily produce the best and least expensive goods and the greatest economic happiness.

Savigny, referring to history, wants to destroy the erroneous assumption that "under normal conditions all law results from legislation, that is, from explicit prescription by the state." Once such an assumption prevails, it results necessarily in the demand to replace the system of particular and deficient laws by a common and rational law posited by the state. The political economists want to disprove from history the erroneous assumption that free individuals have always been capable of self-regulation in trade and commerce—provided the state protected their lives and property. Rather, they contend, restrictive measures were taken by the authorities, and, given the respective cultural level, these restrictions as a rule, have been beneficial. This historical interpretation easily leads to the postulate that, likewise, with regard to the national economy of today, state intervention be not opposed in principle but that its efficacy be considered as a problem in each specific case—the argument being that the merit of state intervention can be established only by the empirical-inductive method, that is, historically. Thus the historical school of law sees the "organic" element in the people—"the quietly moving forces" [*die still-wirkenden Kraefte*]—and regards the state and its arbitrary action as moved by a rather "mechanical" force. By contrast, the historical school of economics tends to consider the contractual relations of isolated individuals as merely mechanical relations and insists on the "organic theory of the state," sympathizing with the doctrine that the individual can "exist only within the state" and regularly confounding the matter with Aristotle's *zoon politikon*.

We notice here ideas that are matched crosswise. The work of Savigny, as well as that of Adam Smith and the physiocrats, resulted from a reaction against the wisdom of the statesmen who thought they governed the nation according to rational principles, be it in a feudal or a parliamentary regime, during a revolution or in an empire. Both favor societal forces. Savigny wants to counter the government with the rational spirit of the jurists; Adam Smith, with that of the merchants and industrialists, including the farmers. Savigny believed that the unimpeded rationality of the jurists, if intensified through the study of Roman law, would be an essentially conservative force, counteracting the "idea of uniformity" which "in Europe for so long has had an impact of unlimited scope, powerful beyond description" and which "aims at the destruction of individuality in all sectors of life." Adam Smith regarded the entire historical development of economic life as "unnatural." Influenced totally by Quesnay, he was under the illusion that the abolition of all state favors and restrictions would benefit most of all agriculture, this being the most productive trade and, further —as he hints—morally superior to manufacture and commerce. In this particular sense, also Adam Smith must be considered a conservative. He, too, regards the state as a revolutionary force. And yet his ideas are rooted in natural law, as are those of the Physiocrats, while the historical school was violently opposed to natural law. The core of natural law is as follows: it assumes free individuals confronting each other, and the will of the state, resulting from their will, placed above them; and it postulates a correctly calculating reason at work in the contracts between individuals and in state legislation. The doctrines disagree on the boundaries between society—the ensemble of individuals—and the state, the collective person. The historical schools, on the one hand, oppose historical opinions contained in the system—a matter not to be dealt with in the present context—on the other hand, they oppose what they call the rationalistic construct. In doing so, they do not distinguish between rationalism inherent in the object, that is, objective rationalism, and rationalism employed in the method, that is, subjective rationalism. The political economists doubt the rationalism of society, the jurists criticize the rationalism of the state. However, hardly asked and certainly not solved is the question whether there can be any other science in this field (beyond mere description) than one employing a rationalistic construction.

It is my contention that society and state tend intrinsically toward rationalism, that is, toward free utilitarian thought—be it individual or collective—and that the same rationalistic trend belongs to the essence of science, occurring here as the trend toward the free construction of efficacious concepts. Furthermore, I am contending that the "historical" approach represents, apart from whatever else it may mean, also the transition to a new type of rationalistic approach toward the facts of social life. In my opinion, the characteristic feature common to all variations of rationalistic thought and volition is a principle of domination *(Herrschaft)*. Consequently, rationalism aims in every field at expansion and even generalization, be it extensive or intensive. Furthermore, to facilitate domination, the rationalistic approach necessarily subdivides its field, rendering the objects of domination as equal and as independent from each other as possible, so that the units can be combined and arranged at will and brought into systems. But first and foremost, reason itself must get disentangled, emerging victorious and absolute from the network of affiliations in which it is caught up.

Rationalistic Processes in Modern History

The rationalistic tendencies themselves, then, are facts of history, and among the most important. They are manifestations of the movement which runs through the entire social development of all modern peoples, if in various forms. It surmounts most easily the obstacles arising in its very own field, namely, science. Other resistances are harder to overcome. The movement has to defeat all sentiments and interests bent on preserving each historic stage. It is always revolutionary. Its own structures become conservative as soon as they solidify and to the extent to which they have grown rigid. On the other hand, all stabilized powers were once revolutionary, because rational tendencies are never entirely absent wherever a social development occurs. However, different tendencies prevail in different epochs, and this makes for the sharp contrast between epochs. All rationalistic tendencies are being assimilated as long as the prevailing tendencies aim at permanent settlement, the formation and conservation of customs, and faith in the reality of the figments of imagination. But these tendencies diminish as soon as the rationalistic tendencies gain superior strength, liberate themselves, and become dominant. Distinguished from all isolated manifestations of rationalistic trends, there are now evolving the forces that represent social reason per se: society, state, science. All three are merely concepts labeling the tendencies that prevail in the different sectors of social life: in the economic, political, and intellectual spheres. In the economic domain, the rationality of individuals is unleashed by their desire for wealth, which to a larger or lesser degree is present in all men, that is, by their desire to utilize and increase existing possessions. In the political realm, the same effect is brought about by the natural desire or the felt obligation to rule, more precisely: by the task of utilizing and expanding a given power over human beings. In the intellectual field, it is curiosity that engages thought most immediately. Here the most important task is to utilize and extend the calculability of events, the command of nature.

These tasks and tendencies are interrelated. To a certain degree they promote each other. Conflicts between them are secondary.

The societal (*Gesellschaft*-like) process is essentially one of rationalization, and shares fundamental characteristics with science. It elevates the rational, calculating individuals who use scientific knowledge and its carriers in the same way they use other means and tools. An establishment in trade or commerce is comparable to a mechanical construction [*Mechanismus*], the entrepeneurial will being the motor. A mechanism is characterized by the relative independence of its parts and by their concerted action. Theoretically, there is no limit to the scope of such coordination and concerted action of tools arranged by careful design; experience shows its steady increase. Likewise unlimited is the growth of cooperation between human volitions and powers, which is intimately related, in the field of productive work, to the application of tools. The increase in machinery as well as the enlargement of businesses and factories is cause and, at the same time, effect of the victory of the most powerful wills in the competitive struggle. It is irrelevant whether these most powerful wills are actually individual wills or whether they are associated and merely act like individual wills. For, as the particles of unorganized matter join or are being joined to achieve mechanical effects, so it is with human wills and powers, if we consider them apart from their organic context. Their dependent, subordinated, regulated cooperation takes place in factories and shops. Their free, coordinated, associated cooperation can be directed toward any goal, but because the volition is commercial, the goal is essentially commercial also. Another goal is the extension of businesses or factories through the acquisition of further establishments—usually by purchase.

Association can take three forms:

1. the fusion of entire enterprises or establishments. Such an association is often free only in name, while in actual fact a larger establishment absorbs smaller ones;

2. the combination of entire legal persons, that is, of their total capital, for the pursuit of common enterprises;

3. the association of individuals who designate certain limited portion of their capital for common enterprises.

Primarily, the individual businessman or the collective enterprise cause movement, namely, a change of place. The merchant moves himself, objects of every description, human beings of all kinds. Motion is especially important to him for the delivery of information, orders, samples, and so forth by land and by water. He aims at the greatest possible speed, because being first brings him profit. Yet he also generates motion in people who remain in the same place, causing them to move their arms and legs; he becomes a manager of work processes by gathering workers—formerly isolated—under his command, and by directing and arranging them in a common workshop, to parcel out among them a unified production process. This is merely a special form of the purchase of commodities. Purchase in advance amounts to placing orders, ordering turns into order taking and finally into production under the capitalist's own name, production of his own merchandise.

Primarily, societal (*Gesellschaft*-like) rationalism means the unleashing and promotion of production and trade, under the general protection of the law. Its champion is the propertied class, which always consists of three sectors, owning (1) real estate, (2) the means of production, (3) money, that is, capital. In all three sectors, those individuals matter mainly who own the respective means in abundance, next those who are fiercely determined to increase their smaller share. The third sector embodies the general concept of the whole class, money being capable of transformation into real estate or means of production. Money is the absolute means. Real estate and means of production are calculated in terms of money insofar as they are considered as means for the acquisition of money. In a historical perspective, therefore, the merchant is the genuine carrier of rationalism and progress in society. He is accompanied by the less active and less visible money-lending capitalist. At the same time, the businessman represents rational man in general—understood as the human being whose total effort serves as a means to one clearly defined end, namely, his personal advantage, and who consequently degrades everything —objects and men alike—to the level of means. The owner or tenant of a landed estate and the manufacturer become increasingly similar to the merchant the more they aim at the production of commodities, that is, the more their activities become a business. The merchant, on the other hand, can pass into both forms, but more readily into that of the manufacturer. This is so because the manufacturer is socially close to the merchant, and as a rule, both are urban, and because in manufacturing the production of commodities lends itself better to limitless expansion.

The generalization of the commercial or business type is of special importance for social history. It marks a trend that counteracts the division of labor as expressed in its original form in the division of society into estates [*Staende.*] Ruling estates are being replaced by a ruling class. The old aristocracy of the soil, the "landed interest," merges with the new aristocracy of the capital, "the monied interest."[4] The ecclesiastical aristocracy is caught in the middle and is being pushed down from its superior position. A rule of priests becomes the more irksome the more it loses its counterbalance in the form of a secular patriarchalism. Nevertheless, it can maintain its strength to the extent that it either remains powerful through landed property or turns commercial and capitalist itself.

Economic Development and Social Change

Furthermore, the commercial and capitalistic direction of economic processes changes and finally reverses the traditional

[4]   Cf. Knapp, *Die Landarbeiter in Knechtschaft und Freiheit,* dealing with the transformation of the manorial system into one of commercially operated large estates in German territories.

forms of the division of productive labor.[5] It does so in three respects:

(1) *The Commercialization of production.*—The merchant or manufacturer becomes the boss of the combined shops each of which was formerly run by its particular master. Now there is no longer any need for the "practice that makes for mastery," for the taste and cultivation of the mind that in the nobler lines of work used to turn the master artisan into an artist. The businessman is the true jack-of-all trades. His art consists in assigning work, that is, eliciting it from artists and other workers. Very often, however, the individual manufacturer turned merchant serves in actual fact as the technical director of the work processes which he initiated. If acting in this capacity, he does specialized work. But we have to differentiate here between two aspects of his activity. Either he can be concerned with producing goods for consumption, aiming therefore at a product of perfect quality, or he can be preoccupied with producing goods as commodities for exchange, aiming, therefore, at the largest possible quantity of commodities made as marketable as possible. The work of the technician qua technician is intellectual work of the highest caliber. But if done under the second aspect, it is only an offshoot of the businessman's work. Although it may involve a considerable amount of mental work, business activity per se is never a social activity, in contrast to the production of goods as goods and the rendering of service as service—even in a fully developed exchange, or market, economy. Production of goods and services, however, loses that natural quality to the extent that they

5   In recent years, rich in sociological inquiries and discussions, attention has focused anew on the division of labor, a *locus communis* in political economy since Adam Smith. It has long been noticed that the term refers to very different social phenomena, and there have been efforts to define the concept more precisely, to differentiate between various kinds of the division of labor, etc. To be noted in particular are G. Schmoller, "Die Tatsachen der Arbeitsteilung" and "Arbeitsteilung und sociale Klassenbildung," *Jahrbuch* XIII, XIV; K. Buecher in *Entstehung der Volkswirtschaft*, p. 119 ff. As far as I can see, neither author has so much as touched upon the *involution* of the division of labor which I am treating in the present article. Nor has Emile Durkheim in his book *La division du travail social*, which deals at length with the moral aspect of the division of labor.

are being pressed into the service of commercial speculation,[6] thus turning into the production of commodities or quasi commodities. This is precisely what happens as they progress along rational lines. Speculation is certainly no particular skill; it is nothing but egoistic thinking—a common human trait.

(2) *The Transformation of the social divison of labor.*—For this very reason, the fully developed production of merchandise tends to negate the division of labor by transforming it and providing it with new features. The trend presented under point (1) is directed against the subjective side of the division of labor while leaving the objective side intact, and even intensifying it. The manufacturer having turned merchant and speculator is no longer a "divided" producer, that is, a specialized and highly competent producer of particular goods. He concentrates his effort on a highly differentiated, most specialized category of commodities, with the intention of unloading them on the market in the largest possible quantity and either as perfect as possible (which is unessential) or as marketable as possible (which is essential). He is not limited in his capability to produce a broad range of goods. But his capital is limited, and the production of specialized goods serves his purpose better, to the extent that it avoids competition and responds to specialized demands. The objective division of labor, as a rational and new method, differs decisively from the old one, which had developed historically. The latter stems from an originally undifferentiated process of labor, which subdivides and becomes structured and, by virtue of this very process, preserves its unity. The former is being devised by entrepreneurs, each of whom selects a part without any other concern for the whole than the intention to convert their respective merchandise into money—money representing all other commodities. All commodities taken together can be considered a whole. It is an ideal whole, a thought product, namely, the joining of all commodities in the market.

The natural whole, by contrast, is an active entity; it is the real economy of a commonwealth, be it a household or a farm, a village or a town community, or an entire people with its national economy. What today is called a national economy (*Volkswirtschaft*)

[6]   Cf. Goldschmidt, *Handbuch des Handelsrechts*, 2d. edition, pp. 408, 412. See also K. Marx, *Kapital* I, 4th. edition, p. 113, note 4.

"is based . . . on an abstraction"; this national economy "lacks a subject."[7] The true condition of the objective division of labor in the context of a national economy becomes apparent when we realize the following: national economies, particularly the large and important ones, are not self-sufficient, but are necessarily part of a larger, theoretical whole, namely, the world economy (*Weltwirtschaft*): the capitalist mode of production results with necessity in an international division of labor. As the economy in one country becomes predominantly industrial, it needs to be supplemented by the economies of agricultural countries. However, the international division of labor stands in striking contrast to all natural division of labor. The latter may be compared with the organic life process, as contrasted to an utilitarian kind of exchange.[8]

The international division of labor takes place not between the countries but between the manipulators of capital. It is not at all important for the objective capitalistic specialization of labor to separate specialized workshops which are linked solely by means of the market; that is but a historical continuation of the precapitalist stage. Rather, capital tends toward integration of the specialized establishments—and the more so, the more it grows, becomes unified, expands, and emancipates itself from the control of its individual owners. The last traces of the subjective division of labor vanish whenever the individual capitalist is transformed into a corporative capitalist, by way of joint-stock companies. This transformation is also the most convenient way to increase indefinitely the capital employed for identical objectives and—contrary to the objective division of labor—to combine heterogeneous enterprises in a system where they lose their independence. The coalition of homogeneous enterprises, for instance, in trusts or cartels, represents a different process although it moves in a similar direction. The process is different because it eliminates competition, but not the division of labor; after having reached its peak, competi-

<hr/>

7   The terms are taken from A. Wagner, *Grundlegung* I, 3d edition, p. 354.
8   Cf. Ferdinand Toennies, "Herbert Spencer's Soziologisches Werk," in *SStuKr*. I, pp. 75–104. (First publ. in *Philosoph. Monatshefte* 1888, p. 71 f.)

tion among giant enterprises is abandoned as irrational and harmful; it moves in a similar direction because here, too, the enterprises lose their independence as they combine in a system; their specialization—while possibly facilitated—no longer represents the division of labor on a national or international scale but merely a differentiated part of the parent system. So far the very process of combination can be observed only in its significant beginnings, although it has long been foreshadowed by the indifference of capital regarding the ways in which it is being applied.

The combination of an industrial mode of production and agriculture on large estates is rooted, in part, in earlier conditions.[9] Even if it is not a matter of latifundia which defy the division of labor by virtue of their accumulated wealth, the boundaries between agriculture and industry are, nevertheless, getting blurred, as agriculture gears itself to the world market and increases its internal division of labor. The more agriculture concentrates on growing marketable products and turning them, as much as possible, into commodities ready for export, the more it develops into an industry and becomes alienated even from its orginal purpose of feeding at least its own labor force. But more remarkable in our context is the tendency of centralized capital to abandon the principle of self-restriction basic to the modern objective division of labor. It is already being violated in many instances. The principle "Never produce anything which you can buy" is now being replaced by the principle "Never buy from others what you can produce yourself"[10]—a principle which, once in operation, is capable of limitless consequences. Eventually it would lead to the concentration of all major industries within a smaller or larger economic area under the command of one unified capital. The absurdity of

[9] T. W. Teifen, "Das soziale Elend und die 'Gesellschaft' in Osterreich," *Deutsche Worte* XIV, 1.
[10] Cf. Sidney Webb, lecture, delivered before the Economics Section and the "*British Association,*" Oxford 1894; comments on Webb's lecture by E. Bernstein in *Die neue Zeit*, 1894/95, p. 22 ff.) ; J. A. Hobson, *The Evolution of Modern Capitalism* (London, 1894, p. 93 ff.) ; Ludwig Sinzheimer, *Ueber die Grenzen der Weiterbildung des fabrikmässigen Grossbetriebes in Deutschland* (Stuttgart, 1893), pp. 20–30. Cf. K. Marx's earlier and comparable observation in *Kapital* (4th ed., p. 312).

private property in this very capital would be so heightened thereby that it should become obvious even to the most casual observer. The second principle, then, paves the way for a total national economy planned by society; and this in defiance of the intentions of the individual "bosses," who thus usher in what they abhor.

(3) *The Transformation of the internal division of labor.*— The ultimate and most powerful effect of capital upon the division of labor occurs within the enterprise which is controlled by capital. It parallels the entire social division of productive labor, and is almost from the outset what the latter becomes only in the course of its development: artificial, that is, generated, or at least appropriated and established, by explicit and arbitrary human action. The appropriation is the most convenient form of transition from one system to the other; it occurs whenever the production of use values (for individual customers), which require extensive cooperation, turns into the production of commodities (for the market). Karl Marx, in his classical description of the "dual origin of manufacture," uses as an example the (horsedrawn) carriage, "the joint product of the work of a large number of independent craftsmen."[11] He might just as well have mentioned the house, produced as a commodity of a compound of commodities, although in this case we do not encounter a consolidated, permanent workshop. As long as the house is being built for a specific proprietor or for a municipality, the customer benefits directly from the divided labor— which remains on the level of production commissioned by the customer (*Kundenproduktion*), as Karl Buecher has aptly labeled it. Here the division of labor is not only social, meaning that it sustains independent enterprises, but it also essentially retains its communal (*gemeinschaftlich*) character because it is not yet conditioned by the market-oriented production of commodities. But the speculative production of houses turns the craftsmen in the building trades from household suppliers into servants of capital. While they retain their divided functions, these are no longer relevant to the social division of labor. The market knows only the building industry.

11   K. Marx, *Kapital* I (4th edition, p. 300).

The other root of manufacturing is much more important in our context because it is the true orginator of a new and artificial division of labor, employing it as a means to the end of maximizing the effect of cooperation in favor of quantity or, to put it the other way around, minimizing the amount of labor required for a given product (labor is measured in terms of working time to be paid for). The manufacturer considers the workers, whom he has hired and assembled in his workshop, as his tool and strives to make that tool as effective as possible. Thus he concentrates it and makes it as uniform as circumstances permit. Being unable to weld together physically the workers' bodies, he must be content to amalgamate them conceptually, fashioning a joint worker (*Gesamtarbeiter*) though not a joint man. He does so by directing their combined effort toward a common object—a piece of merchandise to be produced as rapidly as possible. This production process is partly divided into natural stages, and partly it is subdivided arbitrarily. The resulting segments are assigned in part to the natural units (namely, individuals) and in part to the artificial units of the joint worker (namely, groups of individuals). The same individual—and consequently the same group of workers—performs for ever the same segmental operation, acquiring virtuosity in the particular skill that it demands. Formerly the individual worker made a complete product, but could produce its parts only successively; now he becomes a component of a collective worker who produces all these parts simultaneously.

The difference between this artificial division of labor and the natural one has been well noted by more recent authors, while Adam Smith, in his time, nearly overlooked it—which did not prevent his chapter on the division of labor from becoming famous. Yet, as far as I can see, only Karl Marx expressly stresses that the two kinds of division of labor are different not merely in degree but in substance.[12]

While in manufacturing, the "divided" worker always uses a specialized tool for his specialized work, a further change takes place as capitalistically controlled production progresses. Now the

[12]   K. Marx, *Kapital* I (4th edition, p. 319).

"combined" worker is confronted with a combined tool, namely, the machine or, eventually, a system of machines—belonging not to the worker but to the employer, who also owns the worker's labor power. This presupposes an analysis of the work process, dissecting it into its smallest constituent parts, and, as a consequence, the reduction of divided labor to the handling of the simplest tools possible. "The combination of all tools and their subordination to one single motor power constitutes a machine" (Babbage, *Economy of Manufacture*, 172). Once the machine has grown beyond a certain size, the individual can no longer manipulate it. He can merely perform a particular service at it. Consequently, the artificial division of labor disappears, the machine taking over the specialized labor previously performed by man. Heating the machine, supervising, regulating, feeding, cleaning it, in short, servicing the machine may still be called labor, but it is general, unqualified labor and does not differ subjectively from "personal" services. No human master, however, imposes such steady attention, such monotonous movements as does the "mechanical monster whose body fills entire factories and whose demonic force, first hidden under the almost solemnly measured motion of its giant limbs, erupts in the feverish, frantic whirl of its countless organs of work."[13]

Rationalization Continued: The Processes of Gesellschaft May Result in New Forms of Gemeinschaft

We have seen that societal (*Gesellschaft*-like) rationalism, as it becomes manifest in trade, leads to the reduction and eventual elimination of the subjective division and specialization of labor. It returns men to a state where they are undifferentiated and alike with regard to the work they are able to perform. At one extreme we find the capitalists being unspecified and alike, at the other extreme the workers. If the trend runs its full course, in each of the two categories everybody will be able to do everything, the capital-

---

[13] K. Marx, *Kapital* I, p. 345. Extensive quotes from such authors as Ure, Hobson, Schmoller and Justus Moeser follow in the German text, but are omitted here.—Eds.

ists through their command over property and the workers with their bodies, that is, with their labor power, which is considered detachable from the person. Theoretically, women and children within each class participate fully in this equality, although in practice there are modifications and limitations. Between both groups, however, we find the actual managers of productive labor. According to the nature of their work, they belong to labor, representing its highest potential and its natural authority. But social organization makes them serve capital and gives them the appearance of representing capital. In their capacity as *actual* managers they direct the workers, along with the lords of capital, and they rule the working class in the interest of capital. *Ideally*, however, they serve the labor process and consequently the laboring class of which they are a part; if the working class stood in an unmediated relation to the production process, the managers would emerge from it as an organic part of the working class. But we have to make certain distinctions here. Management is divided into commercial and technical managements corresponding to the two aspects of production, namely, the generation of exchange value and use value. To an overwhelming extent, commercial management is determined by its capitalistic nature. As long as that persists, commercial management will dominate over technical management.

If the capitalistic nature of commercial management could be abolished, the relationship would reverse itself, commercial management being reduced to the technical level of bookkeeping and correspondence between the cooperating production plants. The entire group thus wavering between the social classes can be called the group of intellectual workers (*geistige Arbeiter*). They distinguish themselves by new qualifications, not so much in regard to skills as in regard to knowledge. Societal (*Gesellschaft*-like) rationalism, which otherwise is a great leveler, has given this class a very specific physiognomy within the economic process.

From this vantage point one can consider societal (*Gesellschaft*-like) rationalism in its other form, which up to now exists only ideally. It is the logical consequence, as well as the sequence in time, of the first form of societal rationalism which has spoken its last word, as it were, by bringing about the situation outlined above, namely, the advent of coalitions of competing establishments and of combinations of related enterprises; furthermore, the transformation—thanks to technology—of the previous system of the division of labor within the workshop. The capitalistic class tends not toward extension but toward contraction. This is so despite speculations that it is about to broaden its base. Such speculations can arise and persist as long as there is merely a slow pace of social change. They may gain renewed vigor as often as social change slackens or quickens its pace, both changes of pace being capable of a reconciliatory effect upon the mind. Splitting up large estates into individual lots; cooperative involvement of large numbers of people in industrial enterprises; improving the workers' standard of life through parsimony, birth control, or finally, strikes concerning wage levels, carried on by trade unions, and so forth—all these are being suggested, more or less in good faith, as a remedy against absolute plutocracy. But ideas of this kind carry no weight in the present context because they lack any principle of fundamental change comparable to the one contained in rationalism, which signals a relentless trend.

The working class aims at generalizing its condition by pursuing the results of capitalistic development to its ultimate consequences, with the hope of thereby reversing their effect. It conceives of a future in which the most progressive relation of the capitalists to production will have been made universal. The capitalists' income is purely unearned revenue or profit from trade. A considerable portion of the income of technical managers, likewise, is derived from profit. The capitalistic establishments have become quite independent from their owners, as is demonstrated especially by the joint-stock companies. Nevertheless, they are being managed as if their objective were the enlargement of their owners' fortune and income and its true object, which includes the production of goods, *were* merely a means to this end.

From the perspective of an entire nation or an international working class, there is no such relation of means and end. Rather, the production of goods has its intrinsic value, as far as these goods answer human needs. Goods do not require being changed into money and then changing back the money into goods. This is a detour employed by the capitalistic class, to the end of distributing profit as much as possible to its own advantage; it brings about an increasing involvement of productive labor in the boundless world economy; an adequate food supply for a large population comes to depend exclusively on the fluctuations of international trade, so easily upset in its balance. Yet, a nation that wishes to act intelligently should regard it as its first and foremost economic task to produce the indispensable supplies by its own labor. Although the population has increased and will continue to increase, sufficient food for all could be secured regularly, considering the technical and scientific means provided by our civilization. Industry would in part serve this purpose directly, and in part it would be linked up with it or be based upon it. Manual work, and thereby the arts and crafts, would be reinstated in its rightful place with regard to all goods that need not be produced on a mass scale in order to secure the fundamental requirements of a satisfactory standard of living for the total population. There would be ample time for that kind of work because "crude" labor will be taken care of completely by the machine, the scope of machine work no longer being limited by considerations of private profit but solely by taste and moral judgment. The means of production would be common property. Consumer goods would no longer be produced as commodities, nor would their quantity and distribution be determined any more by the consumption and exchange needs of a tiny minority enjoying the good life. Rather, consumer goods would be distributed according to the principle of justice, proceeding from equality to adequacy. That is, every family employed in the nationwide production enterprise would be entitled to a certain amount of goods representing its share in the annual product of collective labor. It would be up to the individual family to produce with its own tools and means and according to its own taste and mentality —or to obtain through exchange—whatever additional goods it desires for the adornment of life. The effort of the working people, which so far has been stood on its head by the reasoning of the egotists who drained its blood, will be put back on its feet through the reasoning of the people themselves and will thus regain the security of being firmly planted in its natural soil.

These considerations and the enormous problem that they pose take as their point of departure the ascertainable facts and are meant to draw their consequences. The facts are not only those of technology and the scientific mastery of nature but also those of the social order which—having been transformed by technology and science—prepares the way for its own abolition (*Aufhebung*) by precipitating the course on which it is set. The independent establishments on whose privilege and utility that social order is based become less and less numerous because of the increased prevalence of giant-sized enterprises; the remaining few depend no longer on the enterprising spirit and the efficiency of the go-it-alone businessman. Furthermore, they lose their individual character by either joining trusts or combining with other enterprises to form larger systems. Competition in selling one's labor power as a commodity is most readily recognized as absurd and consequently abandoned. The overwhelming majority of the population within a country or a culture area no longer being split by the competitive interests of private business, the field is wide open for considerations of the common interest, and the forces of rationalism are being concentrated on its pursuit.

The further the division of labor—demanding a specialization of skills—recedes, the further disappears the necessity that man be chained for a lifetime to the same segmental job. A change of work becomes psychologically desirable and morally imperative. The differentiation of occupations makes it impossible for the industrial worker to return, temporarily, to agriculture. But as agriculture, too, comes to depend increasingly on machines, and "familiarity with a variety of machines" emerges as "the one and only industrial occupation,"[14] the intermittent return to agriculture becomes a matter of course—all to the good of the worker. A telling controversy has arisen about the effect of fully developed machine labor on the human mind. The prevailing opinion admits that, through its monotony, it exhausts the worker, that it ruins the artistic creativity of a people, and that its moral commands are at least extremely one-sided—such as orderliness, exactness, perseverance,

[14]   P. Lafargue, *Die Neue Zeit*, VI, p. 138.

adjustment to a constraining regularity. Yet, on the other hand, we find also an insistence that machine labor has a favorable effect on the human mind. Here the contention is that the increasing size, power, speed, and intricacy of the machine renders more difficult the job of supervising and servicing it, and requires good judgment, close attention, and technical knowledge. "The machines demand . . . a certain loving care on the part of the worker, his understanding of the ideas of technology incorporated in them . . . ; being miraculous works of the human mind, the machines yield the best results when the laborer working at them rises to the level of intellectual work." As the productivity of the individual worker increases, "his responsibility is increasing also . . . This implies the necessity of a gradual improvement of the laboring classes' standard of living."[15] It is obvious that, in the nature of the matter, favorable effects on the mind are possible, that they are latent in the system but are being curbed by the capitalistic form of production, which, however, the system tends to cast off in the course of economic development—owing to the growing necessity of high wages and short working hours. Thus, in every respect, reason demands that mankind, having so well mastered the forces of nature, now master its own works, which so far it has been obliged to serve.

[15]   G. v. Schulze-Gaevernitz, *Der Grossbetrieb*, pp. 167 f., 171. Cf. also Schoenhof, *The Economy of High Wages* (New York, 1892), and L. Brentano, *Ueber das Verhaeltnis von Arbeitslohn und Arbeitszeit zur Arbeitsleistung* (Leipzig, 1893).

20

THE INDIVIDUAL AND THE WORLD

IN THE MODERN AGE

THERE ARE TWO POINTS OF VIEW from which to look upon the modern age and the preceding one, which we customarily call the Middle Ages. The modern age is the continuation of the Middle Ages. It is marked by increased size and density of the population, especially in the cities, a highly developed commerce linking the continents, the growth of large-scale industry, the tremendous advance of science and, tied to science, of technology; it is an age that augments and refines people's needs, their mores, their living patterns, further removing them from the crudity, poverty, and simplicity of the original folk culture—in brief by "modern age" we refer to all that we know and find so often praised as the progress of civilization. For this is the way of looking at it that

Translated from *Fortschritt und Soziale Entwicklung* (Karlsruhe: Braun, 1926), pp. 5–35; slightly abridged. The paper was first published in *Weltwirtschaftliches Archiv* 1 (1913) : 37–66.

Toennies refers in this paper to some of the most prominent social scientists of his day. Of these, Jacob Burckhardt, Henry S. Maine, Albert Schaeffle and Alexis de Tocqueville are widely known. Wilhelm Roscher was the head of the "older" historical school of economics in Germany, Gustav Schmoller was the unquestioned leader of the "newer" branch of that school of thought. Heinrich Dietzel and Lujo Brentano belong to the same group of scholars although the latter's importance rests more with his assertion that trade unionism should be considered as a complement rather than as an impediment to the premises of economic liberalism than with his purely historical work. John A. Hobson was a pioneer of the welfare school of economic thought in England. Eberhardt Gothein was an economic historian, Richard W. Dove a historian of law.

strikes us every day in many ways. Yet, within this development, as well as apart from it, the modern age is something altogether different from the Middle Ages. It contains and signifies a reversal, an upheaval, and a renovation, a new principle that turns the difference into an antithesis (*Gegensatz*). The modern age is revolutionary —in every sense, not in the political sense alone.

The modern age, as we understand it, is not a mere name for the last four centuries of European life. It is a concept whose essence and attributes begin to unfold way back in the Middle Ages. As the Middle Ages have remained alive in the modern age, so is the modern age already alive in the Middle Ages.

It is only in the light of sociological concepts that this process can be correctly understood.

The Modern Age as the Antithesis of the Middle Ages

The reversal consists in the fact that a countermovement sets in and gradually comes to prevail—a movement which, because and insofar as it orginates in the first, the main movement to which it is opposed, must be deduced from the first and explained by it.

The first, the main movement, is the trend to specialization, to differentiation and individualization, which necessarily results from the adjustment of an original equality and universality to different living conditions.

First, the universal is the unity of a *people* structured in tribes and clans that are aware of being linked by consanguinity and by a real or fictitious descent from common forebears. Such a people multiplies, migrates, mingles with other peoples, and displaces them; it conquers territory, settles on it, and in many places becomes one (*verwaechst*) with its abode. This is how peoples come to differ, depending on the influences of the climate and the nature of the land; how they come to be one thing in the south and another in the north, one thing in the mountains and another in the plains, one thing on the banks of rivers and another by the seashore. Corresponding differences arise regarding the cultivation of the soil, the utilization of natural resources, and other activities. Already in gray antiquity an exchange of products was thus conditioned, even over great distances; there has always been an extensive field for commercial activities, even though it remained somewhat limited for a long time. Political and religious motivations and institutions combine with these activities to preserve the cohesion and the communality of a people. And yet, all this is far outweighed by the tendency toward independence, toward the individuality of regions and places—an individuality which, however much the general life keeps pouring into it, constantly tends to isolate itself, to delimit itself, to be self-sufficient and self-contained. This tendency becomes all the more pronounced the more remote such places and regions are, the poorer the soil, and the less tempting, therefore, to the conqueror and the trader. But even fertile lands that allow a denser settlement may be closed to them, naturally or artificially; naturally, if they are difficult of access and if they lend themselves to widely scattered habitation, artificially, inasmuch as they resist the intrusion of strangers, an effort in which comparative affluence may be helpful. On the whole, multiplication, diversification, and the refinement of needs will proceed slowly but constantly under these conditions, owing to population growth, to the improvement of roads and the means of transport, and to advances in the division of labor. Working against stability are wars and endemic diseases, although in certain regards even these will stimulate the process.

Second, the universal is the culture of the past, which remains effective even if it should be in remnants only. For the European Middle Ages the cultural base is Roman; within the Roman mold, the deeper Greek culture is continued; in the last phase of Roman development, an Eastern propaganda religion with a claim to universality is included. At first, therefore, these cultural goods are preserved and impersonated by the priests of the Roman Church. As guardians of a great tradition which is considered a sacred tradition, they continue to represent a common will, a common spirit, and thus exert their authority as the teachers and masters of young barbarian peoples. This universality, too, is differentiated in territorial and local developments, but slowly and only in a minor part. In the end, these very elements of the civilization of antiquity play a powerful role in shattering the walls of the Church; soon even the religious "confession" is multiplied and diversified, and becomes petrified in narrow territorial confines as the credo of "national churches" or scattered congregations. But however deeply the universality of the Christian religion, and especially that of the Roman Church, may be rooted in the Middle Ages, there are a variety of aspects in which it does concur with the new universal, inimical though this may be to the spirit of Christianity. The very internationality of the structure of the Church promotes the internationality of trade, and thus of capitalism.

The local differentiations reach their peak in the establishment of free, powerful, wealthy and self-assured cities. It is at those peaks that they start turning into their opposites. For the movement is never completed. The ruling upper strata do not fully participate in it. They remain in contact with each other; they persist in the universal and represent it, especially on account of their superior historical memory and the fact that they are the keepers of documents. However, the countermovement is never entirely absent. No region, no place is entirely cut off from communication. They all have neighbors and maintain relations with those neighbors; they intermarry, observe holidays, exchange gifts with them, they buy and sell merchandise; besides, there are antagonistic contacts that may turn into outright hostilities and frequently will bring them about. Priests come from afar, as do judges, traders, and other travelers. Some of the natives themselves go abroad, most likely the nobler ones, and on their return they will disseminate the knowledge of, and often the admiration for, strange things. They imitate them, and are themselves imitated by friends, neighbors, and subordinates. The result is an equalization, a leveling, though it may take a long time for the essential and preponderant tendency to differentiation to be finally overcome.

The strongest force working toward this is the interest of individuals who meet as isolated individuals but will combine, if their interests coincide. Individuals do this, possibly without regard to the groups to which they belong by occupation or descent; they are essentially free in the choice of the means to their ends.

The countermovement thus represents a return to universality,

or at least a tendency in this direction. But though the new universality appears to have many points of contact with the old one, it
is essentially different. It issues from the individuals and is in the
main their thought, their idea. The new universal is an ideal construct, whereas the old universal is a reality manifested as such in
the emotions and the thoughts of men.

First and foremost, this reality is primarily (a) the bond of kinship which is alive and maintains itself in the consciousness of a
people, more intensely in that of a tribe or even more so in that of
a gens or clan. Further, it is (b) the land that is jointly inhabited
and appropriated whether it is believed to have been their homeland from time immemorial or whether it has been conquered and
settled by force. The homeland as well as family cohesion is the
source of the concepts of joint title and joint rights which continue
in the village community, the superimposed manorial law and feudalism notwithstanding. Third, however, the old universality and
communality are realized (c) in the deities that are conceived as
real and in their abodes; the faithful pay homage to them. All of
these universalities are differentiated, localized, and thereby intensified. The individual human being, notably the common man, that
is, the one who does not belong to the ruling classes, feels bound
by the rules, customs, and religious precepts that surround and
condition him. The closer they are brought to him each day and
hour, the more entwined they are with the habits of his life and work,
the stronger will be his sense of their binding force. The division
of labor, the separation of classes and estates, the hearth and home
where the individual finds himself embedded—all of these have
this effect.

It is *in* these unions (*Verbindungen*) and *out of* them, but even
more so *alongside* them, that the "individual" evolves in the particular sense that has become a sociological concept: both the individual and individualism. As a rule, to be sure, we do not talk about
individualism as if it were a view, a turn of mind, an idea, or an
ideal, whether we hold it to be true and good or false and reprehensible. Of late, it has become fashionable to treat individualism
as a mistake corrected by the deeper insights of today, a mistake
that has brought about many good things, for instance, the uni-

versal acceptance of personal liberty, but that must also bear the blame for evils, such as the predominance of capitalism. Such opinions give expression to an intellectualist prejudice, as if thought were the primary function of the human mind—a prejudice closely related to the pride in the nobility of men and to its theological transfiguration. Even the concepts of socialism and communism that are regarded as the antithesis of individualism, are primarily presented as "systems": imaginary structures and constructions that may, for instance, lead to the strange proposal (by H. Dietzel), to call such systems "socialism" if they are derived from the social principle (*Sozialprinzip*), while the other construction, rooted in the individual principle (*Individualprinzip*) and having the central idea of realizing the common good of all individuals, should be termed "communism."[1]

In a most vigorous contradiction to this approach, I referred in the first edition of my book *Gemeinschaft und Gesellschaft* (1887) to communism and socialism as "*empirical* forms of culture." That is to say, I do not regard them primarily as systems of thought but as systems of life, as realities that rest on man's *essential will* in which thought is included as an organ, or else on thought alone, that is, on *arbitrary will*, which is guided in the first place by thought or reason—but always referring to the thought and volition of their own subjects, not to mere theory that approaches the facts from the outside. As far as the concept of "communism" is concerned, this was not a neology; it is accepted usage to speak of the conditions of property in early stages of civilization as "original communism," "family communism," "agrarian communism," or "primitive communism." Likewise, the institutions under which certain religious communities, like the Oneida or the Dukhobors live, or used to live, in the United States and elsewhere are usually called communism. And does socialism exist only as an idea, a dream, a wish, a goal of human endeavor? Is the cry of "sheer socialism" not raised on all sides and in all countries against all kinds of legislative innovations, against the protection of the working man and social security, against nationalization and com-

[1]　H. Dietzel in *Z. f. Lit. u. Gesch. d. Staatswissensch.*, vol. I, 2 art. "Individualismus" in HW[3], p. 591.

munalization? Suffice it to cite so astute a sociologist as Schaeffle, who wrote in the third volume of *Bau und Leben des sozialen Koerpers* (1878):

In Church and state, in education and science, socialism is already tangibly present. What the modern or economic form of socialism represents in regard to the productive and distributive processes of actual social impact is a change that has been taking place in other fields for centuries; the rational meaning of socialism is the transformation of family (private) capital into collective capital, of private services into social services, of private labor into professional labor, of private wages into professional salaries.

And even to this economic socialism, Schaeffle would not have paid such comprehensive attention "if it were not now present among us in flesh and blood." He points to the many communal, state, and federal agencies of an economic nature, from national forests and shipyards to arsenals and governmental magazines, the Reichsbank [comparable to the United States Federal Reserve System—Eds.] and the postal service; today he would be pointing to the draft bill or the (German) government's oil monopoly. In England, the concept of municipal socialism has become as widely accepted as that of state socialism has become everywhere. I summed up my own views as early as 1887, when I wrote that the natural and—for us —past but always fundamental structure of civilization is communistic, while the current and evolving one is socialistic.

And what of individualism? "There is no individualism in history and culture, except as it emanates from *Gemeinschaft* and remains conditioned by it, or as it brings about and sustains *Gesellschaft*. Such contradictory relation of individual man to the whole of mankind constitutes the pure problem." In these words of the preface to the first edition of *Gemeinschaft und Gesellschaft*, I indicated the same view which still seems to me to be the right one today.

I am now modifying the first proposition, however. Now I say: It is in communal unions and organized groups and out of them, but to an even greater extent alongside them, that the individual and individualism evolve—and these are the carriers of *Gesellschaft*.

Like all phenomena of the social entity, individualism manifests itself in economic, political, and moral life. And in each, it evolves in the same threefold fashion: *in* the communal unions and organized groups, *out* of them, and *alongside* them.

Gesellschaft Grows within Gemeinschaft

Within communal unions and associations, the development derives from individuals in positions of power, from the men who thus enjoy the greatest freedom from the outset, as they seek to expand their power and to make it as absolute as possible. To them, the association itself and their subordinates become mechanical tools or means to personal ends.

First and foremost, of course, to the end of *economic* enrichment. Most characteristic in this respect for the transition from the Middle Ages to the modern age is the transformation of the traditional form of the lord-vassal relationship (*Grundherrschaft*) to a master-servant relationship (*Gutsherrschaft*). The lord of the manor had a calling, as knight and ruler; the owner of an estate has a business, he directs an agricultural enterprise. The lord of the manor, too, could itch with acquisitiveness, and there is proof that he did so often enough: he could abuse the powers of his office and seek to raise the services and levies of his peasants, he could devastate their fields as a hunter, and could milk the peasant dry by means of judicial fines, as it happened in England in Wycliffe's day. All these manifestations of tyranny would often lead to peasant uprisings, in Germany at the very threshold of the modern age. They kept recurring again and again: in weaker variants, they continue in our time. But such excesses either leave the social fabric unchanged or constitute mere steps on the way to its destruction. The destruction occurs, indeed, when the peasant is forced off the land or bought out or turned into a modern type of serf, or when the abolition of this serfdom finally transforms him into a free but landless rural day laborer.

The lord of the manor may also become a rentier without either calling or business, one whose individualism shows not so much in direct economic action as in other fields. The dependent peasant will then be a tenant or a sharecropper—the first chiefly in

Great Britain and Ireland, the second mostly in the Latin countries of Europe. Most characteristic of this development is the feudal lord's dissolution of his external relationship to the soil. He no longer lives on his inherited land amidst his vassals; at most he keeps it as a luxury place for the summer or as a hunting lodge, while maintaining a regular residence in the city, as the nobility of northern Italy did in the Middle Ages. Or he goes to live at court, to bask in the sun of princely favor but also to obtain economic advantages, such as sinecures or prebends, and political influence with which to protect his prerogatives—a course typified by the seventeenth- and eighteenth-century French nobility. To be sure, the customs and prejudices of the noble estate restrained its individualism, yet the nobles "lived apart from the middle classes, with whom they avoided to assume contacts, and from the lower classes whose goodwill they had forfeited, and as a result the nobility stood isolated from all the remainder of the nation" (Tocqueville). "Only the nobleman whose fortune was insignificant would still reside in the country" (i.e., in a village). But even these "tree falcons" (*hobereaux*), as they were called, displayed an "absence of the heart" that was imposed on them by the conditions of their social status and that Tocqueville described as more lasting and more effective than physical absence. The British squire, too, has in large part turned into a mere landlord, although a number of them have retained some judicial and administrative functions. In general, the months the landlord spends at his castle mean little to the great mass of the rural population. Many a landowner lives permanently in Paris or in Italy, or otherwise travels abroad as an independent gentleman of leisure; rent collecting is done by his officials. Where the tenants remain poor peasants farming miniature plots, as in Ireland, this absenteeism becomes all the more oppressive. The great landowner of countries not yet emerged from a semi-barbarian state, such as Russia, Poland, or the Balkan countries, is likewise characterized to a high degree by life abroad, as is the American dividend millionaire.

In the *political* area, it is chiefly the prince who makes his weight felt as an individual within the traditional organization he is heading. His aim is to make his sovereignty as absolute as the lord of the manor wants to make his property. He may pursue this aim in the belief that it lies in the general interest, in the interest of the state, as whose servant he regards himself; but, at least if he is an average human being, it is more likely that he will simply wish to enjoy his personal power and to indulge in personal pleasures. For state purposes as well as for the needs of his court, he must strive to squeeze or suck money out of his subjects. Political and economic arbitrariness are inseparable. This is why "finance" was equated with simony, secret tricks and wicked schemes by Luther, and with usury and fraud by others. The most successful secretary of the treasury is the new type of statesman who in Italy has assimilated the principles of Machiavellianism. At first, of course, these were intended for the "tyrant," for the illegitimate usurper who would seize control of a city or a whole country: they are the rules of Caesarism. But they are no less valid for the lawful heir to a throne who in contest with the estates of his realm enforces his will as the supreme law. In part, the *raison d'etat* serves to cloak personal ambition; in part, it is consciously advanced as the maxim of the new political society and thereby in effect comes to be all the more revolutionary, that is, all the more destructive of traditional rights and moral convictions. Hence the currency debasements, the issues of paper money at compulsory valuations, the forced loans, government bankruptcies, and other artifices that corrupt a national economy. Like the prince, so must the state—that is to say, the statesman—wage his fight for self-preservation and self-aggrandizement as much as possible as a free individual. In other words, he must choose to be guided by a loose morality that will at best pay some heed to public opinion.

The organized groups of *moral-spiritual* character, of which the churches are the most influential in our history, exert the strongest control over the individual conscience. But this does not preclude the exploitation and extension by the men who head these organized groups of their power over human souls—on the whole, that is, by the priests of their power over the faithful laymen. As a rule, the clergy is superior in sagacity, or at least in knowledge of the mysteries and the miraculous workings of the cult—in other words, of the means to win or lose the favor of supernatural powers. On this ground alone, priests tend to be more conscious individuals, men who will take the liberties required for successful action. They will break through the barriers that inhibit others, will ignore the qualms of conscience that arise from generally valid moral rules that are confirmed by religious commandments. This may seem to be more difficult for a man supposed to personify the divine commandments, but in reality it is made easier by the fact that he is called upon to interpret and apply the commandments that are given into his hands as raw materials which he may, in some measure, shape at will or, in any event, at the will of his superiors.

In the Roman Catholic Church, this loose morality grew out of penitential practice, as a rich casuistic literature discussed the problems of conscience and increasingly permitted following the laxer view even if it was supported by weak authority. This probabilism was tailored to fit the individual case, the requirements of individuals, especially those in high places, and in the modern age the Jesuits became in many ways its most important representatives. In Catholic countries—for the first three centuries (until 1800) still the main culture carriers—they became the methodical heresy hunters, the champions of papal supremacy and, at the same time, insofar as the two were compatible, of princely absolutism. Generally, they became the ecclesiastic politicians who knew how to adapt spiritual power to modern living conditions that were at odds with it, and how to save or to restore the power of the old ruling classes in the growing modern society as well as in the growing modern body politic. This could be done only by modern means, that is to say, by means of capital; and so we find the Jesuit order playing a large and successful role in world commerce and increasingly in industry. The order used its international connections to build up a vast commercial traffic with countries outside Europe, with Lisbon as the center.

The missions were transformed into trading posts, and a thriving business was carried on in cotton, hides, Paraguay tea. . . . In California they acquired large mines, and their factories and sugar refineries were scattered all over Spanish America; in the eighteenth century their trade in colonial products from the French West Indies came to be of primary importance; the Jesuit colleges became magnificent places of exchange where a traveler could establish credit and whose business deals were not subject to any curbs on the rate of interest. (Dove, "Orden, Geistliche" in *Staatswissenschaftliches Woerterbuch.*)

This is an important example, demonstrating that no matter how clearly capitalism and commerce are forces of the modern age, they also serve as tools and weapons for combating the modern spirit, and that the individualism of the profit motive is not exclusively individualistic and personal in its application. Conceptually speaking, it makes no difference whether I serve a joint-stock company or the Society of Jesus. The Middle Ages had already made the priest a pliant muscle within a large social organism by prohibiting his encumbrance with wife and child. The celibate is always more intensely individual than the family man, and as an individual the unwed cleric is no less at the hierarchy's disposal than a soldier at the general's. "I have neither parents nor family," Loyola bade his disciples say; "to me, my father and mother, my brothers and sisters have died; I have no home, no country, no other object of love and reverence than the Order." As Gothein puts it so well, "It might seem puzzling how one can curb a man's will and reduce him, by his own decision, to an automatic instrument of his superiors, and at the same time require that he expertly trains a variety of talents and develops a personal capacity to make decisions. Yet every modern military education solves this puzzle." (*Kultur der Gegenwart* II, Vol. I, p. 174).

Besides having its place above the people, however, not only a large organization such as the Society of Jesus but a professional entity like the clergy constitutes in itself a community headed by single individuals. It is those individuals who guide and enforce the "policy" of the whole, more or less in the interest of this total entity, but also in their personal interest. In doing this, they may be consciously untruthful, and to highly educated individuals the power which a vicar of divinity naturally wields over the minds of the faithful is a great temptation to use it for the benefit of such a community, and thus for their own benefit. This temptation was so much greater when bishops, notably the supreme bishop, were temporal princes as well—a duality that has so far persisted through most of the modern age. It may be an invention, and yet it is a significant invention which quotes a pope as saying that the legends of Christ are extremely useful for governing human souls. Conscious hypocrisy is rarely recognized as such, but it is one of the crown jewels which on occasion adorned even the three bands of the tiara. Wherever man seeks to buttress and to expand his rule, he will encounter the *raison d'etat* that has always been unscrupulous in choosing its means, or at least has more or less thoroughly overcome its scruples. Financial power, in particular, indispensable for such purposes as for all other desired ends, will ruthlessly develop all the arts of dealing with men: judicial and administrative exploitation, the sale of offices, and the debasement of currencies have been extensively practiced by spiritual and temporal dignitaries. These ills are aggravated wherever favoritism, nepotism, and the influence of mistresses weigh upon the courts. In these respects, an immense influence on national mores and economies has been exerted, especially by monarchic governments, for it is in those that individual needs and individualistic actions have the widest scope, the freest play.

Gesellschaft Grows out of Gemeinschaft

Thus far we have considered individualism within the confines of traditional organization, and it appears that in essence it served to maintain these organizational structures even though their maintenance required changes in form. Manor and guild, feudal monarchy, the Church and its orders—all these are medieval in essence; the modern age works against all of them, undermines and subverts them, attacks them by way of opinions, of laws, of competing institutions. They are thus on the defensive, but since the best defense always and everywhere is the attack, we find all of them advancing as well. Their aggressive tendencies are carried by the systematic consciousness of leaders who know how to adapt themselves, and thus their domains, to the new living conditions; and the main requisite of this adjustment is to know the weapons of one's adversaries and competitors and to learn how to use them.

For a more strongly and originally developing individualism is one that seeks to escape from traditional bonds, one that strives for liberty and liberation, one that breaks the chains which hamper its movements and thoughts.

This individualism ranks foremost among the great movements and cultural processes that mark the modern age: the economic, political, and moral-spiritual processes.

In the economic field, the individualistic development is nothing but the decay of the constitution of the medieval community and the medieval guild, that is, of village and town communities as social forces and realities.

Authoritative and cooperative elements are combined in both constitutions. As a rule, the authoritative element predominated in the communal constitution and in the village community, and the cooperative element in the guild constitution and the town community. Individual liberty rebels against both.

No comparative history of the evolution of the European peasantry has yet been written. There are rudiments, as various authors have described the liberation of the peasant in particular countries. But this does not tell us how much the peasant's own wish and will, his own need and effort contributed to every such liberation, to his release from feudal privileges as well as to that from joint duties and privileges. The peasant is not an economic individual by disposition; but he certainly, and increasingly so, has become one over the centuries. Always and everywhere there must have been some peasants whose stronger acquisitive urge and more conscious pursuit of their own interests made them stand out in comparison to their fellows. Rights of occupancy, which were customarily better protected, the proximity and the influence of lively towns and markets—on the whole, what one may call favorable *opportunity*—all these must at all times have done as much to promote this advance into acquisitiveness as legislative and other activities of the central power, with its fiscal interest in placing the individual upon himself. The peasant develops a certain amount of individualism in his struggle for his rights, in litigation against the lords of the manor and against neighbors. He wants to defend tradition, but bit by bit, notably with the aid of urban lawyers, he learns to interpret tradition in his own way. This trend receives a strong stimulus when the ranks of the landholders themselves are complemented by townspeople, a not infrequent occurrence in the Low Countries as early as the fifteenth century, in France during the eighteenth century, and everywhere in recent times. The size of the unit, on the one hand, and, on the other, such specialties as wine, tobacco, and other staple crops could not but favor the intrusion of a money economy. The restraints of mixed holdings, of neighborhood rights, of pasture privileges came to be burdens on a more intensive cultivation. In England and Scotland, the breaking up of common land by enclosures resulted in enlarged private holdings and in the institution of compact, tenant-farmed units which would gradually grow in size with the turn to a scientifically rationalized type of farming. It is this process—and the displacement of the venerable three-field economy by a system which ever more frankly aimed at the achievement of a net profit and thus, as "free" agriculture, adjusted to every shift in market conditions—which characterizes the still far from complete European development.

In colonial countries, above all in the United States, the farmer has been a businessman right from the start. The farming unit comes to resemble a manufacturing enterprise; agricultural machinery is an American invention. As Hobson puts it, American agriculture tends more and more toward a form in which capital plays an increasingly important role, and labor a relatively less important one. In America, as in Europe, the industrialization of agriculture is not necessarily tied to an enlargement of farming units; by intensive cultivation, smaller areas will be better utilized. However, grain cultivation and a free agriculture which is not dependent on animal power will increasingly demand the establishment of giant farms requiring larger and larger capital investments. Up to that point, of course, the individual manager type will be preserved in agriculture, whether as owner, tenant, or supervising official. Schmoller found that "time and again in agricultural enterprise, even in the most modern, one had to fall back on the individual operator with his wife and children, his farm hands and maids-of-all-work." Schmoller remarks that those who love socialist slogans will describe the modernization replacing this system as the intrusion of capitalism into agriculture; but even those who hate murky slogans will be hard put to find a more illuminating term. It is obvious, however, that in Europe—with the exception of Great Britain—the peasantry and peasant economy have retained major significance, though considerably burdened and hampered by such silent partners as the mortgagee and frequently the holder of promissory notes. In any case, we see the peasant also learn how to become more of a businessman, and how to cultivate the capitalistic production of goods in cooperatives at least, if not yet as an individual. The growing mobility and free divisibility of the land are powerful contributing factors. Property changes hands at a rapidly increasing pace, especially where ground rents have been raised by legislation, and it does not always change into the hands that manage most economically, but often from one speculator to the next. The process affects peasant property as well; sooner or later it can be expected to result in amassment, and it already has had that result insofar as landholding is prized as a patrician luxury and a safe investment. As a source of income, urban real estate far surpasses the rural one, and the commodity quality of the land (*Boden*) is more strikingly apparent in the urban context. The millionaire peasant and the real estate speculator are closely akin. It is in this area that individuals and individual capital holdings will combine in development companies and mortgage banks.

Even so, economic individualism will more quickly and deeply take root in the field of industrial production, and the application of industrial techniques to agriculture is merely a consequence. Another significant tendency is to make agrarian products similar to industrial ones—that is to say, to bring them into forms that are easier to transport as merchandise and more palatable as consumer goods.

The great event to which modern industry owes much of its development is the breakup of the institution of the guild. This had been preceded by centuries of decay, arrested now and then by ossification. Within the institution, discontent surely would seldom arise among the masters, at least not if they attained that rank in time or ahead of time; it came from the journeymen who waited to become masters and who could grow old without achieving independence. Their religious fraternities turned into journeymen's leagues which protected their interests even against the masters, an opposition known to have flared into strikes, indeed into revolts. The journeymen's drive for freedom of trade is not as apparent in history as it might have been expected if they had had a press and other literature; but very early we find traces of a kind of second-class journeymen who did not learn, and were not supposed to learn, the secrets of their trade. In the building trades, these soon came to be numerous. They probably supplied a majority of the "free masters," artisans in small towns and in the countryside who rarely struck it rich, and whom the ban on keeping apprentices and journeymen hampered, even in the cities where they were tolerated. Commonly called bunglers, quacks, troublemakers, interlopers, and often suffering violent persecution, these elements kept multiplying anyway and enjoyed the favor of the authorities and the consumers. As their numbers grew, so did the restiveness within the guilds themselves at their compulsory features—although this opposition movement furnished only auxiliaries for the struggle that terminated the compulsion. Now and then such restive craftsmen were indeed more likely than the guildmasters to think of new techniques and thus to become small manufacturers; in France, new inventions were exempted from the guild regulations as early as 1568. The tendencies that assail the guild system from within a trade must be strictly distinguished from tendencies that fight it from without; and those, in turn, from the ones that undermine it by victorious competition. The result is—as Brentano reports from England—that the guilds slowly wither away without being legally abolished.

Not far removed from the fight for freedom of trade is the progressive ascendancy of individualism in the legal-political sphere, when it rises out of the old political groupings against the ruling estates and the powers that be. The catastrophic event within this uprising is the French Revolution. On the basis of the unfettered civil society—having emerged previously under the tutelage of princely absolutism and a mercantilistic economic policy—the French Revolution establishes the bourgeois state, which does far more for the prevalence of national unity than the *ancien régime* had been capable of doing. In every respect, the sovereignty of the people continued the trends laid out by the sovereignty of the king. The course was set; it would be completed with the absorption by the state of all public law, all public affairs. Within its own centralized power, the state recognizes nothing but the departments and agencies it has established, and within those, the individuals—who are accordingly divided into officials and clients, just as the army, the extract of the state, is divided into officers and men. In the prerevolutionary state, the regulative principle predominated even in the economic system: the guilds were allowed to exist as privileged corporations but shorn of all public significance; their functions were pruned; preference was given to the industry that grew beside them and to the commerce that reduced small craftsmen to dependency. The reason is that these branches of business brought highly welcome funds into the country and into the state exchequer. Thus freedom of trade and free competition were but the last words of a tendency that hitherto had been virulent in a somewhat different manner. The physiocratic argument, denying the possibility of a net yield in industry, underlay the revolutionary legislation needed to achieve industrial power. The physiocrats were more enduringly refuted by Lancashire than by Adam Smith, for the facts speak louder than the most brilliant of writers.

Political individualism means that all citizens are equal. This in turn requires the abolition of any rights of dominion which may be traditional within a state; in essence, therefore, individualism goes against the old ruling estates and the cities as carriers of independent political power. The process has often been called the atomization of the social organism. Roscher takes the view that if the advance of central governmental power entirely dissolves the "smaller groups," if they no longer have a life of their own and if the subjects confront the state as a mere disconnected pile of individuals, the people will, as it were, be pulverized. He relates a favorite metaphor of Napoleon III: that, by dissolving the old estates, the nation had been ground into sand grains, which in isolation are mere dust but can be turned into a rock by a strong state power. As a matter of fact, the picture expresses what any statesman must be driving at, the goal of any purposeful internal policy.

Yet the individualistic evolution is not halted by this "socialistic" tendency. It proceeds within the tendency and alongside it, also in the sense that it is an emancipation.

The labor movement makes demands upon the state, but simultaneously remains a movement aiming at the equalization of the rights of the individual workers with the rights of the individuals of the propertied class. The idea is to win equality of private and political rights, in the state and in the communities. Although achieved in principle and indeed stabilized, private equality constantly has to assert itself against obstructions; the same applies far more to political equality, which to frustrate to the utmost possible extent is one of the arts of government. Beside the labor movement there is the feminist movement, another struggle for emancipation, for private and political rights; the struggles for private rights, too, are essentially political struggles. The emergence of women as individuals surely is a giant final step in the disintegration of age-old communal ties (*Gemeinschafts-Zusammenhang*); it decomposes what had remained an authoritative core in domestic relations. Yet here, too, it is far less the doctrine, the theory, the view that is at fault, if for once we may use this accentuated expression; it is not even women's own will and endeavor so much as life itself, that is, the national economy, capitalism and commercialism, communication, and the need to earn a living. Women already are individuals in economic life, and we see them become more and more so; the fact that they become political individuals as well is a consequence that may, like other consequences, bear within itself the seeds of a sound restoration on a new basis. As pointed out by Tocqueville, a historian who makes profound sense in his research into the nature of revolution, which is the nature of the modern age, "Our forebears did not have the word individualism, which we have coined for our use; the reason is that in their time there was no individual who was not a member of a group, none who might have been thought of as standing by himself alone." Tocqueville has hit the nail on the head here, as on many another occasion.

The social and political struggles are so closely intertwined with moral-spiritual ones that as a rule we regard the latter as the primary phenomena and undertake, for instance, to derive the

French Revolution from the French Enlightenment; also, as mentioned before, we usually view individualism as chiefly an intellectual trend. In fact, the greatest and most momentous phenomenon of the modern age in this very field is the disintegration of a powerful body that has had, and in large part even has retained, an immeasurable import and effect on economic and political life: the disintegration of the Roman Catholic Church. It ruled the Middle Ages, and on the threshold of the modern age it split, with frightful civil wars occurring as a result. From these struggles emerged the modern state, a state which, even where the old Church carried the day, could more freely and strongly confront it—at first in the form of "confessional," that is, Church-related, absolutism. The new national churches tried to restore a divinely warranted authority, though their own roots lay in the denial of that authority, in freedom of conscience, in the right of free examination and interpretation of religious texts.

Time and again the devout individualism of original Christianity would come forth, both within and against the new churches, in pietistic trends and in free congregations (*Gemeinden*) of a more or less revivalist persuasion. Time and again the new churches did as the old ones had done: they would enter the service of princes— in order to dominate them—and in general would seek their points of support among the temporal ruling strata. And yet, the more vigorously Protestantism remains what it is meant to be, the more outspokenly bourgeois is its nature. This is more true of Calvinism than of Lutheranism, more of pietism than of orthodoxy, even though a part of the nobility, its ladies in particular, did feel drawn to pietism by humility and sentiment. A stronger factor was the consonance of pietistic separatism with aristocratic individualism and its claim to be segregated from the common herd; spiritual edification had to vindicate the desire to have one's holy communion, one's holy confession, and one's burial rites to oneself. By and large, however, German pietism was urban, as was British nonconformism. From thoroughly petty bourgeois origins, it rose along with the petty bourgeoisie itself and then turned more or less into Enlightenment and theological rationalism. In its main lines, the struggle for religious liberation parallels the economic and political liberalism of the modern age, and they mutually advance each other. Accordingly, the great colonial country in which political and economic liberties came to unfold most freely is also the country of sects; the Puritans found refuge in New England, the Quakers in Pennsylvania; and the body politic in the American union is essentially neutral, as are its several states. The principle of tolerance, which the more modern type of absolutism had already practiced in Europe, worked the same way: the admission of foreign co-religionists regularly meant an expansion of free trade and commerce.

Gesellschaft Grows alongside Gemeinschaft

The third question to be considered here is how the individual and individualism in the modern age rise and evolve alongside the traditional groupings, again beginning with the *economic* field. There it is the trader who always conducts himself more or less explicitly as an individual toward the other strata, as a person more clearly aware of his own self-interest. He is less settled than the others and, being less tied to the soil, he is not so much tied to place and country either. Travel is part of his business; he visits the marketplaces where all kinds of people meet; even after trade has located in fixed abodes, the trader is often a foreigner. His constant concern, of necessity, is to improve communications. The greater their progress, the more numerously, actively, busily will the traveling merchants be moving to and fro, at home on highways and on waterways, gravitating from the confinement of their towns or villages toward the great field of economic endeavor spreading before their eyes; navigation in particular must serve them. A variant of the merchant is the modern manufacturer—already in the "putting-out" system the merchant is a manufacturer. To run his business, the manufacturer must always be a merchant, and he becomes more and more of a merchant with the mechanization of industry, with growing plant size, with more pronounced capitalistic organization. Less concerned than the merchant pure and simple with unrestricted freedom of trade, the industrialist would rather restrain trade wherever he views it as working more to his detriment than to his advantage; but, like the merchant, he does seek as large a market as possible, at least for his own products, and he therefore joins the merchant in opposing those local and territorial barriers which particular areas would use, and are partly still using, to shut themselves off from the outside world. The merchant, too, tends to be patriotic and conservative if the state power protects and helps him against foreign competition; accordingly, he must set special store by sea power, for trade follows the flag. The representatives of big trade and big industry together form the core of the bourgeoisie that is made up of individuals grown conscious of their property and of their interests. This new economically ruling class confronts, first of all, the nobility and the clergy as the old ruling estates, but then also the old "third estate" consisting of the peasantry and of the artisans and other townsmen. The bourgeoisie is willing and able, through the disposition over capital, to subjugate them all or to attract them to its retinue, to train them in the imitation of its methods and techniques. It thus produces a variety of aides and allies from its own ranks, and it is joined by people who come from other circles.

The merchant approaches the people more or less from the outside, as an alien individual, and everywhere the very strangeness of a stranger has a similarly individualistic effect. It makes for businessmindedness, for the pursuit of one's own advantage; among brothers, comrades, or friends, these tendencies are less likely to find a fertile soil. One stranger meets another at trade fairs and wherever commercial intercourse brings men together, where even men who can communicate only with great effort or through interpreters will feel close to each other simply because they like to trade and to do business—in other words, more probably in towns than in villages, and far more likely in metropolitan centers than in the small country towns where the occasion arises only now and then, if at all; also more probably in colonial countries than in old and closely settled regions. Working always in the same direction are original alien descent and the original or acquired alien religion that often goes with it. This is why such elements usually incline to trade and to free and fairly large-scale industry.

In Europe and in the countries that were colonized from

Europe, the most striking case is that of the Jews. A scattered remnant of the old urban civilization of antiquity, a homeless religious nation dispersed over the whole area of imperial Rome, held together by the belief in their God as by bonds of kinship stretching over vast distances, the Jews were predestined for the role of intermediaries. They knew, appreciated, and possessed money in the form of diverse coin, and consequently the merchandise which the growth of cities and traffic made more and more generally desired was at their disposal. They were hated, feared, and persecuted as medieval civilization had to be ready to do battle with the forces hostile to it, until with the progress of this battle—in other words, with the modern age and initially in Protestant countries—the day of tolerance finally dawned for the Jews. The result was emancipation, meaning legal equality, though counteracted now as before by sentiment and opinion. The conception of what Jews are came to blend so completely with trade, that is, with capitalism, that many traits which we regard as Jewish are in fact characteristic of trade in general—notably of dealings in money and capital—although Jewish peculiarities will often enhance them. On the other hand, their alienation from the "host people" will be preserved and exacerbated as modern communications concentrate masses of Jews in the great cities and as the character of alienation and of the struggle of all against all becomes more general in those cities and in the modern world at large. What shows most clearly in the case of Jewry, however, is also apparent with regard to others that are racial or religious strangers, and even between various Christian creeds, with the smaller groups enjoying the same advantage which marks the Jews: that among themselves they form a community, a sort of conspiracy, increasing their inclination to be somewhat reckless against any but their fellows. Typical as a people are the Swiss, as a sect, the Quakers—both good businessmen also inasfar as their moral-religious principles are reinforced by the insight that honesty is the best policy.

In the *political* field, the universal cultural society prevails beside and beyond all special organized groups. To begin with, this universal society links as with an international bond all individuals who by property and education are disposed to acknowledge each other: within each state it appears as a party. Yet from the commercial circles, in which it originated, this cosmopolitanism shifts more and more to their counterpart: it is the proletariat that develops and cultivates the idea of a superstate, an idea long disseminated by those other circles and now assuming the contours of the socialist world republic. In fact, bourgeois society, in its earlier form which retains individual liberty, already has created a superstate in the essentially international North American union, the most characteristic political structure of the modern age; its future development in a sense will decide the future of European mankind as well. Yet there are also organized groups of a social and economic nature, both national and international, that achieve political power and significance beside the state and may well use them against it.

The third power, the moral-intellectual one, that has arisen beside and above the old contexts and organized groups, likewise is international in essence: it is *science.* In Catholic countries, as in Protestant ones—though more strongly in the latter—it has a steadily disintegrative effect on popular beliefs, on traditional views and mores, but at the same time a newly constructive effect on specifically modern life. Science is the force which transforms men who will give it their wholehearted devotion into free individuals in a higher sense, into freethinkers. It teaches cognition and understanding of the world which, as a unit, is in essence, and thus as a whole, incomprehensible even though all of its parts appear necessarily connected and variously reflect the one law of persistence in change. Comparison is the essence of the scientist's activity, the metrical and numerical expression of relations and equations his supreme goal. As his tools, he must fashion artificial concepts; he must reduce the phenomena to artificial units and subsume them under common denominators. In social life, such artificial units are our concepts of the individuals themselves, because it is the individuals whose isolated existence and evolution we imagine for the sake of explicating all the contexts and combinations from which they arise, as well as all those they produce as new forms.

Economic man, political man, and scientific man *are* these imagined individuals. They touch at many points and interact continually. They share a desire to visualize their ends clearly and to adjust their means accordingly. The course they feel they have to follow is one of cool, calculating thought. They are rationalists and empiricists at once. They take their material from experience and shape it by rational thought. Their thinking serves their willing, but this thinking freely disposes of their motivations—that is to say, it may demand acts of will that can be performed only with inner reluctance and may evoke pangs of conscience. Rational striving by nature is reckless and egotistical, even if the strivings of economic man simultaneously may aim at his family's welfare, those of political man at the welfare of country and state, those of scientific man at the welfare of mankind.

The new universal which the isolated individual relates to, which he affirms in order to acquire it, to conquer it, to control it, is naturally unlimited. It is the world, or mankind, which the merchant in commercial relations, the statesman in world conquest and in the attempt to either subjugate or at least to govern his fellow citizens, strive to make dependent on themselves, and which the man of science wants to understand and even to shape, if, indeed, he intends to be intellectually creative.

Man at the Intersection of Two Worlds, Facing Progress and Decline

Individual man occupies the intersection of two diagonals, which we may conceive of as linking the initial and terminal points of a cultural development. He arises from *Gemeinschaft,* and he forms *Gesellschaft. Gemeinschaft,* essentially, is limited and tends toward intensity; *Gesellschaft,* essentially, is unlimited and tends toward extension. It *is* "the world." The isolated individual essentially is a world citizen. Jacob Burckhardt defines cosmopolitanism as a supreme stage of individualism, a stage whose dawn he thought he was perceiving as far back as in thirteenth-century Italy. Not until the seventeenth century does the term "citizen of the world" seem to have been used to describe a widely traveled, unprejudiced person. The eighteenth century brought the idea of cosmopolitanism to full flower; the nineteenth saw its appearance overshadowed by nationalism, although in fact vastly broadening its real base. The modern nation, notably as represented by a major state, is in large measure a fulfillment of the cosmopolitan quest, though, on the other hand, it curbs that quest and may be viewed as the result of a compromise among contradictory tendencies.

A nation, as distinguished from a people, is a modern formation. Precisely as such, it is an artificial structure, a thought product that has emerged from the consciousness and the political will of many. In the common use of the word, of course, this does not clearly show. We hardly ever even think of nations in pure, unadulterated fashion. The thought, or concept, of a nation is mingled with a variety of emotions that really belong and adhere to the concept of a people.

To be sure, modern nations do have a basic stock of inhabitants who think of themselves as belonging together by descent, and some of the smaller ones—the three Scandinavian nations, for example—are indeed nothing but enlarged, broadened ethnic units [each of them] held together by the same language, by related mores, and by a unified religious creed. But even among the small nations, there are others, like the Belgian and Swiss, composed of people of greatly divergent origin as well as of different languages and creeds; and the small nations are not the typical nations. The great nations are more or less racially mixed. They keep absorbing foreign elements, notably in their capitals and other metropolitan areas. In part they have conquered and annexed territories inhabited by different nationalities; or they attract foreign workers who will fill gaps in the native labor force or undersell it. There are also more and more wealthy foreigners taking up permanent or temporary residence, with the privilege of naturalization after a certain waiting period granted to everyone who is not deemed a risk to national security. In addition, there is the increase in tourist travel. Large cities grow more and more international and metropolitan. By and large, the modern state is indifferent to descent, but less indifferent to wealth and to the conventional marks that serve to embellish the crudity of wealth: to the right religious denomination, to mastery of the state's official language (or of one of its several languages), to displays of a submissive mentality, and to avoidance of whatever might give offense to the circles that set the tone. Compliance with all these conditions is more pronounced among many foreigners than among most natives; this may be particularly so regarding those who are not really the natives' kind, like the Jews, notably if they discard their inherited faith and duly demonstrate their "national" allegiance in the sense of an adjustment to the ruling powers.

In the New World, the international character of modern nations is more strikingly evident than in Europe, and so is their being conditioned by a common government. The American nation is a compound of settlers come from random nations, of Indians they have assimilated or mixed with, and of freed Negro slaves and their illegitimate offspring. Sir Henry Maine remarked that almost all civilized states derive their national unity from past or present submission to some monarchic power. "The Americans of the United States, for instance, are a nation because they once obeyed a king." I would say that to a far greater extent they are today a nation because they respect and acknowledge the union's democratic constitution as their common element of life. In Europe, to be sure, princely power and greed laid a strong foundation for the process of nation building. The princes used to regard territories as latifundia of which they would seek to gain possession by cunning or force, by marriage or inheritance. This quest, however, would scarcely have met with invariable success, if the quest of a strong and steadily more vigorous stratum, the nascent bourgeoisie, had not coincided with it. That stratum—always headed by the merchants and the manufacturers (with whom progressive farmers make common cause) and by their paid and volunteer attorneys—requires a free and expanding sphere of business. What a trust magnate sees in the state or in the empire is a special association for *his* purposes, contributed to by all citizens—and the foremost of these purposes is to guarantee him a large market and action all around the globe, protectively or even aggressively, in behalf of his interests. However, if the power of the state opposes the power of his company, he must submit to the state or make a deal with it.

There are many points of view from which we can observe the individual and the world—how they mutually challenge and qualify each other, how the nations interpose themselves, as it were, as substitutes for "the world"—and these observations are important to an understanding of the economic, political, and intellectual history of the modern age. Let me stress here only one significant aspect out of many.

The course of development is manifested most clearly with regard to the social values which we may understand as the joint property of mankind in the widest sense of the word. Many things, material as well as ideal goods, remain common to many people; others come to be shared by them—ideal goods by the exchange of thoughts and doctrines, material ones by contracts of varied type. To begin with those, we know that the prevailing tendency is to separate and differentiate, to arrive at an increasingly precise definition of private property. The process is most striking regarding real estate; pure and absolute ownership of landed property is a specifically modern phenomenon. Yet personal ownership shows still more precisely in movable goods, especially in those that can be divided at will and turned into other goods—in other words, in money; property comes to be conceived of quite abstractly as "means," as a person's capacity, unlimited in principle, to dispose of things. As a rule, the person is an individual; but parallel to the evolution of individual means runs the one of social means controlled by associations of individuals. The associations are designed to serve a great variety of ends, above all the profit-making ends of business. Capital is combined so as to be more effective in a unified mass. The enlargement of the territory within which economic activities take place means that common goods will increase in any event, to satisfy common needs—most of them depending on the one need for the greatest possible universality and facility of communication and exchange. In part these common needs will be met by private enterprise, but a larger part requires public, that is, joint arrangements. These can come about in considerable quantity without upsetting the character of a social order based on private capitalism; indeed, they support and promote this order. For no private order is possible without the state and its activities, without a multitude of public institutions and goods.

Analogous to the property of private persons is the territorial sovereignty of states. We use the term international property to describe the relation between state power and state territory. It follows that every state has the right to bar strangers from its territory; and yet, under modern international law, the national territory, as a rule, is open to everyone, for transient as well as permanent residence and for the acquisition of property, including real estate. Potentially the earth is jointly owned by all, that is, by all those who know how to win their place on it. In a more distinct and definite sense, this is true of the fluid portion of the globe, or at least of the great mass of that portion which makes up the high seas. It was the early modern age, the same period in which the more precise individualization of national territories was sought and mostly achieved, that saw the application of the principle of the freedom of the seas. . . .

A distinguishing mark of the modern age in all fields is the invention of suitable means to an end, of means of universal communication and exchange in particular; and in a definite sense these will always be the joint property of mankind because and insofar as they serve universal human ends. In this respect, all norms and rules have a tendency to become international in character.

We have reason to be proud of the mighty European civilization of the nineteenth and twentieth centuries, for all the sufferings and sighs it costs us. It has taken much out of our lives: calm, dignity, contemplation, and a great deal of the quiet beauty we may still sense here and there in a village or in a small town. But it has filled our mental as well as our emotional life with tremendous tensions that lift us above all humdrum routine and even above our delight in beauty and virtue, because we have the great intellectual delight to see farther than any past age was capable of seeing and to find ever new satisfactions for our curiosity and love of knowledge. These tensions uplift us because we bless ourselves for our cognition of the causes and effects of things, for facing the world in all its beautiful and ugly manifestations with admiration, even with some measure of understanding. However, modern civilization is caught in an irresistible process of disintegration. Its very progress dooms it. This is hard for us to conceive, and harder still to acquiesce in it, to admit it and yet to cooperate with it willingly and even cheerfully. We must bring ourselves to look upon tragedy, wrestling with both fear and hope so as to rid ourselves of them, and to enjoy the cleansing effect of the dramatic course of events. Scientific analysis can do this if it has matured and transformed itself into philosophy, that is, into wisdom.

21

THE ACTIVE FORCES OF
SOCIAL DEVELOPMENT
IN THE MODERN AGE

EDITORS' NOTE. *Toennies' last publication,* Geist der Neuzeit, *from which this chapter is taken, presents unusual difficulties to the interpreter. Apparently more a collection of notes written at different times during Toennies' scholarly career than a completed piece of work, it is in part repetitive of what the author had said previously, in part merely indicative of what was on the author's mind. Much must therefore be read between the lines; much that is fragmentary must be filled in. To the seminal ideas that are outlined belongs Toennies' rejection of the conventional trichotomy of (Greek and Roman) antiquity, the Middle Ages, and the modern age. Instead, he suggests that there is continuity between the world of antiquity and the subsequent European cultural development and, further, that each and every era within the entire history of human civilization, figuratively speaking, passes through stages of youth, maturity, and aging, with earlier stages showing a predominance of* Gemeinschaft-*like features, giving way to a predominance of* Gesellschaft-*like features with the passage of time. This development is thought to be inevitable, given the fact that man is by nature an individual who cannot help but relate his experience as well as his needs and desires to his own ego and to seek alliances for self-protection and self-enhancement. But the process by which the more and more non-communal and more and more associational individual develops has been most pronounced in recent centuries, partly within communal relations, collectives, and corporations, partly out of these, liberating the individual from them, and partly beside them, initiating associational relations, collectives, and corporations; and all this in an economic, political, and moral-spiritual context. With this sixfold differentiation in mind, Toennies attempts to develop a typology of individual man in the modern age. Going beyond what he already had formulated in the paper on "The Individ-*

ual and the World in the Modern Age," he outlines the types and role performances of the lord, the subject, the layman, the stranger, and the upstart. These are what one may call real types; the normal concept or ideal type behind all these is the individualist.

This is the background upon which the chapter that is presented here ought to be understood. What makes it particularly interesting is that in it Toennies draws a brief sketch of a possible sociology of war. He sees war as an outgrowth of the individualistic spirit and the "great wars" of the modern age as the culmination of the inexorable drift toward Gesellschaft *in a "late" historical development.*

Growth of Population

THE PARTICULAR forms of social life in our period or civilization, of which the modern age represents only a relatively small section, have been fertilized and nourished by an earlier period of a highly developed and widely dispersed civilization of *Gesellschaft* character in classical antiquity. For all that, the new and present civilization has arisen from simpler rudimentary conditions, from which it has grown into more and more varied and complex ones. This development has been determined essentially by the increase and the expansion of populations, by their differentiation and by the division of labor. In the modern age—though, in an analogous but less distinct form, already in classical antiquity—it was commerce, hence capitalism, that rose to dominate this development. Under this influence the standards of urban life became more and more generally accepted, and urban life moved further and further away from what may be called its elementary basis in villages and rural communities. This process carried with it and entailed immense consequences for the economic as well as the political and the spiritual-moral constitution of peoples.

Let us consider in this light the historical events of the modern age, first of all, those that have been, and still are, of the greatest significance for the progress of general social, including economic, conditions.

Translated from *Geist der Neuzeit* (Leipzig: Buske, 1935), pp. 167–81; one brief subdivision is omitted.

Historical events of this nature are the dynamics of population, chiefly the basic change that depends on the relative magnitude of the incidence of birth to the incidence of death and, in its positive sense, on the excess of the former. This change is not a steady one, nor is it insensitive over against external causes. On the whole, the change is more favorable, or positive, in rural areas than in towns, even more so in large cities and metropolitan areas. In the former, marriages are more fertile, largely because of the lower age at marriage and the earlier opportunities for children to contribute to the support of the family, and for parents to bring up and look after their children. In the town, infants and toddlers succumb more easily to infirmities and injuries. Certain checks, however, do operate under rural conditions. Peasant holdings must try to remain efficient when they are passed on in inheritance. Marriage in the holding is therefore often possible for only one among several sons, and a large increase of population is avoided because one does not want to see the holding subdivided or heavily mortgaged. Large increases do not matter among the poor—for they have nothing to pass on; but, among them, their very poverty acts in a negative sense, that is, as a check.

In the towns, the relative position of the craftsmen whose work is steady and whose status inheritable, on the one hand, and the unpropertied people, on the other hand, is comparable, although in the more recent centuries a particular check arose from the compulsory membership in craft guilds so long as this rule remained in force; the opportunity of establishing a family was restricted by that traditional institution, which became even more rigid as it grew older. Consequently, the abolition of compulsory guild membership brought about a marked liberation in the natural increase of population. Previously, increases had been widely kept under control, in rural areas purposefully by the interests and the influence of manorial lordship, while in the towns the difficulty of achieving a position as master of a craft meant that nuptiality was to some extent restricted to marriages between older journeymen and the widows of masters or their daughters no longer in their first youth. Freedom of marriage became a fact simultaneously as a matter of social and economic conditions and as a legal right. This freedom now exists to the greatest possible extent in all European countries as well as in colonial areas. But it actually remained subject to economic restrictions—and this means the standard of living in the widest possible sense: depending, as it does, not only on the fertility of the soil and climatic and meterological conditions relating to harvests and crop failures but also, because of the growing complexity of the world economy, on the rising uncertainty of making a living; and, therefore, in the first instance, on the scarcity or the unstable opportunities for employment and the implications of this instability for wage levels. While as late as the eighteenth century the towns grew but slowly, or sometimes even suffered a decline in population as a consequence of the rigidity of the craft guilds, the liberation process, together with the extraordinary improvement in technology, forcing the pace in the development of the capitalistic mode of production, has led, throughout the nineteenth century, and most markedly in its last third, to that rapid urban growth that ushered in a truly metropolitan epoch. This process continues into the twentieth century. At this point a new trend becomes discernible, largely owing to internal resistances. These gained in strength through rising needs, including those of a cultural nature, making smaller families desirable; statutory restrictions on child labor worked in the same direction. This trend was reinforced by the impact of the enormous event of the [First] World War. Ultimately, this is more likely to lead to a decline than to a further increase in population, chiefly in large cities. Hence, it becomes possible, and has in fact been attempted, to make scientific forecasts. These turn out to be unfavorable regarding the growth of population in those countries on which the European civilization is based, and favorable regarding countries which have had, and still have, a lesser share in western civilization.

Technology

The economist Schmoller correctly observed that technology itself is among the causes that determine population density. Technology in general means everything that man can do: what he accomplishes, acquires, and produces. It is, first of all, the work of the human arm, the hands, and the fingers; but always, and increasingly as it passes into the fingers, it is the work of the human intellect, or what is designated as his mind or spirit. Gradually this capacity gains the upper hand. As in the individual manual worker the technical intellect moves hands and fingers, so (in the words of Goethe's Faust) one mind moves a thousand hands. If one considers under this aspect the development of human skills, one notices as a technology practiced from time immemorial, though certainly acquired only in the course of untold generations, the accomplishments of the hunter and the fisherman, the domestication of animals by breeding and training, the locomotion by means of the wheel and the boat, and, finally, the achievements in agriculture, in mining, and in the building of tents and primitive shelters. Relatively late, man developed the technology of handicrafts, which enabled him to build in timber and in stone, to make utensils and—as needed for many other kinds of work—tools and appliances. Thus it was that in classical antiquity and even before it some countries of the East had reached such a high degree of perfection that large numbers of people could live and work together, partly by means of direct production of the means of subsistence, partly by means of the exchange of these with other commodities; which in turn enabled the narrow stratum of lords and masters to live in splendor adorned by a variety of arts; some of these also benefited the common people, particularly by means of the services rendered to their invisible masters, the gods and demons. All of this was connected with many other technologies, which contributed and continue to contribute to the improvement and the facilitation of social life.

For it is in technology that a fund of skills is being passed on and inherited. Very little of it gets lost, certainly not forever, although some techniques may be forgotten; but others are being rediscovered. At any rate, the fund is being enriched by new inventions and, indirectly, by discoveries. Inventions, to a large part, are made in the immediate context of work, and they are as often as not due to an endeavor on the part of the worker to ease, shorten, and speed up his task. The famous example Adam Smith gave for the technical improvement of the steam engine by an automatic

device (*Wealth of Nations*, Book 1, Chapter 1) is still the best illustration. In general, however, those improvements and refine-
ments in appliances that resulted directly from work had a deeper
significance in that they adorned and refined the product itself. All
genuine arts are closely connected with a passion for the ornamental,
and are therefore based on esthetic discernment, which forms an
important part of the human mind. This does not, of course, render
superfluous those rudimentary areas of activity where work is, first
and foremost, action of the arms and legs; these are determined
less by the needs of the worker himself than by the purpose pursued
in the production line, which is known only to, and determined by,
foremen and managers. Here is a connecting link to warfare, where
even in early times a fairly comprehensive cooperation was practiced. This explains why military technology has always been a
technology concerned with the management of masses of men and
material by mechanical means and, in that connection, with the direction and planned application of fire power. Military technology
has always been a field of rapid technical progress, since it must
adapt itself with speed and flexibility to an external purpose. The
purpose is predominantly destruction as opposed to production, but
that purpose has retroactive effects on production, since it consists
in the special application of produced instruments, namely arma-
ments, and thereby calls for intensified production.

In the same way as the activities that are essential for commerce,
so are the activities that are essential for war, including those of the
political leader, responsible for the conduct of war, rationally conceived activities of a very high order. As such, they are an expression of rational, or arbitrary, will (*Kuerwille*), which plainly subjects all means to the ends it has settled upon in a deliberately
planned procedure. The predominance of this rationalism is an
outstanding feature of the enormous progress that has been made
in the modern age in advance of the Middle Ages and, indirectly,
of all previous ages—progress in production and progress in destruction. In terms of human creativeness, this means negative
as well as positive progress. However, within each of these two
spheres progress may be called positive.

The Great Commerce and the Great War

Commerce is a decidedly peaceful, that is, a socially positive, activity. But it has a good many things in common with war,
the clearly asocial activity, and these common features are joined
in the concept of rationalism: first, the tendency to accumulate
means, in one case, means of production, in the other, means of
destruction, and the problem of moving them geographically, so
that they can achieve their purpose. Second, mastery over these
means requires planning and calculating thought and, accordingly,
system and orderliness and, in the disposition over manpower, its
distribution and deployment. Third, both trade and war involve a
large expenditure of effort, which is most directly represented in
the investment of money. As in commerce, the disbursement of
money aims at an increased return of money, so is the expectation
in the conduct of war that the expenditure should pay off, whether
in the form of a successful territorial conquest or in the form of
ample recompense through the payment of tribute exacted from
the opponent after his defeat, especially if defeat forces upon him a
relationship of lasting dependence. Fourth, the danger that the enterprise may fail or miscarry is a common element in both activities, and that risk is being accepted.

Neither commerce nor war is a modern invention. Yet both have
immeasurably developed their dimensions in the modern age. Large-
scale commerce and large-scale war are modern phenomena. And
they are linked in a variety of ways. The typical war of the modern
age is a commercial war, fought for the purpose of literally driving
the competitor from the field—the field of competition—or of
guarding against his further gain in strength, or of forestalling him
in the penetration of a territory that is of commercial value. These
political interests not only grow with the expansion of world trade
but their growth is accelerated as commerce extends to the field of
finance and worldwide banking; they reach their highest intensity
when commercial interests become the dominant force in the production of commodities, in transport, and in communications, all
of which are gradually being integrated in the capitalistic system.

Parallel with the commercial runs the political development, that is, the growth of the modern state. It leads to the combination and unification of a great variety of existing political units into larger, integrated units with a centralized administration. The starting point of the new political entity is the expanding power of the city, which becomes the core of the power of the state; then the larger state arises from the association of smaller states, some of which may have originated in cities, while others may have been the outgrowth of other previously existing political units that were united through the willpower of an outstanding prince or king. Conditions for an association of this kind are favorable when a natural basis exists of ethnic and racial affiliation, or of spatial affinity and neighborliness, or of a variety of common customs and interests, including common religious observances. But the formation of a large state may also be the result of the acquisition or takeover of weaker political units by a stronger unit using force. Both types may operate in combination or reinforce each other.

Again, it is by means of commerce and war that the modern age has been an agent of continual social and political change. Capital and the state are joining hands when reaching out toward faraway lands and across the seas: they bring under their dominion, by means partly of their commodities, partly of their armed forces, whole territories and their inhabitants, even those that set great store by their own independence.

Capital and the state are joined by science as the third specifically modern social force. Science, though fundamentally different from the other two, has many and strong ties with them. These are essentially ties of reciprocal give and take, just as capital and the state, in their reciprocal relationships, continually in many ways, to be sure, obstruct but predominantly strengthen and promote each other. Science, too, must aim at unification and systematic order by simplifying and strengthening its methods; for its law, too, is the economy of effort.

In the modern age, as in former periods, scientific development goes hand in hand with capitalistic and political development; in quite fundamental ways it is conditioned by the efforts and successes of commerce and warfare. Commerce promotes thought and knowledge, and thought, as computation and calculation, is an essential element of science. And knowledge, which is a combined product of thought and experience, is being advanced as experience widens with the movement from one place to another, which is the typical movement of the merchant. The effects of warfare are similar. Its campaigns are movement over territory, admittedly with a destructive aim yet always mindful of the need to maintain and feed its armies; and, once it succeeds in an invasion, it must give thought to maintaining and developing the conquered territory. In the pursuit of these aims, warfare is accompanied by commerce acting in its own interest. But warfare by itself, too, means more thought and more knowledge—thought, insofar as it calls for the comparison of favorable and unfavorable effects of armed action, particularly the losses in men and material it must incur in comparison with the losses of the enemy, at which it is aiming; and knowledge insofar as the strategist must constantly observe how his own actions and those of the enemy are reciprocally conditioned in their very aim of impeding each other and how the changing chances of the final outcome of a struggle may be assessed.

In this way commerce and war depend continually on, among other things, scientific progress and on changes in scientific outlook. The activity that has always been closely related to commerce, and in certain ways has been dependent on it, is movement from one place to another, and especially one such movement, namely, navigation. Now, since early times, navigation has had to rely on the observation and knowledge of the skies; and improvements in astronomy in the modern age, as formerly, have greatly facilitated it. Further, we must remember what has been said previously about the connection between commerce and technology; what is most striking in this respect is the powerful development in mechanical technology, based, in its turn, on the science of mechanics, which got under way in the last centuries of the Middle Ages, to reach perfection only in the modern age. An extraordinarily wide area of constantly renewed activity was opened up thereby for the investment of capital, which led increasingly to the amassment of activities, mass employment of labor, mass production of commodities. As an aid to mechanics and a physics based on mechanical principles, the more recent development of chemistry must here be noted, which, in turn, opened the way for a better understanding of those processes of life that are inaccessible to mechanics alone. In addition, biology has been instrumental for the observation and the understanding of the processes of growth and propagation in plant and animal life. The new knowledge also became relevant for commerce and for war; for commerce as all kinds of products of the earth and their derivatives called for attention and exploitation; and for war as war materials became increasingly, as time went on, not only mechanical but chemical ones; and finally, as the life sciences, particularly the sciences of human life and its conditions, grew in importance even in tasks oriented toward the destruction of life.

Commerce and war, capital and the political state, on the other hand, support and promote scientific endeavor, partly through the realization of what science is achieving and may achieve for them in the future, and partly in quite a different context, which is determined by different factors. Outstanding among these is the enhanced valuation attached to science and the arts as the wealth of nations increases. Let us look here at the more immediate connections. Scientific research closely resembles commerce in that both push into what is distant and pursue what is novel; commerce, for the sake of the profit that so often may be gained by better knowledge; scientific research, for the sake of knowledge itself, even though, in its striving for what is distant, it will put up with a dependence that results from useful endowment. But always scientific endeavor is stimulated by the exchange of ideas and of research results between those working along similar lines, particularly between scientists working under a variety of conditions in different countries. And, as of commerce, so it has always been a function of war to foster progress by intensifying communication between the inhabitants of different countries.

The Large-Scale Enterprise

The forces of the modern age successfully assert themselves in each one of these main areas of activity, although they are constantly held back by surviving medieval attitudes. But they persistently surmount them and gain superiority. First, in the economic area, the distinct character of the Middle Ages is determined by comparatively simple conditions of social life—conditions, in which rural life and agriculture markedly predominate, and continue to do so despite the growth and flowering of numerous cities. Even the most important cities do not exceed fairly moderate limits, but they acquire and maintain a high degree of independence, so that they rise to the status of free republics within the framework of the larger empire to which they belong as subjects. Initially, the city is dominated by the patriciate, whose wealth and power are rooted both in tradition and in landed estate. But the patricians are gradually being replaced by a class of craftsmen, which draws its strength from the guilds, is capable of defending itself as well as to produce, and, in alliance with the lower orders, represents the community and the people. However, the beginnings of production of marketable goods for profit become more pronounced in a variety of ways. For instance, the technical requirements of work in mining favor the development of large-scale enterprise. Generally, the large-scale enterprise is typical of the modern age. It stands for the pronounced domination which commerce exercises over the freedom of rural and urban labor, including such industrial labor as is domiciled in the countryside. Even when industries are established in rural areas, they are essentially urban in character. The large-scale enterprise run on industrial principles gradually adapts and transforms to its image also the agricultural enterprise; but being a less suitable, because less flexible, form of capital investment, its relative economic importance may decline to the point of insignificance.

The Great Power Struggle

As the large-scale enterprise has proved superior to the small enterprise in industry and agriculture, and eventually in commerce, so are in political life the great powers superior to the smaller ones. The great power is, together with the growth of the concept of the sovereign state, one of the most momentous results of the social forces at work in the modern age: and with the superpower, a centralized governmental bureaucracy, which is faced by the problems of general social welfare (*salus publica*). Its administration is under pressure not only from the old "estates" but increasingly from the bourgeoisie; the middle classes have become influential with the rise of commerce and industry, particularly heavy industry, and strive for a commanding political position. But along with the bourgeoisie, and at the same time opposed to it to the point of revolt, grows the working class, the proletariat that has been created by the former. The opposition is both political and economic in character. Its chances of capturing political power are enhanced by those very ideas of political liberty and equality which had inspired the middle classes and, in drawing strength from the support of the working class, gained them a decisive influence in political life.

In this respect, as much as in others, it is obvious that the social forces at work in the modern age are still in their formative stage and have not yet played their part to the end. An attempt at forecasting the final outcome may approximate near certainty inasmuch as a scientific understanding of the phenomena of social life can be achieved by reliable methods, that is, the closer it approximates and resembles knowledge in the natural sciences.

The modern state, in the course of its expansion and consolidation, leads to warfare as an expression of conflict between states, whether between two single powers, or between a coalition and a single power, or between coalitions of powers. The modern age is the age of the great war, in contrast to the Middle Ages, in which only minor feuds and conflagrations were frequent, even if they gradually assumed a wider scope. Further, the great wars are a matter of planned execution, as they are more and more going to be a matter of applied military technology and of the mass destruction of human life and material assets. In addition to external wars between different states, civil wars have emerged as conflicts on a large scale. In brief, war in all its aspects has become an essential element in the development of the modern state; and, because of its immense cost, warfare has brought in its wake the growing importance of public finance and fiscal policies.

Warfare is mainly provoked by the territorial expansion of a particular state, whether in the form of direct occupation or indirect domination. Direct occupation is often being sought for reasons of nationalism, or under the pretext of it, particularly when a case can be made for larger or smaller areas having formerly been part of the territory of the aggressor, or, even more so, when the inhabitants are of the same nationality [or ideology—EDS.]; other reasons for an attempted expansion are a supposedly necessary shortening of frontiers, or the acquisition of one or several ports, or the gaining of direct access to the open sea. On closer investigation, it frequently turns out that the real reason for such tendencies lies in the needs of trade; for commerce is unthinkable without its natural aim to expand and to raise its profit, so that it jealously watches the expanding trade of other countries and understandably enough fears, as the consequence of such expansion, the decline, if not the cessation, of its own trade. For this reason, modern wars predominantly have been economic wars. In addition, a victorious war, the more severe the conditions of the peace which are imposed on the loser, is the more likely to be pregnant with a new war; this is comparable to what happens in primitive societies in which tribal revenge may endlessly continue as the consequence of an inflicted death or injury—until a superior power grows strong enough to enforce a public peace. A good example for the latter process can be observed in the transition from the Middle Ages to the modern age. At the threshold, as it were, of the modern age, when the central power in the Holy Roman Empire began to disintegrate, an attempt was made to terminate incessant feuds, and a "general public peace" (*allgemeiner Landfriede*) became the law of the land; however, the subsequent warfare between the larger territories with the empire, nevertheless, took the form of a lingering civil war. The recent centuries of the modern age witnessed also in the rest of Europe outside Germany and in the United States, this great European colony beyond the seas, serious internal conflicts which, more often than not, made all the heavier the burden of external wars these countries had to shoulder.

Since modern wars regularly arise from urban interests, in particular those of trade, they signify as much as does the central state power, which owes to warfare much of its consolidation, an increasing preponderance of the city over the countryside. Yet warfare, and the government wanting war or being forced into it, needs the countryside and the rural economy for two fundamental reasons. First, the countryside is the producer of soldiers of greater physical strength and endurance, who are more ready to fight; this counts for much, especially so long as armies are recruited by voluntary enlistment. The second reason is that the armed forces must be fed by its own country until, having gained enemy ground, they can be fed by the occupied territory; further, the dependence on their own country's resources is intensified once exchange and communciation with other countries are exposed during the war to temporary or permanent interruptions. As rural areas suffer from enemy invasion, often even from the passage of their own military forces, more directly than the towns; as their fields are laid waste, their draft animals pillaged or killed, their houses and barns burned, and their manpower often pressed into service in the army and navy despite the principle of voluntary service: it would be but natural if the rural population revolted against a war that chiefly serves urban interests—and to an extent this does indeed happen. But such a tendency is being counteracted by the circumstance that it is the rural folks who not only are more fit for military service, hence better soldiers, but who also are more easily taken in by government-inspired propaganda which persuades them of the necessity and the justice of a war that is about to break out. Vistas of lasting prosperity, hand in hand with the prospect of immediate gain, are conjured up before them. In one case, only the necessity of war cannot be gainsaid, that is, when a plain act of aggression must be resisted to protect the nation from the terrifying peril of foreign domination which would amount to nothing less than bondage. However, by crafty blandishment and political artifice, it is easy to create the conviction that a war is just; the true reasons and causes of a war of aggression as an instrument of power politics, as a rule, will be discovered only by means of historical research long after the generation of those who were cruelly deceived has passed away.

The City as a Factor in Spiritual and Moral Development

The nature of the relationship between the city and the countryside manifests itself most clearly in the spiritual-moral sphere of social life. The city stimulates intellectual life, because living conditions in the city bring people closer together and offer greater variety. City life is also a fertile ground for intellectuality, because calculation and computation are necessary skills in a monetary economy, that is, in commercial activities. The style of rural life is rather that of the *Gemeinschaft* mode, being steadier and quieter; with all that, it is not lacking in conflicts and disputes over mine and thine, even within families; and personal hatred, jealousy, and vindictiveness often lead to grievous acts of violence. The style of life in the city is more impersonal and matter-of-fact, and so are its conflicts and controversies; but with the greater emphasis on monetary transactions and private property and, consequently, on claims and debts, controversies become more frequent and more intensive, and more often require settlement by formal judicial decision.

Of great significance in this respect is the change in the attitude to the ruling powers, that is, in historical perspective, to rule by the gentry. The country folks, on the whole, willingly used to submit to them, accepting as they did their superiority and indispensability, which was felt to be divinely ordained. Inseparable from the devoutness of the common people, religion has always provided the stongest support for sheer domination. In the city, too, religion is an influential authority; moreover, city life is a favorable ground for its artistic as well as its intellectual refinement. But with refinement, doubts and better insight are promoted also, so that a sharp contrast comes into view: pious devoutness as an essential trait of rural, critical thinking, of urban life.

This viewpoint enables us to compare the general turn of mind that predominates in contemporary life with the way of thinking that is widely attested to and documented for the Middle Ages. The distance separating them is an appreciable though almost immeasurable one. One can perhaps say that it is the urban disposition, guided by, and relying on, scientific thinking, that by this time provides the keynote; long since it has exercised a pervading influence also on the more fundamental and natural way of thinking that used to be the mark of the countryside. The difference between then and now, that is, between science and simple faith as well as superstition, appears at its most striking when one considers the immemorial belief, common to the human race, in the existence and the appearance of ghosts and specters.

Bibliography

FERDINAND TOENNIES' major writings are arranged chronologically in three sections: History of Ideas (p. 334); Sociology (p. 335); Sociography (p. 339). Sections of the translations of his works (p. 341) and of selected writings about Toennies (p. 341) are arranged alphabetically by translator and by author, respectively.

ABBREVIATIONS OF COLLECTED PAPERS
> *SStuKr* I, II, II = *Soziologische Studien und Kritiken, Erste bis Dritte Sammlung.* Jena: G. Fischer, 1925, 1926, 1929.
> *FSE* = *Fortschritt und Soziale Entwicklung.* Karlsruhe: Braun, 1926.

ABBREVIATIONS OF GERMAN PERIODICALS
> *AGPh* = *Archiv fuer Geschichte der Philosophie*
> *ARWPh* = *Archiv fuer Rechts- und Wirtschaftsphilosophie*
> *ASGS* = *Archiv fuer Soziale Gesetzgebung und Statistik*
> *ASPh* = *Archiv fuer Systematische Philosophie*
> *AStA* = *Allgemeines Statistisches Archiv*
> *ASwSp* = *Archiv fuer Sozialwissenschaft und Sozialpolitik*
> *DStZ* = *Deutsches Statistisches Zentralblatt*
> *DiJG* = *Dioskuren, Jahrbuch fuer Geisteswissenschaften*
> *JbNS* = *Jahrbuecher fuer Nationaloekonomie und Statistik*
> *KVHS* = *Koelner Vierteljahrshefte fuer Soziologie*
> *PhM* = *Philosophische Monatschefte*
> *SchmJb* = *Schmollers Jahrbuch fuer Gesetzgebung, Verwaltung und Volkswirtschaft*
> *VWPh* = *Vieteljahrsschrift fuer Wissenschaftliche Philosophie*
> *WwA* = *Weltwirtschaftliches Archiv*
> *ZGSt* = *Zeitschrift fuer die Gesamte Staatswissenschaft*
> *ZGStr* = *Zeitschrift fuer die Gesamte Strafrechtswissenschaft*
> *ZV* = *Zeitschrift fuer Voelkerrecht*
> *ZVpS* = *Zeitschrift fuer Voelkerpsychologie und Soziologie*

History of Ideas

"Anmerkungen ueber die Philosophie des Hobbes." *VWPh* 3 (1879): 453–66; 4 (1880): 55–74, 428–53; 5 (1881): 186–204.

"Studie zur Entwicklungsgeschichte des Spinoza." *VWPh* 7 (1883): 158–83, 334–64.

"Leibniz und Hobbes." *PhM* 23 (1887): 557–73.

Editor. *Thomas Hobbes, The Elements of Law Natural and Politic.* Edited with a preface and critical notes, to which are subjoined selected abstracts from unprinted mss. of Thomas Hobbes. London: Simpkin Marshal & Co., 1889; reprinted, Cambridge University Press, 1928, and Frank Cass & Co. Ltd., London, 1970, with introduction by M. M. Goldsmith.

Editor. *Thomas Hobbes, Behemoth or the Long Parliament.* Edited for the first time from the original ms. London: Simpkin Marshall & Co., 1889; reprinted Frank Cass & Co. Ltd., London, 1969, with introduction by M. M. Goldsmith.

"Neuere Philosophie der Geschichte: Hegel, Marx, Comte." *AGPh* 7 (1894): 486–515.

"Historismus und Rationalismus." *ASPh* 1 (1894): 227–52 (now *SStuKr* I: 105–26).

Thomas Hobbes: Leben und Lehre. Stuttgart: Frommann, 1896; 2d. ed., *Thomas Hobbes, Der Mann und der Denker,* 1912; 3d. ed., *Thomas Hobbes, Leben und Lehre,* 1925. Reprint with epilogue and bibliography by K. H. Ilting, Stuttgart, — forthcoming.

Der Nietzsche-Kultus, Eine Kritik. Leipzig: Reisland, 1897.

"Zur Theorie der Geschichte: Exkurs" (Review of Rickert, *Die Grenzen der naturwissenschaftlichen Begriffsbildung*). *ASPh* 8 (1901): 1–38.

"Herbert Spencer (1820:1903)." *Deutsche Rundschau* 118 (1904): 368–82.

"Hobbes Analekten I." *AGPh* 17 (1904): 291–317.

"Hobbes Analekten II." *AGPh* 19 (1906): 153–75.

Schiller als Zeitbuerger und Politiker. Berlin: Verlag der "Hilfe," 1905.

"Simmel als Soziologe." *Frankfurter Zeitung.* October 9, 1918.

Marx, Leben und Lehre. Jena: Erich Lichtenstein; Sozialistische Buecherei, vol. 5, 1921.

"Ferdinand Toennies," in *Die Philosophie der Gegenwart in Selbstdarstellungen* 3:203–44. Leipzig: Meiner, 1923.

"Die Lehre von den Volksversammlungen und die Urversammlung in Hobbes' Leviathan." *ZGSt* 89 (1930) : 1–22.

"Historischer Materialismus," pp. 770–75, in ed. L. Heide, *Internationales Handbuch des Gewerkschaftswesens, 1931.* Berlin: Werk u. Wirtschaft, 1930.

"Hobbes und Spinoza," pp. 226–43, in *Septimana Spinozana.* The Hague: Martinus Nijhoff, 1935.

"Hegels Naturrecht, Zur Erinnerung an Hegel's Tod." *SchmJb* 56 (1932) : 71–85.

"Contributions à l'histoire de la pensée de Hobbes." *Archives de Philosophie* 12 (1936) : 259–84.

"Lettre de M. le professeur F. Toennies, Kiel," pp. xlvi–li, in *Actes du VIIIᵉ Congrès International de Philosophie à Prague 2–7 Sept. 1934.* Prague: Orbit S.A., 1936.

Sociology

"Gemeinschaft und Gesellschaft, Theorem der Kulturphilosophie." Ms. 1880–81, first published, *Kant Studien* 30 (1925) : 149–79 (now *SStuKr* I: 1–32).

Gemeinschaft und Gesellschaft, Abhandlung des Communismus und Socialismus als empirischer Culturformen. Leipzig: Reisland, 1887; reprint, 1904. Subtitle since 2d. ed., *Grundbegriffe der reinen Soziologie.* Berlin: Curtius, 2d. ed. 1912; 3d. ed. 1920; 4th–5th eds. 1922; 6th–7th eds. 1926. Leipzig: Buske, 8th ed., 1935. Darmstadt: Wissenschaftliche Buchgesellschaft, reprint, 1963, with prefaces to 1st, 2nd, 4th and 5th, 6th and 7th and 8th edition added.

"Herbert Spencers soziologisches Werk." *PhM* 25 (1889) : 50–85 (now *SStuKr* I: 75–104).

"Werke zur Philosophie des sozialen Lebens und der Geschichte." *PhM* 28 (1892) : 37–66, 444–61, 592–601; 29 (1893) : 291–309 (now *SStuKr* III: 133–95).

Review of Georg Simmel, *Einleitung in die Moralwissenschaft. Zeitschrift für Psychologie und Physiologie der Sinnesorgane.* 5 (1893) : 627–33.

Review of Georg Simmel, *Die Probleme der Geschichtsphilosophie. Zeitschrift für Psychologie und Physiologie der Sinnesorgane.* 6 (1893) : 77–79.

"Jahresbericht ueber Erscheinungen der Soziologie aus den Jahren 1893–4,

1895–6, 1897–8." *ASPh* 2 (1896) : 421–41, 497–517; 4 (1898) : 99–116, 230–49, 483–506; 6 (1900) : 505–40; 8 (1902) : 263–79, 397–408 (now *SStuKr* III: 196–336).

Ueber die Grundtatsachen des socialen Lebens. Bern: Steiger & Cie., Ethisch-socialwissenschaftliche Vortragskurse, Zuericher Reden, VII, 1897.

"Philosophical Terminology" (Welby Prize Essay, 1898), trans. Mrs. Bosanquet. *Mind* n.s. 8 (1899) : 289–332, 467–91; n.s. 9 (1900) : 46–61.

"Zur Einleitung in die Soziologie." *Zeitschrift fuer Philosophie und Philosophische Kritik* 115 (1899) : 240–51 (now *SStuKr* I: 65–74). (French transl. *"Notions fondamentales de sociologie pure."* *Annales de l'Institut International de Sociologie* 4 [1900] : 63–77.)

"The Present Problems of Social Structure" (paper read at the Congress of Arts and Science, St. Louis). *American Journal of Sociology* 10 (March 1905) : 569–88.

"Ammon's Gesellschaftstheorie." *ASwSp* 19 (1904) : 88–111 (now *SStuKr* III: 372–93).

"Sociologie et Psychologie." *Annales de L'Institut International de Sociologie* 10 (1904) : 289–97.

"Die Entwicklung der Technik," pp. 127–48, in *Festgabe fuer Adolph Wagner*, 1905 (now *SStuKr* II: 33–62).

Strafrechtsreform. Berlin: Pan Publ., Moderne Zeitfragen, no. 1, 1905.

"Eugenik." *SchmJb* 29 (1905) : 1089–106 (now *SStuKr* I: 334–49).

"Zur naturwissenschaftlichen Gesellschaftslehre: Die Anwendung der Deszendenztheorie auf Probleme der sozialen Entwicklung." *SchmJb* n.s. 29 (1905) : 27–101, 1283–322; 30 (1906) : 121–45; 31 (1907) : 487–552; 33 (1909) : 879–94; 35 (1911) : 375–96 (now *SStuKr* I: 133–329).

Philosophische Terminologie in psychologisch-soziologischer Ansicht. Leipzig: Thomas, 1906.

Das Wesen der Soziologie. Schriften der Gehe Stiftung. Dresden: Zahn & v. Jentsch, 1907 (now *SStuKr* I: 350–68).

Die Entwicklung der sozialen Frage. Berlin: Goeschen (Sammlung Goeschen), 1907. 4th ed., *Die Entwicklung der sozialen Frage bis zum Weltkriege.* Berlin-Leipzig: de Gruyter, 1926.

"Ethik und Sozialismus." *AswSp* 25 (1907) : 573–612; 26 (1908) : 56–94; 29 (1909) : 895–930.

"Entwicklung der Soziologie in Deutschland im 19. Jahrhundert," in *Festgabe fuer Gustav Schmoller*, 1908 (now *SStuKr* II: 63–103).

Review of G. Ratzenhofer, *Soziologie, Positive Lehre von den menschlichen Wechselbeziehungen*. *SchmJb* 32 (1908): 329–32 (now *SStuKr* III: 348–52).

Die Sitte. Die Gesellschaft, ed. by Martin Buber, vol. 25. Frankfurt: Ruetten & Loening, 1909.

"Comtes Begriff der Soziologie." *Monatsschrift fuer Soziologie* 1 (1909): 42–50 (now *SStuKr* II: 116–22).

"Wege und Ziele der Soziologie, Rede zur Eroeffnung des Ersten Deutschen Soziologentages," pp. 17–38, in *Verhandlungen des Ersten Deutschen Soziologentages vom 19.–22. Oktober 1910 in Frankfurt a.M.* Tuebingen: I. C. B. Mohr, 1911 (now *SStuKr* II: 125–43).

"Ueber Anlagen und Anpassung." *Frauen-Zukunft* 1 (1910): 483–91, 567–76 (now *SStuKr* II: 155–68).

"Individuum und Welt in der Neuzeit." *WwA* 1 (1913): 37–66 (now *FSE*, 1–35).

"Soziologie und Geschichte." *Die Geisteswissenschaften* 1 (1913): 57–62 (now *SStuKr* II: 190–99).

"Rechtsstaat und Wohlfahrtsstaat." *ARWPh* 8 (1914): 1–6.

Der englische Staat und der deutsche Staat. Berlin: K. Curtius, 1917.

"Der Begriff der Gemeinschaft." *Zeitschrift fuer soziale Paedagogik* 1 (1919): 12–20 (now *SStuKr* II: 266–76).

"Zur Theorie der Oeffentlichen Meinung." *SchmJb* 40 (1916): 2001–30 (no. 4: 393–422).

"Die grosse Menge und das Volk." *SchmJb* 43 (1919): 1–29 (now *SStuKr* II: 277–303).

Hochschulreform und Soziologie. Jena: Fischer, 1920.

Kritik der Oeffentlichen Meinung. Berlin: Springer, 1922.

"Macht und Wert der Oeffentlichen Meinung." *DiJG* 2 (1923): 72–99.

"Zweck und Mittel im sozialen Leben," pp. 235–70, in *Erinnerungsgabe fuer Max Weber: Die Hauptprobleme der Soziologie*, vol. 1. Munich: Duncker & Humblot, 1923. (Now *SStuKr* III: 1–39.)

"Zur Soziologie des demokratischen Staates." *WwA* 19 (1923): 540–84 (now *SStuKr* II: 304–52).

"Hobbes und das Zoon Politikon." *ZV* 12 (1923): 471–88.

"Einteilung der Soziologie," pp. 885–98, in *Atti del V. Congresso Inter-*

nazionale di Filosofia, Napoli, 5–9 maggio 1924. Naples: S.A. Editrice Francesco Perrella, 1926. *ZGSt* 79 (1925) : 1–15 (now *SStuKr* II: 430–43).

"Begriff und Gesetz des menschlichen Fortschritts" (paper read at the congress in Rome, April 1924, of the *Istituto Internazionale di sociologia e di reforma sociale). ASwSp* 53 (1925) : 1–10 (now *FSE*, 36–44). Translated in *Social Forces* 19 (1940) : 23–29, by Karl J. Arndt and C. L. Folse, "The Concept and Law of Human Progress."

"Kulturbedeutung der Religionen." *SchmJb* 48 (1924) : 1–30 (now *SStuKr* II: 353–80).

"Richtlinien fuer das Studium des Fortschritts und der sozialen Entwicklung," pp. 166–221, in *Jahrbuch fuer Soziologie,* vol. 1, 1925. (Now *FSE,* 45–100.)

Soziologische Studien und Kritiken. Jena: Fischer, *Erste Sammlung* 1925; *Zweite Sammlung* 1926; *Dritte Sammlung* 1929.

"Troeltsch und die Philosophie der Geschichte." *SchmJb* 49 (1925) : 147–91 (now *SStuKr* II: 381–429).

Fortschritt und soziale Entwicklung. Geschichtsphilosophische Ansichten. Karlsruhe: Braun, 1926.

Das Eigentum. Vienna and Leipzig: Braumueller, Soziologie und Sozialphilosophie, Schriften der Soziologischen Gesellschaft in Wien, vol. 5, 1926.

"Demokratie," pp. 12–36, in *Verhandlungen des Fuenften Deutschen Soziologentages 27–29, September 1926 in Wien.* Tuebingen: I. C. B. Mohr, 1927.

Wege zu dauerndem Frieden? Leipzig: Hirschfeld, Zeitfragen aus dem Gebiete der Soziologie, third series, no. 2, 1926.

"Demokratie und Parlamentarismus." *SchmJb* 51 (1927) : 173–216 (now *SStuKr* III: 40–84).

"Amerikanische Soziologie" (Review of Walter Lippmann, *Public Opinion). WwA* 26 (July 1927) : 1**–11**.

Der Kampf um das Sozialistengesetz 1878. Berlin: Springer, 1929.

"Soziale Bezugsgebilde in ihren Wechselwirkungen." *Forum Philosophicum* (1930) : 143–69.

"Sozialpolitik als soziale Idee." *WwA* 31 (1930) : 161*–175*.

Einfuehrung in die Soziologie. Stuttgart: Ferdinand Enke, 1931; Reprint, with an introduction by Rudolf Heberle, 1965.

"Gemeinschaft und Gesellschaft," pp. 180–91, in *Handwoerterbuch der Soziologie*, ed. A. Vierkandt. Stuttgart: Ferdinand Enke, 1931. Translated in ed. Loomis, *Toennies, Community and Society (Gemeinschaft und Gesellschaft)*, pp. 237–59 (see below).

"Eigentum," pp. 106–12, in *Handwoerterbuch der Soziologie*, ed. A. Vierkandt. Stuttgart: Ferdinand Enke, 1931.

"Die moderne Familie," pp. 122–31, in *Handwoerterbuch der Soziologie*, ed. A. Vierkandt. Stuttgart: Ferdinand Enke, 1931.

"Staende und Klassen," pp. 617–38, in *Handwoerterbuch der Soziologie*, ed. A. Vierkandt. Stuttgart: Ferdinand Enke, 1931. Translated in *Class, Status and Power: A Reader*, ed. by R. Bendix and S. M. Lipset, pp. 49–63. Glencoe, Ill.: Free Press, 1953.

"Mein Verhaeltnis zur Soziologie," pp. 103–22, in *Soziologie von heute. Ein Symposium der ZV pS*, ed. R. Thurnwald. 1932.

"Sitte und Freiheit," pp. 7–17, in *Probleme deutscher Soziologie. Gedaechtnisgabe für Karl Dunkmann*. Berlin: Junker u. Duennhaupt, 1933.

"Gemeinwirtschaft und Gemeinschaft." *SchmJb* 58 (1934) : 317–26.

Geist der Neuzeit. Leipzig: Buske, 1935.

Posthumous: "Die Entstehung meiner Begriffe Gemeinschaft und Gesellschaft. Fuer Earle Eubank," and "Ueber die Lehr- und Redefreiheit." *Koelner Zeitschrift* 7 (1955) : 127–31; 132–41.

SOCIOGRAPHY

"The Prevention of Crime." *International Journal of Ethics* 2 (October 1891) : 51–77.

"Das Verbrechen als soziale Erscheinung." *ASGS* 8 (1895) : 329–44. "Le crime comme phenomène social." *Annales de l'Institut International de Sociologie* 2 (1896) : 387:409.

"Hafenarbeiter und Seeleute in Hamburg vor dem Strike 1896/97." *ASGS* 10 (1897) : 173–238.

"Der Hamburger Strike von 1896/97." *ASGS* 10 (1897) : 673–720.

"Straftaten in Hamburger Hafenstrike." *ASGS* 11 (1897) : 513–20.

"Die Enquete ueber Zustaende der Arbeit im Hamburger Hafen." *ASGS* 12 (1898) : 303–48.

"Die Ostseehaefen Flensburg, Kiel, Luebeck," pp. 509–614, in *Die Lage der in der Seeschiffahrt beschaeftigten Arbeiter*, II, Schriften des

Vereins fuer Sozialpolitik, vol. 104, part 1. Berlin and Munich: Duncker & Humblot, 1903.

"Todesursachenstatistik." *Soziale Praxis* 13 (1903) : 260–61.

"Eine neue Methode der Vergleichung statistischer Reihen, im Anschluss an Mitteilungen ueber kriminalistische Forschungen." *SchmJb* n.s. 33 (1909) : 699–720.

"Studie zur Schleswig-holsteinischen Agrarstatistik." *ASwSp* 30 (1910) : 285–332.

"Die Gesetzmaessigkeit in der Bewegung der Bevoelkerung." *ASwSp* 39 (1915) : 150–73, 767–94.

"Die Statistik als Wissenschaft." *WwA* 15 (1919) : 1–28 (now *SStuKr* III: 85–116).

"Korrelation der Parteien, Statistik der Kieler Reichstagswahlen." *JbNS* 67 (1924) : 663–72.

"Verbrechertum in Schleswig-Holstein," parts I, II, III. *TSwSp* 52 (1924) : 761–805; 58 (1927) : 608–28; 61 (1929) : 322–59.

"Moralstatistik," in *Handwoerterbuch der Staatswissenschaften*, 4th ed., 1925. (Now *SStuKr* III: 117–31.)

Der Selbstmord in Schleswig-Holstein, Eine statistisch-soziologische Studie. Breslau: Hirt, Veroeffentlichungen der Schleswig-Holsteinischen Universitaetsgesellschaft, no. 9, 1927).

"Das Haarlemer Meer, Eine soziographische Studie." *ZVpS* 3 (1927) : 183–96.

"Die eheliche Fruchtbarkeit in Deutschland." *SchmJb* 52 (1928) : 581–609.

"Statistik und Soziographie." *AStA* 18 (1929) : 546–58.

"Die schwere Kriminalitaet von Maennern in Schleswig-Holstein in den Jahren 1899–1914." With Dr. E. Jurkat. *ZVpS* 5 (1929) : 26–39.

"Ortsherkunft von Verbrechern in Schleswig-Holstein." *DStZ* 21 (1929) : 146–50.

"Sozialwissenschaftliche Forschungsinstitute," pp. 425–40, in *Forschungsinstitute, ihre Geschichte, Organisation und Ziele.* Ed. L. Brauer, Mendelssohn Bartholdy, and A. Meyer. Hamburg: Hartung, 1930.

Uneheliche und verwaiste Verbrecher, Studien ueber Verbrechertum in Schleswig-Holstein. Leipzig: Wiegandt, Kriminalistische Abhandlungen, no. 14, 1930.

"Soziographie und ihre Bedeutung." *Deutsche Justiz* 6 (1930) : 70–77.

"Der Selbstmord in Schleswig-Holstein alten Umfanges, 1885–1914." *Nordelbingen* 8 (1930) : 447–72.

"Leitsaetze und Vortrag in der Untergruppe fuer Soziographie," pp. 196–206, in *Verhandlungen des Siebenten Deutschen Soziologentages vom 28 September bis 1, Oktober 1930 in Berlin.* Tuebingen: I. C. B. Mohr, 1931.

"Zur Statistik der Deutschen Reichstagswahlen." *DStZ* 23, no. 2 (March 1931) : 33–40.

Review of Theodor Geiger, *Die soziale Schichtung des deutschen Volkes.* *ZGSt* 94 (1933) : 527-30.

"Der Selbstmord von Maennern in Preussen 1884–1914." *Mensch en Maatschappij* 9 (1933) : 234–54.

TRANSLATIONS OF TOENNIES' WORKS

Borenstein, A. Farrell, trans. *Custom, An Essay on Social Codes.* Preface by Rudolf Heberle. New York: Free Press of Glencoe, 1961.

Bosse Ewald, trans. *Inledning til Sociologien.* Oslo: Fabricius & Sonner, 1932.

Giordano, Giorgio, trans. *Communità e Società.* Introduction by Renato Treves. Milan: Editioni di Communita, Classici della Sociologia, 1963.

Leif J., trans. *Communauté et Societé: Categories fondamentales de la sociologie pure.* Introduction and translation by Leif. Paris: Presses Universitaires de France, 1944.

Llorens, Vicente, trans. *Principios de Sociologia.* Mexico, D.F.: Fondo de Cultura Economica, 1942.

Loomis, Charles, trans. *Fundamental Concepts of Sociology (Gemeinschaft und Gesellschaft).* Translated and supplemented by Loomis. New York: American Book Company, 1940. British edition, *Community and Association (Gemeinschaft und Gesellschaft).* London: Routledge & Kegan Paul, International Library of Sociology and Social Reconstruction, 1955. *Community and Society (Gemeinschaft und Gesellschaft).* Translated and edited by Charles P. Loomis. East Lansing: Michigan State University Pres, 1957; Harper Torchbook Edition, 1963.

SELECTED WRITINGS ABOUT TOENNIES

Aron, Raymond, pp. 20–28 in: *La sociologie Allemande contemporaine*

(Nouvelle Encylopedie Philosophique), (Paris: Felix Alcan), 1935; English translation pp. 14–19 in: *German Sociology* (New York: Free Press, 1964).

Bellebaum, Alfred. *Das soziologische System von Ferdinand Toennies unter besonderer Beruecksichtigung seiner soziographischen Untersuchungen.* Meisenheim: A. Hain, Koelner Beitraege zur Sozialforschung und Angewandten Soziologie, herausgegeben von R. Koenig und E. K. Scheuch, vol 2, 1966.

Bluem, Norbert S. *Willenslehre und Soziallehre bei Ferdinand Toennies.* Doctoral dissertation, University of Bonn, 1967.

Cahnman, Werner J., pp. 110–11, 540–41 and *passim* in Cahnman, Werner J. and Alvin Boskoff, *Sociology and History* (New York: Free Press, 1964).

———. "Toennies and Social Change," *Social Forces* 47 (1968) : 136–44.

———. "Toennies und Durkheim: Eine dokumentarische Gegenueberstellung," *Archiv fuer Rechts- und Sozialpilosophie,* forthcoming.

Freyer, Hans. "Ferdinand Toennies und seine Stellung in der deutschen Soziologie." *WwA* 44 (1936) : 1–9.

Heberle, Rudolf. "The Application of Fundamental Concepts in Rural Community Studies." *Rural Sociology* 6 (1941) : 203–15.

———. "The Sociological System of Ferdinand Toennies: Community and Society," pp. 227–48, in *An Introduction to the History of Sociology,* edited by Harry Elmer Barnes. Chicago: University of Chicago Press, 1948.

———. "Das soziologische System von Ferdinand Toennies." *SchmJb* 75 (1955) : 1–18.

———. "Ferdinand Toennies' Contributions to the Sociology of Political Parties." *American Journal of Sociology* 61 (no. 3, 1955) : 213–20.

———. "Toennies, Ferdinand," pp. 98–103. *Handwoerterbuch der Sozialwissenschaften.* Tuebingen, 1959.

———. "Toennies, Ferdinand," pp. 98–103. *International Encyclopedia of the Social Sciences.* New York, 1968.

Hoffmann, Friedrich. "Ferdinand Toennies, im Gedenken seiner heimatlichen Vorbundenheit, zu seinem 100. Geburtstag." *Zeitschrift der Gesellschaft fuer Schleswig-Holsteinische Geschichte* 79 (1955) : 301–16.

Jacoby, E. G. "Ferdinand Toennies, Sociologist: A Centennial Tribute." *Kyklos* 8 (1955) : 144–61.

———. "Zur reinen Soziologie." *Koelner Zeitschrift fuer Soziologie und Sozialpsychologie* 20 (1968) : 448–70.

Jurkat, Ernst, ed. *Reine und Angewandte Soziologie: Eine Festgabe fuer Ferdinand Toennies zu seinem achtzigsten Geburtstag am 26. Juli 1935, dargebracht von Albrecht, Boas et al.* Leipzig: H. Buske, 1936.

Klose, O.; Jacoby, E. G.; and Fischer, I., eds. *Ferdinand Toennies–Friedrich Paulsen Briefwechsel 1876–1908.* Foreword by E. G. Jacoby. Kiel: F. Hirt, Veroeffentlichungen der Schleswig-Holsteinischen Universitaetsgesellschaft, N. F. no 27, 1961.

Koenig, René. "Die Begriffe Gemeinschaft und Gesellschaft bei Ferdinand Toennies." *Koelner Zeitschrift fuer Soziologie und Sozialpsychologie,* 7 (1955) : 348–420. Cf. other contributions in *Koelner Zeitschrift,* same issue.

Leemans, Victor. *F. Toennies et la sociologie contemporaine en Allemagne.* Preface by René Maunier. Paris: Felix Alcan, 1933.

Leif, J. *La sociologie de Toennies.* Paris: Presses Universitaires de France, 1946.

Levi, Albert William. "Existentialism and the Alienation of Man," pp. 243–66, in E. N. Lee and M. Mandelbaum, *Phenomenology and Existentialism.* Baltimore: Johns Hopkins Press, 1967.

McKinney, John C., in collaboration with Charles P. Loomis. "The Application of Gemeinschaft and Gesellschaft as Related to other Typologies," in *Community and Society,* transl. by Charles P. Loomis, pp. 12–29.

Nisbet, Robert A. *The Sociological Tradition,* pp. 71–80 and 208–11 and *passim.* New York: Basic Books, 1966.

Oberschall, Anthony. "Toennies' Social Statistics and Sociography," pp. 51–63, in *Empirical Social Research in Germany in 1848–1914.* Paris and The Hague: Mouton & Co.; Publications of the International Social Science Council, 1965.

Oppenheimer, Franz. "Die moderne Soziologie und Ferdinand Toennies." *WwA* 23 (1926) : 187*–208*.

Palmer, Paul A. "Ferdinand Toennies' Theory of Public Opinion." *The Public Opinion Quarterly* (October 1938) : 584–95.

Pappenheim, Fritz. *The alienation of modern man, an interpretation based on Marx and Toennies.* New York: Monthly Review Press, 1959.

Parsons, Talcott. "Note on *Gemeinschaft* und *Gesellschaft,*" pp. 686–94, in *The Structure of Social Action*. 1st ed. New York and London: McGraw-Hill, 1937.

Rosenbaum, Eduard. "Ferdinand Toennies' Werk." *SchmJb* 38 (1913): 2149–96.

Rudolph, Guenther, "Ferdinand Toennies und der Faschismus." *Wiss Z. Humboldt Univ. Berlin* 14 (1967): 339–45. Cf. Rudolph's review of Bellebaum, *op. cit.*, in *Wirtschaftswissenschaft* (1968): 497–501.

Salomon, Albert. "In memoriam Ferdinand Toennies, 1855–1936." *Social Research* 3 (1936): 348–63.

Striefler, Heinrich. "Zur Methode der Rangkorrelation nach Toennies." *DStZ* 23 (1931): 130–35, 163–68.

Takata, Yasuma. "Die Gemeinschaft als Typus." *ZGSt* 83 (1927): 291–316.

Treves, Renato. "Ferdinand Toennies e la teoria della communità e della società." *Quaderni di Sociologia* 12 (1963): 3–24.

Vierkandt, Alfred. "Ferdinand Toennies' Werk und seine Weiterbildung in der Gegenwart." *Kant Studien* 30 (1925): 299–309.

Von Wiese, Leopold. "Toennies' Einteilung der Soziologie." *KVHS* 5 (1925): 445–55.

Wirth, Louis. "The Sociology of Ferdinand Toennies." *American Journal of Sociology* 32 (1926/27): 412–22.

"Zum Hundertsten Geburtstag von Ferdinand Toennies." *Koelner Zeitschrift fuer Soziologie und Sozialpsychologie.* vol. 7, no. 3 (1955), with contributions by L. V. Wiese, H. Plessner, R. Koenig, J. Leif, R. Heberle, G. Wurzbacher, J. Johannesson, and two posthumous papers by Toennies (see above).

Index of Names

Index of Subjects